D1474935

DISCARDED

DISCARDED

CAMPUS SECURITY
AND
LAW ENFORCEMENT

JOHN W. POWELL

BUTTERWORTH PUBLISHERS INC.
Boston   London

COLLEGE OF THE SEQUOIAS
LIBRARY

Copyright © 1981 by Butterworth (Publishers) Inc. All rights reserved.

No part of this publication may be reproduced, stored in a retrieval system, or transmitted, in any form or by any means, electronic, mechanical, photocopying, recording, or otherwise, without the prior written permission of the publisher.

All references in this book to personnel of male gender are used for convenience only and shall be regarded as including both males and females.

Library of Congress Cataloging in Publication Data

Powell, John W   1915–
    Campus security and law enforcement.

    Bibliography: p.
    Includes index.
    1. Campus police–United States. 2. Campus police.
I. Title.
HV8290.P63   363.2'89   80–25430
ISBN 0–409–95028–9

Published by Butterworth (Publishers) Inc.
10 Tower Office Park
Woburn, MA 01801

Jacket illustration by Stephanie Primm

Printed in the United States of America

COLLEGE OF THE SEQUOIAS
LIBRARY

To my wife, whose hard work, support
and encouragement made it possible.

CONTENTS

Section III – SPECIFIC PROTECTION AREAS   **141**

PREFACE

The overall purpose of this book is not only to provide guidance for present campus security and law enforcement administrators but also to assist those entering the campus field. In writing it I recalled my own experience in 1960 when I was appointed head of security at Yale University and unsuccessfully looked for a book or some reference material. Since then many newly appointed administrators of campus security departments have also vainly sought such assistance. One of the motivating reasons for writing this book has been because of the constant statements of campus administrators that such a book is urgently needed.

I have tried to direct my writing not only to those in the field but also to college and university administrators, student government leaders, faculty and staff members, and others who in one way or another have security responsibilities or some interest or concern. Hopefully, this book will provide guidelines and the blueprint depicting what an effective campus security program should consist of and furnish "ammunition" for heads of departments to "prove the point" and acquire administrative support for security requests. In other words, I was always mindful of the fact that it could be used by nonsecurity people to assess the level and effectiveness of security on their campus in comparison to other institutions of learning.

In preparing the manuscript I have drawn heavily on my own experience as director of security and associate dean of students at Yale University (1960-1968) and my close association with heads of campus departments down through the years. I have also utilized a great deal of the knowledge and information gleaned from conducting security studies at over forty colleges and universities. My personal growth in the campus field was enhanced greatly by these studies because at every one of them I learned something of value that could be of benefit to others.

This book has also been written to fill an increasing need for a textbook to be used by criminal justice teaching programs. I am presently teaching a course on "Campus and School Security" and other colleges and universities have instituted similar studies. To the best of my knowledge no book or significant amount of reference material exists in this field at present.

In closing I would like to acknowledge the wonderful assistance of my wife and secretary, Marjorie, who not only encouraged me to write it but kept me working when the golf course or some other more pleasant endeavor beckoned. My thanks to her also for editing, typing, and proofreading my very rough manuscript.

John W. Powell

SECTION I.
THE GROWTH AND
PURPOSE OF
CAMPUS SECURITY

Chapter 1

THE EVOLUTION OF CAMPUS SECURITY

The growth and trend towards the professionalism of campus security has been the most rapid in the private security field in recent years. Campus security has largely been tailored to meet the ever-increasing, difficult, and changing security problems of our times as reflected at our colleges and universities. Effective campus programs have adopted some of the best aspects of law enforcement and private security. The directors of these programs have always been keenly aware that they were serving an intelligent, sensitive, predominantly young academic community.

ORIGINS OF CAMPUS SECURITY

In all probability, campus security started in 1894 when the Yale Campus Police Department was established.

Yale, like many other educational institutions, occupies a large segment of the center of a city (New Haven, Connecticut). Consequently, everything the university does seems to rub off on the New Haven community and vice versa. In the late 1800s, "town-gown" relations were particularly strained because of frequent mass confrontations between students and townspeople that often developed into full-scale riots, which culminated in students and the New Haven Police battling it out. After one of these bloody battles, a town-gown ad hoc committee was formed. The committee suggested that two New Haven police officers be assigned exclusively to the Yale campus as a means of bringing about better student-police relations. When a notice requesting volunteers for such an assignment appeared on the police bulletin board, many officers reacted as if recruits were being sought to be thrown to the lions. However, two New Haven officers, William Weiser and James Donnelly, volunteered.

Officers Weiser and Donnelly walked across the New Haven Green each morning and disappeared behind the walls of Yale. Although their brother officers wondered at first if they would ever see the pair again, they always returned at the end of each day. Weiser and Donnelly apparently began to establish a rapport with students and the Yale community.

Some members of the campus community did not like the idea of the officers leaving the university each evening and "telling what went on at Yale" to their superiors. Therefore, in 1894 the officers were hired away from the city by Yale, and the Yale Campus Police was established with Weiser as chief. However, they still retained their New Haven Police authority (power of arrest), a situation that has existed for Yale officers to this day.

Chief Weiser wrote a book in 1914 entitled *Yale Memories,* in which he stated that his department's most important function was to "protect the students, their property, and University property." This remains an apt description of the function of campus security today. In another section of the book Weiser displayed sensitivity to the need for promoting good relations with students (a sensitivity that is sometimes lacking in campus security personnel) when he wrote, "with good judgment, tact, and just plain horse sense," officers were able to win the respect and friendship of students.

Security During the Early 1900s

During the early 1900s there was little need for security forces on campus, and the local police department was relied upon to handle the few problems that did arise.

The 1920s and 1930s saw watchmen emerge out of the physical plant or buildings and grounds departments. Their main concern was to protect college property. They walked a regular watchman's clock tour at night to act as a fire watch, close and lock doors, tend the boilers, and perform other maintenance tasks.

After the repeal of Prohibition in the early 1930s, watchmen began to take on other functions dealing with the enforcement of student regulations. They were supposed to detect violators of the curfew rules, the ban on drinking on campus, or regulations against members of the opposite sex in dormitory rooms. Very few violators were reported to the dean for disciplinary action, however, because these watchmen, or "campus cops" as they were often referred to, did not or would not report student violators.

Progress During the 1950s

In the 1950s an awareness grew among some campus administrators that they should have at least some semblance of a police presence. A number of schools hired retiring members of the local police department to become chief at a low rate of pay. For the most part these former police officers did not have any administrative experience and merely tried to set up a department similar to the one from which they had retired. They still remained under the supervision of the director of buildings and grounds. Having no budget of its own, the security department remained about the same with the emphasis on protection of college property.

In 1953 the Northeastern College and University Security Association was formed by a group of campus security administrators in the northeast to foster professionalism and the exchange of information.

This development was followed in 1958 by the formation of the National Association of College and University Traffic and Security Directors, which in 1967 changed its name to the International Association of College and University Security Directors and in 1980 to the International Association of Campus Law Enforcement Administrators. This association presently has over 800 institutional members.

The Student Dissent Era

The student dissent era in the late 1960s and early 1970s provided campus security with its greatest impetus toward professionalism. Mass student demonstrations, takeovers of entire buildings, disruptive "sit-ins" in the university president's office, vandalism, arson, and similar incidents made campus administrators realize the need for a trained, higher level security operation headed by an experienced security professional.

Many campuses realized that the present security departments and their supervisors were incapable of controlling these types of situations or furnishing advice on how to prevent or handle them. Consequently, many administrators relied on the usual campus approach of forming committees to decide what to do. Too often, the committees did nothing or gave in to the demands of rioting students. Local and state police, who were not sensitive to the campus scene, attempted to deal with these situations by force and arrest. Consequently, the situations often accelerated and other students and faculty, previously uninvolved, joined the confrontations. All of this dissension and violence culminated with the 1970 shooting of several students by the National Guard at Kent State University in Ohio.

Suddenly an urgent cry arose on the part of presidents and other top college and university administrators for professional security departments able to relate to the campus environment and prevent and control student problems. The overall philosophy, learned from sometimes bitter experience, was that the institution must control these situations *on campus with its own personnel* rather than call in outside police agencies.

During these years many campus administrators and newly hired security directors studied and copied the Yale University Police Department, whose trained young officers had been able to cope with student uprisings successfully without calling in outside police. Some colleges and universities utilized the services of consultants in studying security problems and establishing effective programs tailored to the needs of a campus community.

Campus security during the late 1960s and early 1970s had to be programmed to meet student problems. Therefore, it emphasized a low-key but highly professional approach utilizing well-trained young officers who were either enrolled in college degree programs or who had already achieved a degree. These security officers were attired in smart blazer-slacks outfits bearing the college seal and department name instead of the police-type uniforms of the former watchmen-guards. Professional degree-holding security administrators were very much in demand to head these departments, and colleges raided other colleges for these proven campus security professionals. Security directors no longer answered to the head of physical plant but directly to the president or vice president.

This upgrading of security personnel and, particularly, supervision was accompanied by all the other factors that make for a professional approach. Salaries were made competitive with outside police departments, and the same fringe benefits were afforded to security personnel as those enjoyed by faculty and administrators.

Physical changes also took place. Campus security emerged from the basements and boiler houses where, for the most part, they had utilized office equipment and lockers discarded by other departments. They were relocated into attractive, well-equipped, businesslike office space with lockers and squad rooms for the officers.

New, unmarked police vehicles were purchased for patrol purposes and equipped with two-way mobile radios. Security officers also carried modern, efficient two-way FM radios.

Truly professional departments emerged that could relate to all segments of the campus community. *Service* and *prevention* were the watchwords. However, because student problems were the challenge, these departments continued to depart from the police image that was unacceptable and, in fact, distasteful to students and faculty. (Police were commonly referred to by students as "pigs.") In addition to blazers replacing uniforms, department titles were changed from police designations to such names as Department of Security Services, Department of Public Safety, or Department of Safety and Security. Police titles (chief, captain, sergeant, police officer, and so on) gave way to titles such as director of public safety, security supervisor, or security officer.

Student confrontations and dissent produced a hectic and trying period in the history of American educational institutions, but from this period emerged rapid progress toward a truly effective and professional security approach.

THE CHALLENGE OF CRIME

With the era of student dissent over, relative calm now prevails on campus. However, a new and increasingly serious problem faces campus security today—crime, including theft, assault, rape, and armed robbery.

Professional campus security is firmly established at many colleges and universities today. Some campus administrators, however, still look upon security as a necessary evil and will not face up to the need for a professional but campus-oriented approach to meet the challenge of increasing crime.

The advent of the 1980s will present new challenges to campus security, such as escalating crime, threats to personal safety, and possible acts of terrorism. Campus administrators must more and more face up to the fact that a well-trained, professional campus security department is an absolute necessity in order to insure the safety and well-being of students, faculty, and staff.

Chapter 2

TODAY'S CHALLENGE – CRIME

Universities during the late 1960s and early 1970s were mainly troubled by the alarming trend of social and political unrest that, although of great concern to administrators, did not seriously threaten the safety of the campus population. As campus unrest waned it appeared to be replaced by a new problem—namely, increased crime in the form of thefts, assaults, robberies, rapes, and the selling of drugs and narcotics.

College and university campuses became prime targets for outside criminals who realized that a campus population was made up of mostly young people who had little concern for security or crime and administrators whose main interest was education, not protection or enforcing the law. Therefore, many undesirables invaded college campuses to steal, rob, deal in drugs, and commit sexual acts including rape.

The university environment itself contributed to increased crime because during the past twenty years it has changed from a somewhat cloistered existence removed from the outside community to the unrestricted open campus of today.

This change was also initially fostered by the Supreme Court decision in 1961 in the case of *Dixon* vs. *the Alabama Board of Education* that struck down the in loco parentis concept under which educational institutions had operated for years. Under this concept the university acted as an away-from-home parent in imposing discipline and rules and regulations. This important Supreme Court decision called for students to be accorded the same rights and privileges as any citizen, which required universities and colleges to abide by strict legal procedures.

The "student ward" of yesterday became the "student citizen" and this change was undoubtedly one of the factors contributing to student demands, demonstrations, and dissent a few years later.

The student citizens achieved their rights, but with these rights the parental-type rules and procedures that had protected them in the past disappeared and led to increased crime and security problems. Some of these changes that provided opportunities for the outside criminal or undesirable were completely unrestricted access to campuses, the abandonment of all college regulations and curfews, free access to dormitories at all hours, coeducational dorms, and the demise of "house mothers" and similar adult positions in dormitories, fraternities, and sororities.

Unfortunately, no accurate figures on campus crime exist at any centralized location. The closest we can come to any sort of standardized statistics is the *FBI Uniform Crime Reports.* However, less than 250 colleges and universities contribute to these reports, and these are almost exclusively state institutions.

In speaking about crime statistics we also must recognize that many crimes are never reported. The percentage of unreported crimes is especially high on campus because many young people seem to be reluctant to report anything to the police. Students say, "Why report it? Nothing will be done." Too often they are correct, because their campus security departments have no effective reporting system and little investigative ability.

Enumerating statistical data on crime is of limited value, not only because accurate data do not exist but also because any figures would quickly become obsolete. Instead, this chapter offers a brief assessment of campus crime conditions today.

WHAT ARE THE PROBLEMS?

A few years ago a series of one-day campus security workshops was held across the country, sponsored by the National Association of College Auxiliary Services. One of the questions asked of those attending was, "What do you consider your greatest problem?"

Approximately 375 colleges and universities were represented; over 98 percent of them stated their greatest problem was crime, particularly theft.

From the 2 percent that did not list crime as their greatest problem came a variety of answers. Some years earlier the most common answer would have been, "student dissent." However, not one answer even remotely indicated that students were a problem . . . except that they were careless about locking their doors and accepting some security responsibility.

Only two of the institutions surveyed indicated that parking was their greatest problem. About twenty years ago this would have been the number one problem. Other answers indicated the following concerns:

- Apathy of the community, particularly the administration.
- Convincing the administration of the need of professionalism to fight crime.
- The faculty will not accept their share of security responsibilities.
- The open campus.
- Complete lack of key control.
- No money.

Theft Problem

Students are the major victims of campus thefts, with their dormitory rooms and parked vehicles the principal targets. Ranked behind student victims would be college property, with shoplifting from bookstores near the top of the list. The majority of these thefts are in the petty larceny category (usually under $100).

Who commits these on-campus thefts? A relatively small percentage of students and probably even a larger percentage of certain categories of employees do steal. However, these account for only approximately 30 percent of campus thefts. Outsiders account for at least 70 percent.

On some campuses the theft problem has peaked, and in some cases it has been reduced drastically. A number of factors have contributed to these reductions. The overriding reason has been a more professional security approach, able to provide not only effective patrol and follow-up investigations but preventive measures and educational programs as well, so that the entire community becomes security conscious. Another reason is the changing attitude of the student, who is tired of being "ripped-off" and is now more willing to report and cooperate in the solution of thefts.

Crimes Against the Person

The more serious crimes against the person unfortunately seem to be increasing at an alarming rate. These are the crimes of rape and other sexual offenses, armed robberies (frequently drug-related), vicious attacks often involving knives and other weapons, and similar offenses. These types of crimes soon cause a campus community to boil over and *demand* better security *immediately.*

Many tragic cases have called attention to the dangers of campus crime in recent years.

For instance, a lone female student was studying during the daytime in a classroom at the University of Tennessee. A young male entered the room, locked the door, and forced her at gunpoint to disrobe. He handcuffed her and subjected her to a brutal sexual attack.

A freshman student at Huntingdon College went to a college building about 6:30 P.M. on a spring evening to tutor another student. There she was accosted by an intruder who held a gun at her head and threatened to "blow your brains out" unless she submitted to his advances. She was taken to a remote area on the top floor where she was assaulted and raped.

The brutal rape and murder of two sorority sisters in their rooms at the Chi Omega House at Florida State University in January 1978 sent shock waves through every campus in the country and focused attention on increasing rapes and assaults of women on campus. A wave of fear spread among women students everywhere and campus security departments were under severe pressure to provide additional security for females.

A freshman student at Yale University was raped on her first night in her dormitory room and this was followed by another rape and attempted rape elsewhere on campus. The campus community demanded more protection that resulted in Yale University Police Officers wearing uniforms for the first time, the installation of locks on bathrooms and entryways, peepholes being installed in dormitory doors, and the purchase of expensive electronic access control and emergency alarm systems.

Seton Hall University experienced a robbery in the middle of the afternoon. A lone robber pointed a gun at an employee counting money in the bursar's office, handed her a paper bag, and said, "Fill it up." He walked away with about $10,000 in cash.

A graduate student at Florida State University, who had been an unsuccessful candidate for a doctoral program, walked into the office of his major professor and fired a bullet through his head at point blank range. He then turned the .38 caliber revolver on himself and committed suicide.

An employee at the University of Miami Medical Center was accosted by a knife-wielding robber as she parked her car when arriving in the morning. Her assailant attempted to remove her ring by cutting off her finger, causing a severe infection and partial disability.

I could go on and on listing these horror stories that have affected virtually every campus in the country. Every head of campus security can probably relate at least one similar incident that has caused his campus community to be concerned and demand additional protection.

Let us look at what actually happened on one campus where several rapes and attempted rapes had occurred in a relatively short period at the start of the college year, when no vacation period was near to cool the situation. (Some college administrators reading this will undoubtedly believe it is their campus that is described, because this is a familiar scene.)

The first step after the initial outcry for more security was to form an ad hoc security committee made up of students, administrators, faculty, security, and housing representatives. Bowing to campus pressure, this committee recommended more "bodies" (untrained guards)—an ineffective solution. After the committee had spent considerable time and visited other institutions in an effort to come up with the answers, my campus security consulting firm was called in. Students were led to believe that the so-called experts would immediately solve their problems and prevent future incidents. Nothing could be further from the truth. An effective security program *has to be built over a period of years*; no one can produce it by pushing a magic button. Too many ineffective and expensive "crash" security measures have been taken by such committees.

The time to prepare for an effective, responsible, knowledgeable security program that can protect a campus community is when relative calm prevails. A good campus security program entails much more than bodies and must evolve slowly. Certainly professional supervision and high-caliber, intelligent, well-trained personnel are among the most important factors.

Students are rightfully asking for at least as high a level of security as they would enjoy in the outside community. It is encouraging to see more and more student leaders taking part in campus security programs. Students desire and will increasingly demand professional security protection and response.

LEGAL RESPONSIBILITY TO PROVIDE SECURITY

The president of one university stated, "I look upon my position like the mayor of a city. I feel responsible for the safety and well-being of my university city and the people who study, work, and reside here." A college or university *is* like a city as far as crime is concerned; it experiences all the problems of a city. The only difference from campus to campus is in the degree of crime dictated by the location of the institution (e.g., urban or rural), the rate of crime in the surrounding community, the type and location of dormitories and other buildings, the security operation, and many other factors.

Does a college or university have any legal or moral responsibility to those who work, study, and reside on campus? When an institution accepts students into its residence halls, it must also assume at least the moral responsibility for providing adequate security. The question of legal responsibility, to the best of my knowledge, has never been decided, although a number of institutions have been sued for their alleged failure to provide adequate security.

One of the major suits against a university involved a coed who was forced at gunpoint into a vacant auditorium (which should have been locked) as she crossed the campus one night en route to her dormitory room. What made this case unusual was that a campus security guard had come upon the pair in the auditorium almost immediately. Although it is not clear what happened, lawyers for the victim claim that in spite of the fact that she was "screaming at the top of her lungs," the guard left after having a "quiet conversation" with the attacker, who could have passed as a student. The guard said he thought they were "lovers."*

---

*Incident occurred at George Washington University, Washington, D.C., February 7, 1972.

The female student was sexually assaulted for more than an hour. She filed suit against the sixty-one-year-old guard and the university for $5 million and $55,000 for medical and psychiatric care. Her lawyer pointed out that this was the first time the question had arisen regarding the legal responsibility of the university to provide a secure campus. The suit contended that the guard was "totally unfit for the responsibilities the university had given him." It also pointed out that campuses need "trained policemen" and that "students have a right to expect the university to give them reasonable and adequate security.

A small southern college has also been recently sued for over $2 million dollars for a "lack of adequate security" after a freshman student was raped at gunpoint in a college science building during the early evening hours. This promising, straight A student suffered an emotional breakdown as a result and withdrew from college.*

Most colleges and universities have an understanding with their local police departments that officers do not come on campus unless requested to do so. Where does this leave the students and employees when there is a weak, low-level campus security operation? They are being treated like second-class citizens as far as security is concerned. The institution is virtually issuing an open invitation to thieves, rapists, and other criminals to engage in their acts, with the odds much lower that they will be caught than in the outside community.

DRUGS AND ALCOHOL

Drugs and alcohol on campus have been a particular and often delicate problem for campus security departments to handle. This problem is compounded on some campuses by administrators adopting the attitude because of a fear of media exposure that "we have no problem here." Campus security officers are confused at many institutions as to what their responsibilities are in regard to drugs and narcotics because they are not allowed to investigate or take any action in regard to possible drug violations.

The use of drugs and alcohol on campus leads directly to other crimes ranging from simple acts of vandalism to armed robberies of student pushers. A weak or hands-off security policy towards drugs also invites outside users and especially pushers to come on campus.

The drug and alcohol problem has experienced many changes at colleges and universities during the past half a century. Students in the late 1920s and early 1930s sneaked Prohibition-era bootleg liquor on campus for parties and football games. Alcohol continued to present problems (mostly in the form of vandalism and disturbances) throughout the 1940s and 1950s, but the use of drugs was relatively minor and rejected by most students.

---

*Incident occurred at Huntingdon College, Montgomery, Alabama, April 23, 1979.

The student dissent period of the 1960s seemed to spawn the increased use of drugs and narcotics on campus with marijuana leading the way. The use of these illegal substances appeared to be one other tactic on the part of some students to show their distaste for the establishment and its laws. The youths of the 1960s and at present look upon marijuana in the same light as Prohibition-era students regarded alcohol. They point to the millions of alcoholics in older generations in arguing for the legalizing of marijuana and the right to "do their thing." A pot party is their generation's cocktail party.

We must also recognize that students of today are brought up in a pill society that is increasingly buying the well-advertised proposition that there is a chemical solution for any problem, whether it be physical, psychological, or social.

The late 1960s and early 1970s saw many college students progressing from marijuana to amphetamines (pep pills), barbiturates (downers), tranquilizers, and some to hallucinogens (LSD, and so on), and finally, hard narcotics (heroin, cocaine, morphine, methamphetamine—"speed"). However, the demise of unruly student dissent in the 1970s and students' willingness to work within the system also seemed to signal a decrease in the use of LSD and addictive narcotics. Marijuana remained as popular as ever and still is used freely and extensively on most campuses by students who continue to argue that it is not as harmful as alcohol and is their way of "getting high."

The drug scene has always spawned numerous new illegal and often legal substances that a few students are willing to experiment with but that can be extremely dangerous. Some of these in the past have involved glue sniffing, inhaling laughing gas, inhaling lighter fluid and gasoline, and even digesting large amounts of sunflower seeds and nutmeg. Of more recent vintage, and considerably more dangerous, has been the advent of "angel-dust" and mixing cocaine and ether, a concoction that can be a dangerous fire hazard.

A campus security organization should keep up to date on what is happening in the drug world and be able to recognize the multitude of substances used and the effects of such use. The best approach is to designate and train one or two members of the department, preferably investigators, and make them responsible for handling most cases involving drugs. Training will probably involve sending them to special schools such as those held some years ago for campus officers by the U.S. Bureau of Narcotics and Dangerous Drugs. Membership in the International Narcotic Enforcement Officers Association, Inc. would also provide up-to-date information and an opportunity to attend conferences and seminars devoted to this subject.

A rather alarming return to the heavy use of alcohol has occurred in the past few years. Many campus security administrators have expressed to me that alcohol is getting to be a major problem and contributes to increased acts of vandalism, personal injuries, and disorder. At the same time they indicate the use of LSD and other psychedelic drugs (with the exception of marijuana) has declined dramatically, probably because of the hazards involved that can result in temporary or permanent insanity and even death. Of continuing concern is the taking of barbiturates with alcohol to produce a "cheap drunk."

On most campuses the percentage of students using various drugs and addictive narcotics is small, but as we proceed into the 1980s the use of marijuana continues to be very much a part of the youth culture. Like the recent return of the senior prom and other vestiges of campus life in the 1930s and 1940s, apparently heavy drinking, particularly of beer and wine, will also continue and probably increase.

There has always been a great deal of confusion and lack of clear-cut policy regarding the role of campus security in regard to illegal drugs and narcotics. This confusion and lack of direction from college administrators is caused by some basic issues relating to certain values about which faculty and the administration disagree.

Some of these issues are as follows:

- What is the role of the institution with respect to students' freedom to make their own decisions?
- What right does the institution have to interfere with students' freedom of choice?
- On what basis and to what limits does the institution protect students' freedom of choice?
- What about the legal aspects? Is it the concern of the institution if students violate the law?
- If the law is broken are sanctions to be applied by society's legal process, the university's, or both?
- Is the law in conflict with many educators' belief that experimentation is part of growing up and the educational process?

These issues and others are probably the reason why many educational institutions have never formulated any clear-cut policy in regard to illegal drug use on campus. Many institutions have merely included a statement in the student handbook to the effect that student behavior in this regard is not its special concern, that it should be handled as elsewhere in society, and that the institution will cooperate fully with outside law enforcement agencies. Some institutions have no written policy at all. The tendency on the part of some deans is to handle each case on its own merits and to avoid hard and fast written policies.

Campus security will always face a segment of the campus population including faculty, students, and staff members, who will be vehemently opposed to any action or investigation on campus involving drugs. I recall that at Yale during the 1960s when drugs were becoming a problem and some students were selling marijuana and other drugs and narcotics, the New Haven Police Department indicated to me that they were investigating these student pushers and asked if I wanted to be kept informed regarding their identity and day-by-day developments. My answer was that I would rather not be informed until only a few minutes prior to the drug bust, at which time the highest ranking Yale officer would accompany the New Haven officers to the student's room. I followed this policy because the first question asked by the college master or dean affected was always, "When did you first know about this?" If I had known about it previously most administrators would have insisted upon being advised and some would have "counseled" the student beforehand — resulting in all evidence being removed. The Yale officer on the scene not only assisted the New Haven officers in locating the student but also insured that the arrest and search was conducted as discreetly as possible and that the student's rights were fully protected.

The role of the campus security or police department in regard to alcohol on campus is a relatively easy one compared to its role with drugs. Alcohol is not illegal, and therefore, security is mostly concerned with the aftermath of its use, which involves vandalism and personal accidents such as falling. One of the department's major roles on most campuses is to escort or convince fellow students to take the offender to his room and see that he goes to bed and stays there.

Most of the consequences of overindulgence are rather petty in nature, do not merit an arrest, and can be handled, if necessary, through the disciplinary process. In the case of repeated drunkenness, the student should be referred to the proper counseling service for assistance. This procedure dictates that security report each incident to the proper dean or student affairs person so that they will be aware that a student may have an alcoholism problem.

The role of the campus department in regard to drugs and narcotics is not so easy or clear cut as in dealing with alcohol, because most of these substances are illegal. Here all the weight of campus opinion that we have previously discussed come into play. The most important thing is to *establish a specific policy* and let the entire campus community know exactly what this policy entails. On many campuses this has never been done.

In establishing this policy one clear-cut fact must be considered: The use, possession, supplying, or selling of illegal drugs and narcotics is against the law. If a campus department's personnel are sworn peace officers (as most are and should be), they have the legal responsibility to enforce all laws and cannot selectively decide what laws to enforce or ignore. Therefore, a campus security or law enforcement agency, in my opinion, cannot completely disregard these violations, and campus administrators should not tell them to or imply that they do so.

The campus department should follow the same policy in regard to violations as most outside law enforcement agencies today — namely, that investigations and arrests should be directed at the pusher not the user (unless there are some mitigating circumstances).

Investigations of drug pushers on campus, whether they involve students, employees, or outsiders, are extremely difficult for campus security departments to conduct successfully. First of all, the department faces the fact that these investigations, to be successful, usually involve informants and undercover officers who must "make a buy" from the seller. This type of covert activity, particularly since Watergate, is looked upon with extreme disfavor by a large segment of the campus population. I have never heard of any educational institution providing "buy money" for an undercover campus officer to purchase drugs or narcotics from a pusher operating on campus.

The campus department's role, as I see it, has to be one of full cooperation with outside law enforcement agencies so that open and complete two-way communication on drug matters proceeds on a highly confidential and discreet basis. Most campus security investigations would involve mainly identifying possible pushers on campus and keeping appropriate outside law enforcement agencies informed regarding the results. The actual buy should probably be made by undercover police officers from local or statewide drug and narcotics units, either on or off campus. If subsequent arrests and searches incidental to arrest take place on campus, there should be at least some representation present from the campus security organization. However, if arrests take place off campus, campus officers should not actually be involved except to obtain the facts of the arrest for a report to those on campus concerned and having a need to know.

One of the strong indications of drug involvement by students is an unusually high number of armed robberies on campus. These robberies usually involve the student opening his dormitory door and being confronted by an armed subject (or subjects). This type of armed robbery often means that the inhabitant of that room is dealing in drugs and the robber is after not only money but also drugs kept on the premises. These student pushers have been known to make more money (tax free) during a college year than some of the faculty and administrators.

These procedures, particularly keeping outside law enforcement officials advised of suspect student pushers, will very much go against the grain of many people on campus. However, in the last few years there has been a growing resentment and complete lack of sympathy on the part of students and other segments of the campus community toward drug pushers, especially if they are dealing in hard narcotics. I look for this resentment to grow during the remainder of the 1980s and beyond and to make the college and university officers' position more tenable, and hopefully, result in college campuses no longer being looked upon as safe havens for those dealing in drugs.

Subsequent chapters will attempt to project ideas and procedures to assist in setting up a professional but preventive and service-oriented approach to campus security in order to cope with these crime problems. However, a campus security operation cannot be molded and stamped the same for all campuses. It must be carefully tailored for the individual campus it will serve.

Chapter 3

FIVE APPROACHES TO SECURITY

Five basic types of security operations are presently in existence at college and universities:

1. Low-level watchman-guard operations primarily designed to protect college property;
2. Contracts with guard services;
3. Contracts with local police departments;
4. Proprietary security departments;
5. Proprietary police-oriented law enforcement agencies.

Whatever approach to security an institution takes, administrators will usually defend it as meeting the needs of their campus. In some cases this statement will be true, but in many instances it will not. This chapter analyzes each of the five approaches briefly and comments on the present trend away from a security approach toward a law enforcement or police concept.

WATCHMAN–GUARD OPERATION

The watchman-guard operation, similar to campus security in its early days, is concerned mainly with protection of college property. It is usually administered by the head of the buildings and grounds department. The watchmen-guards carry time clocks, walk regular routes, occupy fixed posts, and usually have little investigative ability. They may wear uniforms, but they have no police powers, weapons, or other law enforcement–type equipment.

Many college administrators and, particularly, faculty members make the mistake of expecting this type of low-level security operation to handle the crime problems of today's campus. They expect these largely untrained, sometimes elderly guards or watchmen to act like professional, experienced law enforcement officers. At the same time, however, they are most vocal in stating, "We don't want a police department on this campus!"

These educators appear to want the best of two worlds—an efficient security operation but not high-caliber, trained, armed officers with full powers of arrest and professional supervision. Unfortunately, there is no middle ground here; colleges must decide whether they will be satisfied with a low-level watchman-guard-operation or whether they need a professional department with full police powers and necessary equipment. However, as will be pointed out later, such a professional approach can be programmed to be in tune with an academic atmosphere.

CONTRACTED GUARD SERVICE

The campus that is interested only in what a security force will cost, and not the way it will perform, will probably be a potential customer for a contract guard agency. Strong money-saving arguments exist for the use of contract agencies, such as a flat rate per hour of service, with no vacation, sick leave, insurance, medical, retirement, or other benefits to worry about. The agencies often represent their guards as trained and professionally supervised employees who will be replaced immediately if the client does not like their performance. This is particularly attractive to institutions under civil service or where employees are virtually locked into their positions because of a strong union.

The question that must be asked here is, "What am I getting for my security dollar?" There is an old saying that you get only what you pay for. This can certainly be applied to contract guard companies, which are in business for one purpose —to make money. They are in a competitive business, selling a uniform with a guard inside. Their product must be sold with a fairly substantial profit, because like other businesses, they have increasing overhead costs for administration, taxes, insurance, uniforms, and a multitude of other expenses. Therefore, they must pay the guard as little as possible and charge the customer as much as possible.

City, state, and municipal institutions are required by law to solicit bids for contract guard service. This bidding is usually done through the purchasing department, which treats buying this service the same as buying equipment. Sometimes the head of security has no say whatsoever regarding the company that is hired. One director of security is presented by his purchasing department with a new contract force each year. These new guards are completely unfamiliar with the campus and their duties. The director's only comment is, "They get worse and worse."

Securing contract guards by bid usually leads to a force that is being paid the minimum wage. It also may lead to a tongue-in-cheek type of contract specifying many things that neither the contract agency nor the institution expects will be adhered to.

Disadvantages of Contract Guards

Although some contract guard agencies are without principle or integrity, the majority of contract companies are trying to provide the best possible personnel at a completely unrealistic salary level. Contract guards are not the answer, however, to providing the progressive, responsive, alert, imaginative, intelligent service needed to combat the main problem on campus today—crime.

Let us take a look at the disadvantages of using contract guards:

1. Contract guards in many cases are unmotivated, unskilled individuals who are working as guards because it is the only position open to them. Some are moonlighters who take this as a second job in order to enjoy a higher standard of living. Some are retirees who, although often sincere and conscientious, are elderly and do this work as a way to keep busy while earning as much extra money as Social Security will permit.

    Others are "police buffs" who have been rejected by municipal and campus police departments for a variety of reasons. These individuals can sometimes be dangerous on campus; once they don a uniform they may consider themselves "Mr. Authority." They are even more hazardous if armed.

2. Contract guards cannot be expected to be police officers or to perform anything more than the most routine watchman-guard functions. They have no police authority (power of arrest, and so on) and are usually instructed by their superiors not to get involved in arrests or any physical action.

3. Contract guards identify with security and police mainly through their uniforms and badges, which present the image of authority and act as a deterrent. However, students are quick to realize that these symbols are only for show, that the guard has no authority and cannot really provide effective protection and response to problems. Students label them "rent-a-cops."

    When female students in a residence hall were asked if they had confidence in the ability of the contract guard to protect them, one girl replied, "Our guard is so old that I would have to protect him."

4. A contract agency's commodity is guards. Understandably, they try to get and keep as many guards on the job as possible. Their answer to most security problems is, "You need another guard." Once assigned to

a post, a guard is apt to remain there forever, even though the need for continuing his services is questionable.

If a guard was assigned two or three years earlier because of some unusual situation (a series of thefts, for example), the present guard may have no idea why he is there, except that his superiors have told him to "sit here."

5. The turnover in contract guards is understandably high. New guards have to learn their duties and the campus, and often they cannot even answer a simple question such as "Where is the president's office?" In one case, a contract guard was hired and instructed to take up a position in the main lobby of the student union at Boston College. The new guard assumed his post but, unfortunately, it was at Boston University. He worked two hours before someone inquired what he was doing there.

6. Contract guard salespeople usually turn the pages of a beautifully prepared pictorial account of their services. Included in this presentation is the photo of an immaculately uniformed young guard and information about the training he has received. Contract guards, however, are not trained police or security officers; their training consists mainly of on-the-job instruction with another guard or supervisor walking them through their duties. Contract companies cannot afford to spend much time training personnel who may not be with them tomorrow.

7. One of the great weaknesses of contract service is supervision. Again, a company cannot afford to provide high-priced, competent supervision unless the client is willing to pay for it. Too often, supervision becomes another way to get more money per hour from the client for a sergeant or lieutenant in charge. Many times these individuals, although wearing more brass and a sergeant's badge, have no real experience or administrative ability.

8. Although state and municipal laws are tightening up on the fingerprinting and screening of contract guards, many abuses still occur in the hiring of individuals. Often a guard is hired pending the record-checking process, which sometimes can take months. There have also been increasing cases of guards involved in thefts and other crimes while on duty.

9. Serious legal problems can result from the actions of contract guards. Most have absolutely no idea of their legal powers and authority, and this lack of knowledge can result in serious errors leading to civil suits or even criminal charges. Most guard companies recognize this fact and are reluctant to arm their guards unless the client insists.

10. The last and probably most important weakness of contract guards is that they simply do not relate to a campus community. Although an

occasional guard may build a good relationship with students and others, they usually have no concept of university life or the aims of the institution they serve.

An effective campus security or law enforcement operation must be part of the educational process. It cannot hope to be successful unless it gains the respect and confidence of the community. Guards must have that all-important "feel" for campus life and must realize that they work in a sensitive community of intelligent people who look to them to make the campus a safe place to work and study.

Contract guards will cost a great deal less than an in-house security program, but they may not provide the campus community with the protection and response to which it is entitled.

The International Association of Campus Law Enforcement Administrators, whose main purpose is to foster professionalism and better security on campuses, will not accept for membership any institution that depends entirely on contract guards for its security program.

CONTRACT WITH LOCAL POLICE

Contracts with local police, which are not too prevalent, can take several approaches. In one case a major state university was located in a relatively small city where the campus population was close to the city. Security for the extensive campus was traditionally contracted at a rather staggering cost with the municipal police. However, there was no special campus unit or attention to campus problems. Service consisted of an occasional patrol car driving through the area and responding to complaints.

The great weakness in this arrangement was that the university had absolutely no control of police actions on the campus and got very little feedback on what was going on, such as results of investigations, arrests, and similar matters. There was also the usual town-gown relationship, with the local police having little patience or sympathy for campus problems, particularly those involving students. Municipal officers would not perform any of the routine security functions such as locking doors and turning lights on and off. The campus community felt it had practically no one really looking after its security interests. Therefore, another another large expenditure had to be made to hire contract guards to take on these responsibilities and create a security presence to reassure the campus population.

This situation existed until the state legislature, in an austerity move, cut the large payment to the city for police service. This drastic action precipitated a major crisis, with city officials screaming for their payment. It had been in existence so long it was no longer considered a privilege, but a right.

Another form of a rather loose contract with the local police is to have them furnish off-duty officers, usually at time-and-a-half pay, to police the campus. This type of arrangement can lead to all sorts of problems. The campus job becomes a secondary one, undertaken purely for the sake of making some extra money. There is usually a constant turnover of officers, many of whom have little rapport with students and the campus community and some of whom even have deep resentments toward them. The off-duty officers are inclined to approach the position with the same police philosophy they have toward their regular law enforcement duties, and the college exercises very little control or supervision over them.

At one campus that hired local officers to take over the night shifts, the job was considered a real plum given only to favorites of the police chief. The officers had pretty much dictated to college officials what they would or would not do. What they did best was to snooze, watch television, and drink coffee in a comfortable college lounge.

Although there may be exceptions, the contracting or hiring of off-duty local police to assume responsibility for security on a campus has not generally proved effective and is particularly disliked by students.

PROPRIETARY SECURITY DEPARTMENT

The predominant campus approach today is still that of a security department with personnel who are called *security officers.* Because of the emphasis on projecting a low-key approach and profile, particularly during the student dissent era, some of these departments have adopted names such as Department of Security and Safety, Department of Security Services, Department of Safety, and similar nonpolice titles. In many of these security departments, however, police and military titles are still used for the subordinate supervisors. Although the head of the department may carry the title of director of security, his supervisors may have the titles of captain, lieutenant, sergeant, and corporal.

On some campuses these departments have retained their security designation but, in effect, have evolved into police operations with full police powers, firearms, police-type uniforms, and other equipment. However, campus administrators and a large segment of the community would object to any change of title that would identify them as a police department.

PROPRIETARY POLICE–ORIENTED
LAW ENFORCEMENT AGENCY

The crime problem has been responsible for a rapid and somewhat drastic change in the philosophy and role of the campus security department during the past few years. This development has sometimes resulted in a complete law enforcement approach, with campus departments becoming prototypes of local police departments.

These departments carry police titles (e.g., University Police Department), and the head of the department is called chief of police, with his subordinates carrying the usual police designations down to police officer. Most of these departments project a strong police image by their type of uniform, equipment, and sometimes their authoritative manner and large number of arrests.

SECURITY VERSUS LAW ENFORCEMENT APPROACH

No more controversial topic exists on campus today than the security versus law enforcement approach to campus security. People advocating a law enforcement approach want no part of the name *security* and proclaim that they are policemen and law enforcement administrators, not security officers or security directors. They argue that their function on a campus is to enforce the law equitably and arrest lawbreakers. They refuse to adhere to the double standard on many campuses that calls for the arrest of outsiders but refers student lawbreakers to the dean—and often takes no action in regard to faculty, staff, or other employees.

A number of these campus police administrators also argue that the days of in loco parentis are over and that students want to be treated like adults and exactly the same as everyone else. However, it must be recognized that in loco parentis is not dead in the eyes of students' parents, who still expect the college to provide behavior guidance and shelter their offspring from certain actions and problems.

People favoring the police approach also point out that an efficient, progressive campus law enforcement department that enforces the law equally and efficiently for all segments of the campus community as well as noncollege violators inspires respect and confidence in the law and is, therefore, a part of the educational process.

This trend towards a thorough law enforcement approach manifests itself at practically every campus security seminar or conference. For example, in 1971 the International Association of College and University Security Directors changed the name of its publication from *The Newsletter* to the *Campus Law Enforcement Journal*. After repeated attempts by an increasing group of law enforcement-oriented members, the name of the association was finally changed in 1980 to the International Association of Campus Law Enforcement Administrators.

People resisting the law enforcement and police designation maintain that a campus department, whether public or private, is not a law enforcement agency but a security department whose main responsibility is to provide security and a safe campus environment. They state that their function is not to see how many arrests they can make but to provide service and prevent problems. The late Larry Fultz, former director of security at the University of Houston, stated at one conference, "Gentlemen, if you think you are law enforcement officers and want to go the police route on a campus, you are only kidding yourselves. You are security officers, because that's what colleges and universities pay you to be."*

Probably the greatest objection to the law enforcement concept with its police image comes from certain segments of the faculty, administration, and staff. This is particularly true in private colleges and universities as well as in community colleges. It also usually follows that the smaller the institution, the greater the objection to having a police department on campus.

In conducting security studies at some campuses, I have been impressed with some university police departments that, while organized the same as any municipal police agency, have been sensitive to the community they serve and have projected a professional image that inspired respect and confidence.

At other institutions the police image has taken over completely and caused the community to look upon the department with distrust and a lack of respect. At one large university I found university police officers sworn in under the local police department, having the same titles, wearing exactly the same uniform and arm patch, driving the same make, model, and color of patrol vehicles with exactly the same flashing lights and marking, carrying the same weapons, and using the same report and other forms. It was virtually impossible to tell the outside municipal officer from the campus officer.

The result was that campus officers identified almost completely with the outside local officers and spent too much time frequenting police headquarters, a short distance from the campus. Many of the campus officers were too concerned with arrests and the most common question I heard in their squad room was, "How many did you bust today?"

When I interviewed students and student leaders it was evident that the department had losts its credibility on campus. As one student expressed it, "The campus cops and the city cops, they are all the same in my book." It was easy to see why he and the campus in general felt this way because some university officers appeared to delight in arresting students for minor traffic and other violations and an attitude prevailed in which campus officers openly stated that their only loyalty was to the outside police department that swore them in and not to the university, even though the university paid their salaries. Therefore, they refused to perform routine functions such as parking and traffic control, locking doors, turning out lights, and other duties that local officers were not required to perform.

Best Aspects of Both Approaches

It is relatively unimportant whether a campus department carries the police or security title. The important question is, "Does it serve the needs of the campus?"

---

*Statement made during a board of director's meeting of the International Association of College and University Security Directors held at the University of Georgia, Athens, Georgia, January 11, 1973.

If it projects the right image and the campus community has confidence in and respect for its operations, then its title and the titles of personnel are irrelevant.

Subsequent discussion will make clear the fact that any campus department today that hopes to handle increasing crime and other problems efficiently must be tailored after a progressive security *and* law enforcement approach, and it must be sensitive to serving a campus community. In other words, it must utilize the best aspects of private security and law enforcement but adapt them to the campus it serves.

In our discussions reference is made throughout to "campus security" rather than "campus law enforcement." This usage is not a put-down of the people who advocate campus law enforcement. The campus security designation is intended here to embody many law enforcement concepts necessary to perform effectively. To many individuals, however, law enforcement still means an emphasis on after-the-fact arrests, while security typifies prevention, protection, and service.

Chapter 4

THE PROPER ROLE OF CAMPUS SECURITY

Defining the proper role and functions of a campus security department is difficult because the operation must be programmed to meet the needs and general attitudes of the campus it will serve. However, any campus department must direct its efforts primarily at prevention and service to be successful.

Often the campus police or security department has removed itself from the mainstream of campus life because of the role it plays. In some cases there is a lack of respect and confidence in the department, or the department has adopted a defensive posture in which it seems to be at odds with the entire campus community. This type of situation can lead to the security force becoming a minority on campus, completely removed from the life, activities, and mission of an educational institution.

A good public relations program is important to let the campus community know what the problems are and what the security department is doing to solve them; and the best public relations agent is still the officer himself, who makes or breaks the department's image through his contacts with people, response, performance, general appearance and demeanor, and involvement in campus activities.

SECURITY AS PART OF THE EDUCATIONAL PROCESS

The role of a campus department, unlike the role of an outside law enforcement agency, is to contribute to the overall purpose of an educational institution — namely, to educate. It achieves this purpose by projecting an image of courtesy, concern, and competence that gains the respect and confidence of the community.

Earning Respect of the Campus Community

The question arises as to how a campus security department achieves this respect and confidence, particularly when students are sometimes apathetic about security or resent it because it represents authority. Security must be sold to the community through personal appearances and rap sessions by the security director and others. Certainly, the director should involve himself in the orientation process so that all students will at least know him by sight. In these appearances the department should be projected as an integral part of the institution whose purpose is to protect and serve students. At the same time, students should be reminded of their own security responsibilities.

A security department can also establish itself in the eyes of the campus community through media such as the student newspaper and radio station. Although at times campus newspapers may misinterpret and misquote, they can also be a valuable means of getting the message to students. After all, a campus newspaper is the principal means of communication with the student body.

A progressive and efficient security program, which provides quick, courteous, and knowledgeable response to student problems, can give students a higher regard for the law and law enforcement in general—an attitude that will carry on after graduation.

Education in Prevention

Another aspect of security as part of the educational process involves educating students and the community to preventive steps they can take to reduce security hazards.

One of the major weaknesses of local law enforcement has been its emphasis on after-the-fact arrest, giving no thought to prevention or to educating the public about its own security responsibilities. Security is everyone's responsibility, but unfortunately many citizens have adopted the attitude of "not getting involved" and blame the police for lack of protection.

Many effective campus departments have been able, through effective performance and rapport with the campus community, to insure cooperation and educate members of the community to their own security responsibilities.

PREVENTIVE PROGRAMS THAT WORK

Educating students and others to security hazards and what they can do to prevent them can be accomplished in a good public relations and publicity program.

As noted earlier, the head of the security department should participate in the orientation process and in rap sessions with students and organizations such as student government, residence hall councils, and others. Campus security departments should also prepare pamphlets for widespread distribution detailing the services the department can provide, while at the same time reminding the students of their own responsibility and how they can prevent problems from occurring. Naturally, these pamphlets also spotlight the location of the department and routine and emergency telephone numbers, for example, "Help is 248-2000 or Ext. 333."

Quick Response to Emergency

The importance of students and others being able to reach security by phone immediately at any hour cannot be emphasized too strongly. Quick response to emergency situations should be an absolute must on any campus, particularly those with residence halls. One of the most common complaints of students is "You can't reach security!" Sometimes this occurs when the security dispatcher also has to handle all after-hours calls to the college. In some small colleges emergency calls are even directed to an outside answering service that in turn is supposed to notify the patrolling officer or guard by radio.

A special emergency telephone number should be available that security will answer immediately. This line should be kept clear at all times and never be used to make outgoing calls. The number should be given considerable publicity on campus in student publications (handbook, campus newspaper, posters, decals, and so forth). All campus phones should also have a small, brightly colored sticker that reads, "In case of emergency call Public Safety, 248-2000 or Ext. 333."

Posters and Pamphlets

Eye-catching posters can also be used to focus on major problems. The Student Marshal program under the Department of Safety and Security at Syracuse University designed and produced a series of photographic posters graphically depicting security problems and telling students "Lock your door," "Lock your bike," "Don't hitchhike," and so on. The posters also stress one theme in large, bold letters: "Think Security!"

Syracuse University and several other campuses also use a large poster depicting well-known fairy tales, captioned "Fairly Grim Tales." Two of the nursery rhymes read as follows:

Cinderella was late for the prince
And resorted to thumbing a ride.
No one has seen or heard from her since —
They say it was homicide.

Mary had a little lamb,
But all lambs look the same.
To prove that Mary's lamb was hers,
She stamped it with her name.

Many campus departments, such as at Tufts and Northwestern Universities, prepare and distribute pamphlets on individual subjects such as bicycle security and safety, fire safety, employee safety, residence hall security and safety, and other topics.

Identification of Valuable Property

Most departments today have some form of "Operation Identification" program that instructs students and others to engrave valuable property with an easily identifiable number (Social Security, driver's license, student identification, and so on). The department loans an engraving tool to the student and registers the engraved property. A decal is issued for the student's door as a warning to would-be thieves.

Preventing Bicycle Thefts

Bicycle thefts are a major problem on most campuses today, and bicycle registration programs similar to Operation Identification programs can also be used to advantage. For example, thefts of bicycles at Yale were skyrocketing until a registration program was instituted employing cross-indexing information on the bicycle (make, serial number, color, and so on) and the name of the owner with a description of the bike. This latter index was necessary because victims of bicycle theft many times could not recall the serial number. A number, which was included on the two index cards, was engraved on the frame under the seat where it could not easily be detected or removed. The final step was to issue a small but prominent decal indicating the bike was registered by the Yale University Police Department.

The program resulted in a substantial decrease in bicycle thefts and a correspondingly substantial increase in recoveries of registered bikes stolen. Of the bicycles stolen, only about 10 percent were registered and carried the decal. The decal itself was, in all probability, acting as a deterrent.

Available Booklets and Films

A number of commercially distributed booklets and films are also available that could be used for preventive crime education on campus. Among the best of these are several crime prevention booklets that can be purchased at low cost and inscribed with the campus security department's name or logo. These booklets were prepared, with the assistance of myself and several directors of campus security, by Channing L. Bete, Incorporated, Greenfield, Massachusetts 01301. The following booklets have been widely distributed to students:

- *Don't Take Chances on Campus*
- *What Every Woman Should Know about Rape*
- *What Every Woman Should Know about Self-Protection*

Rape Prevention Programs

The most acute crime problem on campus today is rape, and preventive education programs must be directed at this problem. Many colleges have pamphlets and other material on this subject and have set up rap sessions and various programs with women's groups. These preventive programs are usually tied into a women's crisis center in which security as well as representatives of appropriate campus departments such as medical and mental health are involved. The entire mechanism of the women's crisis center goes into operation when the victim makes one phone call over an anonymous phone line that is always operational. The victim is then counseled and assisted throughout the entire experience, sometimes including psychiatric help.

An excellent pamphlet entitled *Rape* has been prepared by the Department of Public Safety at the University of Massachusetts, covering everything a woman should know about rape from legal, medical, and other pertinent points of view. This booklet could easily serve as a model for other campus departments.

Getting Security's Message Across

Some campus departments have been very innovative in getting their security message across. Some have used bumper stickers reading, "Prevent theft—lock your door." Others leave eye-catching cards on desks or in rooms stating, "You could have been ripped-off. Lock your door!"

The Department of Public Safety at the University of Massachusetts produced on campus with student assistance an excellent film regarding rip-offs of student rooms. The film depicts the most common types of thefts of student property caused in part by students' failure to assume any security responsibility—for example, the common theft that occurs when students leave their rooms unlocked while taking a shower. This film is widely shown to students and is effective because it was filmed on campus using students and security personnel as actors.

The Department of Public Safety at the Florida State University headed by Security Director William A. Tanner, a well-qualified pioneer in the campus security field, has an excellent campus program that emphasizes prevention. This program combines alert motor and foot patrol of all areas of the campus to reduce the opportunity for crime and immediate, knowledgeable response and follow-up investigation. Through a four-day ten-hour patrol system the campus is afforded additional coverage during the high-crime period between 9:00 P.M. and 3:00 A.M. The department also uses the services of the Tallahassee REACT Club made up of responsible citizens interested in CB radio to watch and report any suspicious activity on or near the campus.

Bill Tanner's department encouraged and coordinated the escort services for young women at night provided by the Inter-Fraternity Council. It also was one of the first campus departments to implement an extensive crime prevention and community education program to reduce the opportunity for crime, to gain the support of the campus community through public awareness, and to educate university citizens in preventive measures so that they become part of their everyday lives.

The department focused on one phase of this preventive program by organizing the Women's Safety program to deal with crimes against women. Since its inception in 1972, specialists in crime prevention from the campus Department of Public Safety have annually alerted over 2,500 women on campus regarding crimes against women and how they can be prevented. Personal appearances before women's groups have been supplemented by prevention-oriented articles in local and campus newspapers, presentations on the campus radio station, and distribution of a question-and-answer brochure focusing on the preventive aspects of campus crime.

An active Operation Identification program is offered to all residence halls, fraternity, and sorority residents, and over 70 percent avail themselves of it. A crime prevention brochure focusing on the theft problem is widely distributed on campus.

Florida State has also sent at least one of its public safety officers to the National Crime Prevention Institute. As a result this college developed the capability to have crime prevention officers conduct security surveys of various facilities and operations on campus with a view toward recommending preventive measures to insure better safety and security. These surveys are conducted in dormitories and especially in high-risk areas such as the cashier's office, credit union, and dining halls where large sums of money are handled.

Duke University has a crime prevention unit that was formed some years ago to combat the increase in crime. This unit, which is patterned after street crime units in local police agencies, uses officers of the Duke Public Safety Department in a variety of ever-changing disguises to patrol the campus. One purpose of the program is to detect security weaknesses and endeavor to eliminate them. The other is to thoroughly publicize the program so potential criminals will view anyone on campus as a possible police officer.

The unit is quite small and all officers have a chance to volunteer for about two months of this duty, which is sought after by most personnel. Officers are assigned to patrol specific areas where crimes have occurred or that appear to be likely targets.

Disguises are changed to fit the environment and assignment. For example, one officer assigned to the Duke Hospital wore a white smock, stethoscope, and name tag and was addressed as "Doctor" by many patients and employees as he wandered through the premises.

The preventive aspects of this type of patrol are particularly evident in the case of suspicious individuals on campus who are watched and, at times, challenged by the officer. (Duke University is private property where trespassing statutes apply.) This type of patrol can result in a crime being prevented and spreads the word to deter those who might otherwise regard the campus as an easy mark. Women officers have been particularly effective in the program, particularly as decoys.

The only objection to such a program on a campus would be similar to those voiced regarding the use of closed-circuit television and informants. A sensitive campus community, especially students, might object to what they might consider spying tactics that surreptitiously invade their privacy. Therefore, it is very important that this type of operation be explained thoroughly to the campus community before being initiated. This explanation should emphasize that the purpose of having these officers in disguise is merely another tactic to be used to prevent crime on campus and provide better coverage and protection.

The Department of Public Safety at Central Michigan University in cooperation with the office of Instructional Design and Development produced a twelve-minute slide/tape program used for freshman orientation that emphasized the basic preventive measures students should take to reduce their vulnerability to thefts and other crimes. This program utilized three large rear-projection screens, three projectors, special electronic switching synchronized with the narration, and stereophonic background music. The total cost for producing the program was about $2,000.00 and was more than offset by a rather dramatic decline in thefts.

The University of North Carolina promoted a University Police Department Awareness Program in which it employed posters, radio spot announcements, and even eye-catching classified ads to involve the campus community in crime prevention. For example, one classified ad read, "STUDENTS—FREE MOVING SERVICE—FAST. It only takes a minute. Leave your door open or unlocked day or night, and everything will be moved out for you. Report suspicious activity to the University Police, 933-6565."

The Massachusetts Institute of Technology (MIT) Campus Police Department, under its experienced Chief James Olivieri, has engaged in an innovative and ever-changing crime prevention program to combat crime in this busy, densely populated area of Cambridge, Massachusetts. This program has involved a well-publicized "Operation Bolt-Down" in which electric typewriters were bolted to desks free for a one-month period. It also involved crime prevention officers' visiting, unannounced and informally, offices and laboratories throughout the institute to spread the message of crime prevention and leave copies of "Crime Prevention Rundown."

Another tactic used with success by MIT and many other campus departments is to have patrolling officers leave "Crime Prevention Notices" at locations where the potential for crime exists. A copy of this notice is illustrated in Figure 4-1.

The MIT Campus Police also sells at wholesale cost hand-held compressed-air personal safety alarms that produce an attention–getting noise.

Every new student entering MIT receives a packet of informative data regarding the Institute. Included in this packet is the MIT Campus Police Information Digest, which provides an overview of the crime problem in the area, how to prevent crime, and a description of the Campus Police and the services it provides. Women students are also given a "Women's Packet" that includes various personal safety pamphlets and a map of the area in which streets dangerous for lone women at night are spotlighted and the Campus Police escort service is publicized. The department is also involved in the orientation of foreign students in regard to crime, personal safety precautions, the law, police procedures, and customs in this country. The department also contributes the "Weekly Police

Figure 4-1. Patrol crime prevention notice. Courtesy of Massachusetts Institute of Technology Campus Police Department, Cambridge, Massachusetts.

M.I.T. CAMPUS PATROL
CRIME PREVENTION NOTICE

DATE: _____

TIME: _____

At the date and time noted, the condition listed was observed by an Officer patrolling the area. We ask you to join with us in the effort to reduce the opportunities for criminal activity by correcting the situation. Crime prevention is everybody's business — please make it yours.

☐ Unlocked/unattended room/office/area.
☐ Valuables left unattended.
☐ Typewriter(s) or similar items not secured to desk.
☐ Open or unlocked windows.
☐ Unsecured Motor Vehicle.
☐ Unsecured Bicycle.
☐ Other: _____

LOCATION: _____ OFFICER: _____

ONE COPY RETAINED FOR PATROL RECORDS. NOTICE NOT A SANCTION.

N° 4995

Blotter" to the student newspaper that lets the community know the extent of the crime problem that week and the areas affected.

Finally, in response to increasing bicycle thefts, a "Bicycle Compound" was allocated in the center of the campus and is monitored by students. This proved to be very popular and substantially reduced bicycle thefts.

Many campus security departments such as at Yale, Wayne State, University of Pennsylvania, and the University of California have installed prominently marked emergency telephone call boxes at strategic locations on campus, which insures immediate communication and response. The sight of these emergency telephones is reassuring to the community and appreciated as evidenced by the relatively few annoyance calls received.

The University of Houston developed a comic book called *The Adventures of Cougar Cop* (the University mascot) depicting the "courageous cougar cop in cacophonous collision with catastrophic crime!" The comic book skillfully depicts the qualifications, selection, screening, and training of Cougar Cop as he becomes a member of the University Police Department, and the booklet emphasizes the service and preventive aspects of the department's functions. The booklet ends with the following "Statement of Purpose,"* written by its former director, Joseph P. Kimble, typifying what campus security is all about:

> University Security recognizes a responsibility to state its organizational purpose. Why do we exist? We exist to serve and protect a social and academic environment that sustains and encourages moral and intellectual growth. We facilitate this goal by being as *proactive* as possible in anticipating and preventing unsafe conditions and protecting individuals from the imprudent or illegal acts of others.
>
> To do this we seek out educated, motivated men and women and train them to function as university police officers. Their commitment (and the commitment of support staff) is to improve the quality of life on our campus. Conflict and resolution is their primary goal, to be realized through mutual cooperation and understanding, or when necessary, through imposition of administrative or legal sanctions. Inherent in the application of sanctions is that such actions shall be ethical, constitutional, and humanistic.
>
> Our operational philosophy of "peace keeping" is a social service that can exist only when it has the support and involvement of the total community. We are committed to the dissolution of prejudice and stereotypes and dedicated to the development of a constructive partnership with *all* segments of the University community.

---

*Courtesy of the University of Houston Police Department and Joseph P. Kimble, Campus Security Manager, DeAnza College, Cupertino, California.

SECTION II.
STRUCTURE AND
OPERATION
OF THE CAMPUS
SECURITY DEPARTMENT

Chapter 5

THE CAMPUS SECURITY DIRECTOR

The director or head of the department is probably the most important ingredient in formulating a successful security program. He or she must be, above all, a good administrator, possess imagination, intelligence, patience, determination, and be tuned in to life on a campus.

The trend today is no longer to hire the retiring local law enforcement officer, FBI agent, or military retiree but to look for the younger security professional who has displayed qualifications of leadership and administrative ability. One of the qualifications at most institutions is that the head of the department have at least a bachelor's degree, preferably in police science and administration. Campus administrators have recognized that younger, college-educated security administrators usually relate better to students and the campus in general. They also feel that, since the director is working in an academic environment where education is the product, he should have a degree and a level of intelligence on a par with those he will be serving.

LOCATING A QUALIFIED DIRECTOR

A good approach for the college president looking for a new security head is to organize a search committee made up of responsible members of the administration, staff, faculty, student groups, and possibly others. This committee's search should be exhaustive and will take considerable time.

Hiring from Other Institutions

The first place the committee should look is at progressive, efficient campus security departments. Many colleges and universities have been able to hire outstanding, proven campus security administrators from other institutions.

Individuals who are second or third in command in professional and efficiently run campus departments are another fertile field for recruiting. These subordinate security administrators are usually young, well-qualified, career-minded professionals in their field who will welcome the opportunity to head their own departments. At the University of Connecticut, for example, two young aides to former Director of Public Safety David P. Driscoll were hired to head departments at Northeastern University and the University of Maryland, Baltimore County. Driscoll has an excellent philosophy regarding losing his assistants. He observes, "If you have an efficient department and train high-caliber, ambitious young professionals to work for you, this is bound to happen."

Advertising Job Opportunities

The question often arises as to where to advertise for a head of campus security. The best approach is probably to contact someone who knows many people in the campus field and has a general knowledge of the proficiency of many departments and their administrators.

Another source is the International Association of Campus Law Enforcement Administrators. An announcement in the association's *Campus Law Enforcement Journal* might produce results. Communications should be addressed to James L. McGovern, Executive Secretary, IACLEA, Post Office Box 98127, Atlanta, Georgia 30359.

Campus administrators should be careful about advertising in too many police or security publications unless they are willing to wade through hundreds of résumés. Unfortunately, many retiring law enforcement officers (and some who are not ready to retire) have very little knowledge about campus security and look upon it as a relatively easy job in a pleasant, serene, often scenic environment. Nothing could be further from the truth! Many former law enforcement administrators who have entered the campus field say, "I didn't know it would be like this. I have never worked so hard in my life!"

Choosing the Candidates

After reviewing résumés the search committee should narrow the applicants down to the few candidates in whom they are really interested. The next step should be a discreet preliminary inquiry regarding the candidate and his capabilities.

This inquiry can usually be accomplished by telephone on a confidential personal basis through other campus security administrators if the applicant is already in the field. Otherwise, it should be made with local individuals who know the applicant. Sometimes this inquiry can be conducted by a third disinterested party without divulging the interest of the hiring institution.

If the present security director is retiring, he should be on the search committee. He will normally prove invaluable in furnishing information and making this preliminary check.

Interviews with Applicants

The next step after the applicants are narrowed down to a few is to determine their availability and interview each of them. One method is to invite the candidate to visit the campus and be interviewed by the entire committee—preferably, after he or she has toured the campus and has some idea of the existing security program.

Another technique is to visit the applicant and observe his present operations. This provides an overview of his present department and his accomplishments as its chief administrator. Most applicants inform their superiors of their interest in a new position, and contacts with these superiors can be another means of evaluating the candidate's potential.

Naturally, it is not practical for the entire committee to make this visit, but two or three representatives can be selected and then report to the entire committee. The visit should be made prior to the applicant's being invited to the campus to be interviewed by the entire committee.

Travel Expenses

The college inviting the applicant for an interview should be willing to pay travel expenses. One university invited a top-flight candidate to be interviewed but informed him he would have to pay his own travel expenses. He replied, "If that's the importance you place on the position, I have no interest."

Before paying travel expenses, however, the institution should make sure that the applicant is really available and interested in making a change. Many candidates have the attitude, "I am not really interested, but I might as well make the trip at their expense." One way of determining the applicant's sincerity is to interview him thoroughly on the telephone regarding his availability and interest in the position. Another is to find out if he has informed his superiors of the new job possibility. Still another is to determine if the applicant would be willing to pay half the travel costs, which later can be returned, particularly if he is hired.

Search committees must also be aware that well-qualified directors might also be using the old technique of applying for a new job to illustrate their worth to their superiors. Quite a few directors have used this technique to secure higher salaries and other benefits when their institutions had reason to believe they might lose them. In some cases, they had no real intention of leaving their jobs.

The Intensive Search

It has been most encouraging to see universities and colleges recognize that the security operation is a very important factor on campus and that the head of the campus department should be chosen with the same care as a college president. For example, Harvard University conducted an exhaustive search for a proper replacement for its retiring Security Officer and Chief of Police Robert Tonis. Approximately one year prior to Chief Tonis's retirement, a search committee was organized consisting of deans, administrators, faculty, students, and others. This committee concentrated on searching out top security and law enforcement administrators throughout the country, particularly in the campus field. They placed advertisements not only in local newspapers but also in the *New York Times, Wall Street Journal,* and other major papers. In addition, notices of the position were carried in *The Police Chief* (published by the International Association of Chiefs of Police), *Campus Law Enforcement Journal,* and numerous other publications.

  Almost 900 individuals indicated an interest in the position. The committee carefully reviewed all résumés, sent letters of acknowledgement, and eventually conducted a series of interviews with prospects who appeared best qualified. A decision was made only after the finalists had been interviewed repeatedly and investigated thoroughly regarding their experience, ability, leadership qualities, general character, and ability to get things done and get along with people.

SALARY AND BENEFITS OF THE DIRECTOR

The salaries for capable, professional campus security administrators have increased significantly in the past few years. These increases reflect not only a recognition on the part of college administrators of the importance of having a professional security approach but also the type of well-educated, capable, career-minded individual entering the field.

  A rule of thumb in determining a director's salary is: Be competitive with other local institutions of similar size that have professional directors. A comparison can also be made with the salaries of law enforcement officials in the area. The location and size of the institution, the size of the department, the director's responsibilities, and many other factors must also be taken into consideration.

AVERAGE SALARIES

Although no salary survey has been made recently, the average salary for the head of a campus department is approximately $26,000. However, there is a considerable span in salaries, with some heads of departments (usually small watchmen operations) making as little as $12,000 a year, while a few others earn in excess of $40,000.

Salaries for security directors at community or two-year colleges with no residents are usually scaled between $17,000 and $25,000. Smaller residential colleges, particularly if they are located in rural or low-crime areas, would also follow this salary pattern. However, colleges and universities of any size, especially those in urban or high-crime areas, will probably not be able to hire a professional director for under $25,000 per year, with the average for these institutions being at least $30,000.

Fringe Benefits

Campus security directors should also enjoy the same fringe benefits, except tenure, as faculty and administrators. These usually involve retirement benefits under the Teachers Insurance and Annuity Association (TIAA) and the College Retirement Equities Fund (CREF) or a state or other retirement plan. It also involves the usual vacation, sick leave, medical and sometimes life insurance benefits. The director should be on a faculty and administrative level and never be classified as an hourly paid worker.

DUTIES OF THE DIRECTOR

Administrative Ability. The director of a campus security operation must first of all be a strong administrator who is able to work closely and harmoniously with all segments of the campus community. His main responsibility is to organize and administer an efficient security operation to meet the needs of his campus and cope with new problems when they occur.

Availability. A director should be available at all times, except possibly when he is away on vacation or seriously ill. The security department should know where he can be reached at all times. Many directors are provided with radio-equipped vehicles for their use when off duty so they can be easily located and respond to emergencies. A radio-equipped vehicle also carries the bonus of enabling the director to listen in to the radio dispatcher and learn what is transpiring on campus.

Crime Prevention. The director must be fully cognizant of crime conditions on campus, develop appropriate preventive and security techniques, and design and employ selective enforcement procedures and techniques in areas of high crime. He must be aware that prevention of crime is one of his most important functions.

Recruiting Personnel. The director will also be responsible for the recruiting and proper screening of security personnel. He will also be primarily responsible for scheduling and deploying personnel so as to realize maximum coverage and performance.

Training. The proper training of new employees and retraining of other personnel will be an important duty and should be geared to campus requirements. Appropriate files should be maintained on each employee's training and the results achieved.

Law Enforcement Liaison. The director will be responsible for effecting proper liaison with federal, state, and local law enforcement officials and agencies to insure mutual understanding and a coordinated, workable relationship. In effect, he will be his institution's sole representative on these matters.

Records and Reports. The director will be responsible for instituting and maintaining an efficient record-keeping system and compiling statistical data on crime and services performed. This should include periodic and annual statistical reports to his superior, reports that can be used to justify the budget the director will prepare.

Morale and Discipline. He will be responsible for maintaining high morale, discipline, and a businesslike, efficient operation. If allegations of misconduct are made, he should conduct an appropriate, thorough, and impartial investigation and submit a written factual report with recommendations to his superior.

Personnel Files. The director will also maintain personnel files on subordinates and prepare periodic performance ratings of his employees. He should set up and administer a fair and equitable promotion procedure.

Security Representative. Lastly, he will be the main representative of the department on campus and as such must be its chief public relations representative. This will include involving himself in campus affairs, participating on committees, making public appearances, talking with students, keeping contacts with the campus and outside media, and acting as the professional leader of security on that campus.

TITLES AND ORGANIZATION OF DEPARTMENT

Although the department's name can indicate a police or security orientation, its procedures and type of operation and personnel are more important than the name in establishing the proper image.

At present, the most widely adopted name is *department of public safety,* with its chief administrator being the *director of public safety.* This public safety concept involves responsibility for all aspects of the personal safety and well-being of those in the campus community. It usually means that the director of public safety will be responsible not only for the security force but also for fire and safety, parking, and sometimes transportation (buses, car pools, and so on). In effect, the chief administrator over each of these operations will be a subordinate answering to the director.

Figure 5-1 depicts an organizational chart for a large state university's department of public safety. This type of organization can be simplified to meet the needs of smaller institutions.

Titles of Subordinates

The titles of subordinates to the director must be tailored somewhat to the campus. Although it is relatively easy for a campus to accept a new title for the head of the department, it is sometimes difficult to change subordinates' titles and the name of the department itself. Many older administrators, faculty, and staff will continue to use the old terms.

Titles that are identified with police functions (e.g., captain, lieutenant) can be retained if that is what the campus has become accustomed to—changing them will probably achieve very little. However, as illustrated in Figure 5-1, there is a tendency to use nonpolice-type designations such as coordinator of line operations (formerly chief of police), shift commander (lieutenant), field supervisor (sergeant), investigator (detective), public safety officer (police officer).

The range of titles should be in direct proportion to the size of the department. Some departments of only ten officers have a full range of titles—chief, deputy chief, captain, lieutenant, sergeant, and police officer. A small department like this would be better served by the simple structure of director, shift supervisor, security officer, and possibly investigator.

SECURITY'S PLACE IN THE
CAMPUS ADMINISTRATION

To whom should the department and its director answer in the campus administrative structure? In the past (and unfortunately, on a few campuses at present) the security department has traditionally answered to the head of buildings and grounds

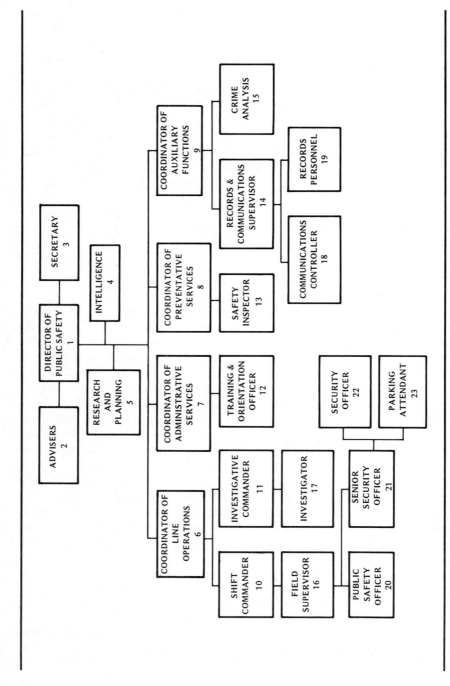

Figure 5-1. Organization by functions of department of public safety. Courtesy of University of Connecticut Department of Public Safety, Storrs, Connecticut.

Key for Figure 5-1.

1. DIRECTOR OF PUBLIC SAFETY—Provides overall administrative control for public safety operation.
2. ADVISORS—Public information; technical information; legal information.
3. SECRETARY—Correspondence; appointments and coordination; maintains records and files.
4. INTELLIGENCE—Gathers and maintains intelligence information.
5. RESEARCH AND PLANNING—Reviews department policy and procedure; studies feasibility of innovative police equipment; recommends measures to improve operation of the department.
6. COORDINATOR OF LINE OPERATIONS—Primary police functions; directs all phases of police security, parking shift assignments, criminal investigations, criminal reports, complaint assignments.
7. COORDINATOR OF ADMINISTRATIVE SERVICES—Budgeting; accounting; purchasing; recruiting and training; inspectional services; personnel management; citizen complaints; secretary of awards committee.
8. COORDINATOR OF PREVENTATIVE SERVICES—Planning of fire, safety and alarm systems; fire safety inspection of university facilities; initiates corrective action for violations; apprehends perpetrators.
9. COORDINATOR OF AUXILIARY FUNCTIONS—Communications operations; records operations; equipment and supply acquisition; equipment maintenance; physical plant maintenance; forms and procedures control; departmental property control; recovered property control.
10. SHIFT COMMANDER—Responsible for the line operation during tour of duty; inspection and review of all line personnel; assignment of duties; execution and maintenance of university safety program; security; parking.
11. INVESTIGATIVE COMMANDER—Responsible for the investigations function; inspection and review of investigation section; personnel; assigns cases; collects evidence; conducts investigations; recovers stolen property; reviews reports; interviews and interrogates; arrests perpetrators.
12. TRAINING AND ORIENTATION OFFICER—Formulate and implement training courses; evaluate, recommend and research training needs; public relations—speaking engagements; personnel orientation; education of personnel; testing development and implementation.
13. SAFETY INSPECTOR—Testing of equipment; maintenance of university facilities; maintenance of inspection system; initiates corrective action for violations.
14. RECORDS AND COMMUNICATIONS SUPERVISOR—Supervises records personnel; trains records personnel, inspection, control and evaluation of departmental records system; annual report editor; supervision of communications and personnel.
15. CRIME ANALYSIS—Analyzes crime trends; maintains and updates maps and charts; reviews offenses and recommends corrective, preventative actions.
16. FIELD SUPERVISOR—Directs, supervises and coordinates personnel; trains and inspects personnel; proceeds to all serious assigned runs for command and inspection purposes; performs all duties of public safety officer.
17. INVESTIGATOR—Arrests perpetrators, recovers stolen property; recommends security and safety measures; interviews and interrogates; gathers and evaluates evidence; prepares reports.
18. COMMUNICATIONS CONTROLLER—Receives, routes and dispatches messages; maintains accurate status of field units; performs communications and clerical tasks.
19. RECORDS PERSONNEL—Copying; typing; filing; file retrieval; file inspection; telephone service; walk-in information service.

20. PUBLIC SAFETY OFFICER—Patrol functions; arrests criminal offenders; conducts preliminary investigations; gathers and evaluates evidence; prepares written reports; enforcement of criminal and traffic laws.
21. SENIOR SECURITY OFFICER—Patrols parking areas and facilities; supervision of parking personnel; reports violations.
22. SECURITY OFFICER—Patrols and inspects parking areas; assists all university persons and guests; reports violations.
23. PARKING ATTENDANT—Provides security of parking lots; assists with parking; reports violations.

Key to Figure 5-1 (continued)

or to the physical plant director. This set-up can result in security officers being regarded the same as other maintenance and custodial employees, sharing lockers with them, utilizing time cards, and taking on the image of the service employees.

Since the average head of plant is concerned mainly with buildings, grounds, and university property, the operations usually remain at a watchman-guard level that is unable to cope with people problems. When this situation prevails, security personnel are often told not to have anything to do with students.

The head of a campus security department answering to the physical plant director might be compared to the chief of police in a municipality answering to the head of the public works department.

Another danger in answering to the head of the plant is that the security operation then rarely has its own budget or separate identity. It is merely another part of the plant operation, similar to the painters, custodians, and carpenters. In the past security was often in the same union as these service personnel, which created major problems when a strike occurred. Certainly its stature on campus was diminished, and consequently, confidence and respect from the community were often lacking.

The head of a campus security department should answer to someone high enough in the university or college structure so that he will have some backing and administrative clout. The title of this individual is not as important as his interest in security, ability to get along with and back the director, and willingness to make decisions and accept responsibility for policy making.

It is important to assess the individual occupying a position before deciding that security should answer to that position. On one campus where a security consultant was called in, for example, the guard force supposedly answered to the executive vice president. However, the vice president had delegated responsibility completely to the director of the physical plant. To compound the problem even more, a new president had just started his duties on campus, and it was evident that the former executive vice president no longer possessed much authority and in fact might be leaving soon.

To continue to have security answer to this executive vice president would result in its remaining exactly where it was, and the consultant's report and suggestions would never be implemented. Therefore, the consultant recommended that the security force answer to a younger, enthusiastic, ambitious vice president of student affairs who had been hired by the new president. The change was made, and security prospered under the new, interested administrator.

In certain rather unusual cases, the head of security may be very happy answering to the physical plant director—if his superior is deeply interested in the department, lets the director accept responsibility for its management, and has sufficient power in the university to get things done.

In most cases, however, the head of campus security should answer to a vice president of administration or someone on a vice-presidential level who also administers other auxiliary services.

COLLEGE OF THE SEQUOIAS

LIBRARY

COLLEGE OF THE SEQUOIAS
LIBRARY

Chapter 6

SELECTING AND TRAINING SECURITY OFFICERS

The effectiveness of any campus security program will depend largely on the security personnel who have the responsibility of carrying out its day-to-day functions. The selection, screening, and training of these employees are major responsibilities of the campus security director.

The term *security officer* will be used here, although the same personnel may also be called public safety officers, police officers, patrolmen, or other similar designations. I hope, however, that the terms *guard* or *watchman* are not used, because they are usually associated with a low-level, contracted, or unprofessional approach emphasizing protection of property.

QUALIFICATIONS

Surprisingly, many campuses have no written or formalized qualifications for security officers. Some of these campuses also lack any screening process. Coupled with the lack of qualifications, this results in the hiring of some security officers who are not only incompetent but are "troublemakers" as well.

For example, at one large university the chief answered to the director of the physical plant, who was a police buff, a strict disciplinarian, and actually ran the department. The chief was largely a figurehead; all hiring and decision making were performed by the director of the physical plant, who based his hiring almost entirely on physical appearance and personality. On several occasions this director had driven into a gas station, been impressed by the attendant's appearance and demeanor, and hired him as a security officer without regard to his qualifications or background. After this director's retirement, the chief had to contend with a group of inefficient, disgruntled, and unmanageable individuals, some of whom were of questionable honesty.

Although federal and state laws are somewhat restrictive in regard to qualifications that may be set, minimum standards should be established to insure that qualified personnel are hired. Qualifications for the security officer position should be clearly defined and printed for distribution to prospective applicants. This material should also briefly describe the responsibilities of the position, salary, and fringe benefits.

Maturity

Some degree of maturity should be required so that security officers are not younger than most students. On the other hand, caution should be used in hiring older personnel who may be physically unable to carry out their duties and may also be unmotivated or unable to relate to students and a campus community. The ideal age limits for a new security officer today would be about 24–35 years, but certainly exceptions can be made in the case of obviously well-qualified candidates.

Education and Work Experience

A higher caliber individual can be acquired by specifying a combination of education and work experience. Officers should have at least a high school education. Additional work experience of five years could be required to attain the desired age. Any years of schooling beyond high school could be applied to the work experience.

Many college and university security departments now require at least an associate degree (preferably in criminal justice or law enforcement), and some require a bachelor's degree. A large number also require that their officers be enrolled in degree programs.

These higher educational requirements make a great deal of sense; they contribute to younger security officers being hired and also insure intelligent personnel who will better relate to all segments of the campus community. Campus security officers serve an intelligent, well-educated population, and they should also be well-educated and intelligent in order to become part of this community.

Physical Standards

Not too many years ago, law enforcement agencies required minimum height standards that ruled out many well-qualified officers. Height is relatively unimportant, but weight must be considered. Obesity has too long been a characteristic (depicted in cartoons, movies, and television) of the police officer and guard. Height and weight qualifications should be in conformance with medical charts. In addition, applicants should be in good physical condition and be required to pass a thorough medical examination given by the hiring institution.

Experience in Related Fields

Prior experience in security or law enforcement is usually desirable but does not need to be a qualification. Many campus security administrators prefer to hire candidates without experience so they can train and indoctrinate them in the proper procedures and duties they will be responsible for handling.

Care should be exercised in hiring retired police officers to insure that they are flexible enough to adopt new methods, procedures, and viewpoints. Sometimes retired law enforcement officers are inclined to have "tunnel vision" and resist change. They may fail to communicate with the community because they project an authoritarian image rather than one of service and courtesy. A *good* retired law enforcement officer, however, is a distinct asset to any campus department — not only because he is experienced but also because he knows how to handle and work with people, is used to working long and irregular hours, and follows orders.

A military background, particularly as a member of the military police or similar unit, is often desirable. Some very fine young but mature campus officers, interested in furthering their career and education, have been hired immediately after their military discharge.

Ability to Relate to Campus Community

In setting out qualifications for applicants, it should also be made clear that they must be of good character, free of criminal convictions, and that they will be screened thoroughly prior to being hired.

The most important qualification in an applicant desiring a campus security position is the ability to relate to students, faculty, and staff and to blend with the campus atmosphere.

RECRUITING

The best recruiting efforts are usually made by security personnel who interest relatives and friends in applying for positions. This method has the advantage because applicants are known personally and recommended by a member of the department who can furnish background information on them. Experience has shown that in a professionally oriented and efficient department, good personnel will recruit equally competent individuals.

Selective advertising can also be employed, as well as personal contacts with other members of law enforcement, campus, and other security fields. Advertisements, however, can generate hundreds of replies, most of them unqualified. A blind ad is recommended if placed in a local newspaper.

If the institution has a criminal justice or law enforcement program, this should prove a most fertile field for recruiting. These programs are educating many young law enforcement and private security officers who may be interested in making a change. Military discharge depots are also a good source of personnel.

Recruiting of qualified personnel was formerly a rather difficult problem, but the difficulty has been greatly alleviated by the present employment situation, particularly for young people, and by the fact that campus security has progressed to the point where it attracts better educated and qualified applicants.

SELECTION AND SCREENING

The most important function in any security or law enforcement organization is the proper selection and careful screening of personnel.

The director of the security operation should make the final decision in regard to who is employed under him. It is a mistake for campus personnel departments to select and assign personnel to a campus security department with little or no input from the head of the department. In some cases the heads of these security departments share the blame for depending entirely on personnel people to recruit, screen, and select security personnel, then criticizing them for hiring incompetent and unqualified individuals.

Security personnel are not like any other employees of the institution. They must be depended upon not only to exercise the best of judgment, often under pressure, but they must be absolutely honest and possess good moral character. They will usually have master keys to all areas, will be exposed to all sorts of situations and temptations, and will in effect be largely responsible for the department's image on campus.

Application Form and Interview

The first step in the selection process should be an exhaustive interview by the director based on a *detailed* application form filled out by the applicant. This form should list the applicant's history of education, employment, addresses, and similar background information. In reviewing this application form and during the subsequent background investigation, the director should make sure the applicant's entire adult life is accounted for. For example, if the applicant shows an unexplained break in employment, he should be asked what he was doing during this period. The application should include a signed statement by the applicant authorizing the release and checking of records pertaining to him.

Although laws have placed some restrictions on divulging arrest records, either the application form or interview must determine whether the applicant has ever been convicted of a crime (other than minor motor vehicle violations). If he has been convicted, detailed information should be acquired.

Written Tests

If the director feels, as a result of this initial interview, that the applicant has good potential, he should be given a written test. This test should be designed to measure the individual's IQ, and particularly, to determine whether he can express himself well enough in writing to compose a coherent, legible report employing correct spelling and grammar. Report writing is one of the major weaknesses of law enforcement and security officers, which is one of the main reasons for the written test with at least one or two questions requiring applicants to express themselves.

Surprisingly, few campus security departments avail themselves of the excellent testing facilities that exist on their campuses. Security officers, particularly those who will carry weapons, should be exposed to some psychological testing to determine their attitudes, stability, and fitness. Only rarely has this been done, however, even though most institutions have the capability to perform the testing at no cost to the department.

Advisory Committees

Some campuses have security advisory committees made up of faculty members, administrators, student leaders, and others. These committees sometimes also interview the prospective applicant and report their observations and recommendations. The effectiveness of these committees in this screening process depends largely on their composition. At some institutions they have been quite effective, while at others they have occasionally recommended the hiring of individuals who were not acceptable to the director. The important point to remember is that the director will have to train and work with the new officer, and therefore the director should have the final say in the hiring decision.

Police Record Check

After the applicant has successfully passed the interview and written or other tests, he should be investigated thoroughly. The first step in this process should be to submit the applicant's fingerprints to police record bureaus covering locations where he has resided or worked. In addition, the prints should be submitted to the state's central record-keeping facility, which would also submit them to the FBI.

Severe restrictions have been placed on police record bureaus regarding the divulging of arrest records, particularly to private security departments. Probably one of the best reasons for a campus department to have police authority is that it will be possible for them to legally submit the applicant's fingerprints for a complete check of local, state, and FBI records.

Not every applicant who has been convicted of a crime should be automatically disqualified, however. For example, an officer in the Yale University Police Department had been hired at a time when very little screening was done of security personal and no record check made. When a new policy was instituted requiring fingerprints of all security personnel to be submitted for a complete check, the officer went to his superior and admitted that, in his youth, he had stolen automobiles and engaged in similar acts that resulted in his serving a term in a reformatory. After his release, however, and particularly since he had married and had children, he had been in no difficulty. The officer was assured that he would not be fired and that his honesty was appreciated. He proved to be one of the most loyal and hard-working officers in the department.

Convictions for morals offenses, however, or for repeated and recent intoxication, thefts, drug-related crimes, and other convictions showing lack of character and instability should be reasons for disqualification.

Background Investigation

The final step in the screening process is a complete and detailed background investigation. In many cases, particularly in private industry, this so-called personnel inquiry is made by the personnel department, usually by means of form letters or telephone calls. This type of investigation is usually not effective, because in today's climate employers and individuals are reluctant to furnish derogatory information in writing or over the telephone. Many companies have a policy of giving the dates of the former employee's employment and nothing more.

There is an old saying, "The only way to get something done right is to do it yourself." This idea can certainly be applied to the screening of applicants for security positions. A trained investigator (in small departments this may be the director himself) should perform this background inquiry by personally interviewing neighbors, references, past employers, supervisors, former fellow workers, and others acquainted with the applicant's ability, personality, character, and habits. Education, credit, and possibly other records should also be checked. The inquiry should cover the applicant's entire adult life and should be performed in person.

Home Visit

A visit to the applicant's home may also be beneficial. This visit reveals not only home conditions and family life but also provides an opportunity to meet and talk to the applicant's spouse. In this talk the irregular hours (nights, holidays, weekends, and so forth) required of a security officer should be described, as well as other phases of the position that impose definite hardships on family life. Many good officers have left security or police work because their wives could not adjust to rotating shifts and a way of life unlike that of any other profession. Therefore, it is important to talk these matters over with the applicant's spouse before making the final decision regarding employment.

The need for thorough screening of security personnel prior to hiring cannot be overemphasized. It is better to work with fewer personnel than to hire officers quickly and regret it later when they prove to be incompetent or worse. It is usually much easier to hire than to fire, particularly when civil service or unions are involved.

SALARIES

To insure the hiring and, particularly, the retaining of qualified personnel, salaries and fringe benefits must be attractive.

The general rule to follow is that these salaries must be competitive with other campus and private security operations in the area and also competitive with local law enforcement. Campus security administrators can use the tactic of comparing their pay scale to other security and police salaries in the area to convince their superiors that salaries need to be raised in order to hire and retain qualified individuals.

Trends in Pay Levels

Describing average salaries for campus security personnel is difficult because no extensive salary studies have been made. A few years ago, however, I conducted a study during a series of campus security workshops in California, Georgia, Ohio, Illinois, Colorado, and Texas. Based on the results of these workshop surveys, as well as frequent contacts with campus security departments throughout the United States and Canada, certain rather clear salary trends appeared.

First, salaries apparently are somewhat governed by the geographic location of the institution. In the South, Midwest, and northern New England, salaries are considerably lower than elsewhere. The highest salaries appear on the West Coast, parts of the Northeast, and in the more urban and large state universities of Illinois, Wisconsin, Minnesota, and Ohio.

Another salary trend indicates that, in most circumstances, the larger the university or college, the higher the salary. Occasionally, however, a relatively small college pays excellent salaries. Usually this situation prevails because of the recognition and concern for security on the part of the particular college president or other top administrators. It may also result from campus community pressures, sometimes as the result of a previously low-paid and low-level operation coupled with a series of serious incidents.

Still another trend is that salaries tend to increase when there is a need for a progressive, efficient security operation because of the location of the institution in a high-crime area.

It is encouraging that during a time of austerity on practically all campuses, security salaries and other budgetary considerations have increased or have not been affected by cutbacks as much as other campus departments. This fact reflects the growing recognition on the part of administration of the need for a qualified, efficient security operation.

Average Salaries for Campus Security Positions

Director of Security, Director of Public Safety. Salaries for qualified professional directors of campus security range from a low of $15,000 per year at two-year nonresidential and smaller institutions to over $40,000 at large universities. The average salary for a director would be approximately $26,000 a year, with exactly the same fringe benefits offered to faculty and administrators.

Secondary Supervision. It is difficult to report any average salary figures for secondary supervisors because their number and duties vary with the size and composition of each department. However, salaries should be fairly adjusted between those paid to officers and to the head of the department and should be set to reflect the degree of supervisory responsibility the position entails.

Security, Public Safety, or Police Officers. Salaries for officers vary greatly from institution to institution. Some are paid by the hour, while others are salaried and paid on the same bimonthly or monthly schedule as faculty and administrators. If possible, all security personnel including officers should be paid on a salary schedule rather than on an hourly basis. This places security personnel in a different category than other hourly service personnel such as kitchen workers, painters, and custodians.

If possible, these salaried personnel should be afforded the same fringe benefits as faculty, staff, and administrators, including vacation and sick leave, insurance, hospital, and medical benefits and retirement plans.

Unions. One of the reasons why unions have been successful in organizing campus service and security employees is that administrators never gave them the recognition, salaries, and benefits afforded faculty, administrators, and staff. Officers in the Yale University Police Department, for example, are salaried employees who receive the same attractive benefits as faculty and others. Consequently, although service personnel were unionized, the University police officers were not interested because their salaries and benefits were superior to those given union employees. There was also a feeling of pride in not being classified as hourly paid custodians or similar service personnel.

The benefits of a nonunionized security operation become most apparent during a strike, when security is urgently needed to keep the institution running on an even keel. Certainly a campus security officer can handle striking employees he knows personally more effectively than can outside law enforcement officers or contracted personnel.

Basic Salary and Overtime. Although officers' salaries vary greatly from a low of $10,000 per year to over $20,000, an average basic salary would start at approximately $14,000 per year and increase in steps over a three-year period to $17,000.

In addition to basic salary, campus officers are frequently utilized at overtime pay to handle the multitude of sports, social, and other events on campus. This overtime work, plus additional salary for night differential pay, can result in considerable extra compensation.

Fringe Benefits

One of the major weaknesses in the private security sector has been a tendency to regard guards or security officers as "second-class citizens" as far as fringe benefits are concerned. These benefits, particularly in regard to retirement, have lagged far behind those afforded employees on an administrative level and sometimes even staff and clerical positions.

The lack of fringe benefits is not as prevalent in the campus field and is constantly improving. If a campus security operation is to be regarded as professional, it must also be afforded exactly the same benefits in regard to vacation, sick leave, medical plans, and similar fringe benefits as administrators, faculty, and staff. Naturally, if a union is involved these benefits will depend on the existing union contract and may or may not be in conformance with other positions in the institution.

All personnel should be afforded the opportunity to enroll in The Teachers Insurance and Annuity Association (TIAA) and College Retirement Equities Fund (CREF), which is the retirement plan offered by the majority of educational institutions. Some institutions offer this plan to their director and higher echelon supervisor but not security officers. However, even this retirement plan is geared for faculty and administrators because it does not consider that the duties of a police or security officer are different from any other campus employee. They involve irregular shifts and hours, working under stress, and at times, hazardous conditions, critical decision making, and they especially require good physical condition and alertness.

Municipal police departments have recognized the demands of police duties and that the police officer's job calls for a younger man or woman. Therefore, for many years retirement eligibility has been based on 20 or 25 years of service rather than a certain age. Inasmuch as most police officers start their employment at an early age, they are able to retire while still in their 40s or early 50s. Even the FBI now has a mandatory 55-year retirement age for its special agents.

Colleges and universities will eventually have to provide similar early-age retirement plans for their police and security officers. For example, retirement after 25 years of service with continued employment after 25 years contingent upon health and ability to perform might be appropriate. This type of early retirement would also be attractive to applicants resulting in more applying and a better selection of well-qualified candidates. It also should result in less turnover while, at the same time, increasing the opportunities for advancement.

Increases and Promotion

Salary increments should be based on performance and not given simply because the officer has put in enough time to reach the next salary level. Each officer should receive periodic efficiency reports that evaluate his overall performance and furnish the basis for salary increases and promotion.

Some departments that require college degrees or enrollment in a degree program schedule salaries to increase as educational credits and degrees are achieved.

The saying, "You get what you pay for," can certainly be applied to security officers and other security department personnel. Qualified, motivated, and efficient personnel must be paid a competitive and decent salary if they are to be hired and retained.

TRAINING

Training has always been one of the major considerations for a campus department. Formerly, campus departments depended largely on a friendly chief of police who would allow campus officers to sit in on his department's recruit and in-service classes. The only training provided on most campuses was on-the-job training in which the new officer would break in with an experienced officer.

Weaknesses of Outside Police Training

Training campus officers in a municipal law enforcement training school has its weaknesses. In the first place, they often receive training in some matters they have absolutely no use for. Another hazard is that at times they are inclined to adopt a police philosophy that is not always acceptable to a campus community. In other words, too much emphasis may be placed on arrest, use of weapons, defensive tactics, and police procedures. Young police recruits sometimes have a glamorized image of their duties, fostered by television and movies, which has to be changed during training—particularly for the campus officer. In some cases they are inclined to judge their performance on how many busts they make rather than how many crimes they prevent and services they provide.

The final weakness of having campus officers attend outside police training sessions is that the campus may lose its new officer at graduation time. This loss occurs when the new officer is placed in a class with recruits from outside departments and police instructors from law enforcement agencies. If the recruit does well in the school, he may be "persuaded" to join an outside department—and the campus loses not only the officer but also the cost of the training.

Planning In-House Training

One of the major responsibilities of any campus security director is to set up and administer a training program tailored to the needs and operations of the department and campus. This should be fundamentally an in-house training program that follows a regular schedule and carefully formulated curriculum. Too many training programs are thrown together because somebody has suggested the need for training. At times the subject matter of these programs is not well thought out but depends too much on "who can we get to talk?"

Larger departments should designate one individual as the training officer who, in addition to other duties, will assume the responsibility for administering the training program.

Some state systems that encompass many universities and colleges have established statewide coordinators of security working out of a central office. One of the prime responsibilities of these coordinators is to set up a uniform training program for all campus officers, involving not only recruiting but also in-service training sessions. This training is usually provided in area schools, thereby reducing the need and expense for officers traveling or staying overnight away from home. The State University of New York and the University of Texas systems provide good examples of such uniform security training programs under a coordinator.

Training Subjects to Be Covered

A typical in-house training program for new officers should cover many of the same subjects as any law enforcement training session for police officers. However, it must also prepare the campus officers to work in and become a part of the educational environment of a college or university.

Initial Training. At the outset the new officers should be made to feel that they are an important part of the community they serve. At the opening session they might be greeted, for example, by the president or a vice president to whom the security department answers. A series of relatively short presentations should follow in which administrators and staff, especially those in student affairs, give some history of the college and its activities.

These individuals should describe their areas of responsibility, security problems encountered, and how they will work with and depend on the security officer. Among those meeting with new recruits should be various deans, the directors of athletics, buildings and grounds, health services, dining halls, housing, student union, and other departments. Student government leaders may discuss the problems bothering students. Naturally, the director of security should also figure prominently in these early sessions in order to provide some history of the department and what will be expected of the new personnel.

During the initial stages of training, recruits should be given a tour of the campus, preferably by a student guide, and furnished with maps and literature regarding past and present campus life and activities. All of this early training will not only assist in acclimating the recruits to the campus and its environment but also in making these new officers feel welcome and an integral part of campus life. The training should be designed to provide recruits with some insight regarding the structure of the campus, to enable them to meet the principals that administer it, to learn how a campus operates, and to understand why their position is somewhat different from local law enforcement or other fields of private security.

Departmental Rules. Considerable training should be provided in departmental rules, regulations, and procedures. A manual of these rules and procedures can be used to advantage here and should be considered an important and continuing training tool for any department. It should be kept up to date, and officers should be accountable for knowing its contents. This manual can be supplemented by the director's issuing periodic written directives and bulletins that should be read and signed by all personnel.

Report Writing. Report writing should be emphasized, with actual cases involving role playing to test the trainee's ability to report factually and accurately. Because report writing has long been a major weakness among police and private security officers, considerable time should be allotted to this subject. Supervisors should continue this training later by closely reviewing and, where necessary, correcting officers' reports.

Image. Sensitive areas such as public relations and other subjects that tend to create a better image of the officer should be stressed. Most educational institutions have faculty members and others well qualified to teach these subjects.

Firearms Safety. If personnel are to be armed, the importance of an effective firearms program cannot be overstressed. Firearm safety should be a very thorough training program given by an accredited firearms instructor. It should involve qualifying on the practical pistol course and continued training at regular intervals. This training should stress the safety aspects and, particularly, *when* the weapon should be drawn and used. The firearms issue, a most delicate one on most campuses, will be treated in detail in Chapter 9.

Criminal Law. Conventional police-type training subjects must also be taught, particularly if personnel have police authority such as power of arrest. An officer must be conversant with the criminal statutes under which he operates. In fact, one jurist has commented that the security officer "is bound to know the law." Therefore, courses should be included in criminal statutes, laws of arrest, use of force, search and seizure, preservation of evidence, and so forth. Training should be provided to insure that an officer will know his limitations and responsibilities as well as what his authority entails.

Many of these subjects can be taught by the department training officer, other members of the department, or faculty members. However, it is usually necessary and often desirable to bring in selected outside law enforcement training officers to handle some of these subjects. The legal counsel for the university may also be asked to discuss some of the legal ramifications entailed in being a security officer. Institutions having criminal justice or law enforcement programs should involve members of that faculty in the training program.

Continuous Training

The fact that training is an ongoing pursuit that must be continuous to be really effective must also be recognized. It should be pursued daily by supervisors issuing instructions at shift changes and giving constructive criticism and guidance to their subordinates.

Also many excellent audio-visual programs in slides and movies are available that can be utilized. Many of these are maintained in funded libraries for the free use of law enforcement agencies.

Every campus security department should also maintain at least a small security and law enforcement library accessible to all personnel. Included in this library, or available in the squad room, should be copies of various periodicals such as the *Campus Law Enforcement Journal, Security World, The Police Chief, FBI Law Enforcement Bulletin, Law Enforcement Communications, Security Management,* and similar publications.

Chapter 7

DUTIES AND SCHEDULING

The duties of a campus officer in many respects are similar to those of a municipal police officer. They both work shifts, serve irregular hours, are on call for emergencies, patrol districts, answer calls for assistance, perform arrests, and take other police actions when necessary. However, a somewhat different philosophy and approach is involved on the part of the campus officer, who serves an educational community of which he is very much a part. Therefore, the emphasis is not on arrest but on prevention and service.

The image of the campus security department is largely formed by the manner in which officers perform their duties, including their courtesy and demeanor. Campus communities desire three qualities in their security departments:

1. Immediate availability and prompt response when called;
2. Knowledgeable, alert, and intelligent handling of problems;
3. Courtesy, friendliness, and willingness to help.

Any campus that has a resident community should provide twenty-four-hour response. In other words, a knowledgeable and alert member of the department should answer calls for assistance immediately and dispatch an officer.

On some resident campuses, security is largely nonexistent or inaccessible after midnight or at other times. On others, an outside answering service takes calls during certain periods—a procedure that is usually very ineffective. Some campuses even use antiquated means of signaling officers such as flashing red lights outside the residence halls, activated by members of the residence hall staff.

Colleges and universities that do not provide twenty-four-hour-a-day service and prompt, efficient response may be risking civil suits if residents are attacked or their personal safety jeopardized.

NUMBER OF SECURITY PERSONNEL

One of the most difficult administrative problems faced by heads of campus departments is how to arrive at the correct number of security personnel to furnish effective coverage and prompt response. Unfortunately, many campus administrators, particularly in state systems, want to fix the number of personnel by a ratio formula according to population (for example, one officer for each 2,000 students and employees). No such magic formula can be utilized to determine personnel needs.

The use of an officers-to-population ratio goes back to the early days of law enforcement when, because of a lack of statistics and other data, municipal administrators set up the ratio system to determine their police staffing. Such a formula is rarely employed today.

Factors in Determining Size

Many factors must be considered in establishing the size of a campus security department. Some of these factors are discussed in the following sections.

Location of the Campus. Is it in an urban, suburban, or rural area? Crime and security problems usually tend to increase the more urban the location.

General Layout and Composition of the Campus. A self-contained campus serviced by its own loop or other access roads is easier to protect than a campus spread along public thoroughfares, where campus buildings are sometimes interspersed with a variety of noncampus buildings and facilities.

Nature and Type of Terrain. Some colleges and universities are bordered by expansive lawns, wooded areas, lakes or ponds, freeways, or other barriers that in effect form a security buffer zone between the campus and the outside community.

Type of Campus Security Operation. Is it a low-level guard operation that must depend largely on the local police for response? Or is it a professional, self-sufficient department that only has to call for outside police assistance to handle certain emergencies?

Degree and Effectiveness of Outside Police Coverage. If the campus is located in an area in which local police coverage is inadequate or inefficient, the department will need more officers in order to be able to handle its security program and problems without outside assistance.

Age, Type, and Architecture of Buildings. Usually, the newer the buildings the easier they are to protect. For example, at one campus almost all the residence halls were large, private homes that had been converted into dormitory facilities. Students were living in about twenty of these wooden structures scattered on the perimeter of the campus. Compounding the problem was the fact that these former residences contained multiple ground floor windows, double glass doors, poor locking hardware, and were very vulnerable to fire. Naturally, this arrangement called for more coverage than if students were housed in one large, modern dormitory.

Electronic Protection Devices. Staffing needs may be reduced if certain buildings and critical areas are protected by alarms or closed-circuit television.

Quality of Supervision. The quality of supervision, as well as the scheduling and deployment of officers to insure maximum coverage, is important. Good supervision and effective scheduling and deployment of personnel will help to reduce staffing needs. For example, on several campuses two officers were assigned at all times to patrol vehicles. Although there are certain instances for which two-officer cars are necessary, in most cases they are a waste of manpower.

Data to Support Personnel Needs

The staffing requirements of any security or law enforcement department must be justified by good, solid, factual statistics depicting the rate of crime, services performed, and workload. These requirements means that the department must maintain accurate statistics and an effective record-keeping system.

Security directors often lament, "They won't give me enough officers to do the job." These directors might be asked, "What have you done to convince your supervisors of the need for additional personnel?" All too often, the head of security has merely asked for more personnel without justifying the need through statistical data and other factual information. With a combination of statistical data, logic, and just plain salesmanship, a new head of security often manages to acquire new personnel, equipment, and office space.

Departmental Budgeting

Some educational institutions still budget security coverage for each department (housing, plant, and so on) directly to that department. This procedure results in various department heads dictating security needs and usually demanding more and more personnel. In effect, the director of security has little control over the number of officers or their duties; he becomes largely a supplier of personnel.

Every campus security department should have its own budget, and the head of the department should be solely responsible for determining the number of personnel, their deployment, and scheduling. However, the director should certainly listen to the needs and security problems of other campus administrators in their areas. If a department needs special coverage that cannot be furnished within the normal budgetary limits of the security department, then a charge-off of the particular event (social, athletic, and so on) can be made.

SCHEDULING AND DEPLOYMENT

Scheduling of personnel is a difficult task for every security and law enforcement department, principally because security is the only operation on most campuses that must be staffed and functioning twenty-four hours a day, every day of the year.

Twenty-Four-Hour Coverage of One Post

Many campus administrators and faculty members tend to think that three-shift, twenty-four-hour-a-day coverage of one post requires the services of only three officers. They do not consider the fact that an officer has two days off each week, plus vacation, sick leave, and holidays. The absolute minimum number of officers needed to cover one post or district twenty-four hours a day is five, and even then some problems can arise in maintaining constant coverage, particularly in small departments. The larger the department, the more flexibility is enjoyed in scheduling. A department of ten to fifteen officers or less has few resources to take up the slack if several officers are off duty at the same time. In a very small department, the number of officers needed to provide around-the-clock coverage for one district or post would be closer to six.

Coverage during Training

One of the major dilemmas encountered in training personnel is how to provide adequate training while still maintaining adequate security coverage. One department has even hired contract guards to maintain at least some coverage while a number of regular officers were engaged in training sessions. (This approach does have the advantage that the campus community usually recognizes how much better their own personnel are than those furnished by a contract service.)

The problem of providing coverage while officers are in training sessions has no easy answer. The usual solutions are to have officers cover additional districts and to schedule training for less busy times during summer and other vacation periods.

Scheduling and Morale

Scheduling has important effects on department morale. One of the main aspects that bothers personnel and can result in the greatest number of gripes is inequitable scheduling, so that some personnel feel they are being discriminated against. Although some of these grievances are imaginary and unfounded, some are legitimate and certainly bad for morale.

One area in which scheduling abuses can occur is in off-duty assignments, which usually involve overtime pay. Most campuses have many of these assignments such as dances and other social events, rock concerts, athletic contests, meetings, and conferences. On some campuses the supervisor gives these jobs to his favorites or to senior officers more frequently than to others, and/or selects the easier assignments for them. (For example, working a rock concert is more demanding than an alumni luncheon.)

One way to insure fairness is to keep a log of these assignments so that all personnel have the opportunity to work them and earn approximately the same amount. In other words, when a request for off-duty service is received, the next off-duty officer in line is offered the opportunity to work it. If the officer declines, the log would reflect this fact as well as the amount he would have earned. The next officer in line would then be offered the assignment.

Shift Scheduling

Most campus departments have a 12:00 midnight to 8:00 A.M. shift, an 8:00 A.M. to 4:00 P.M. shift, and a 4:00 P.M. to 12:00 midnight shift (or approximately these hours). Many departments find it easier and better for morale to schedule these shifts so that the same number of personnel and the same number of posts or districts will be covered on each shift.

The problem with this type of scheduling is that at times it deploys too many personnel on certain shifts, while during other periods insufficient personnel are deployed. For example, the busiest period and the hours needing most coverage on most campuses are from approximately 8:00 P.M. to 2:00 A.M. Sometimes this difficulty can be overcome by scheduling an additional 6:00 P.M. to 2:00 A.M. shift and reducing the other shifts accordingly.

Poor Scheduling Practices

Undefined Assignments. One scheduling and deployment practice that should be avoided is the failure to establish clearly defined districts or posts to which officers are assigned. On several campuses officers merely report to work and are loosely assigned to certain areas with no close check on where they patrol or spend their time. This lack of definition leads to officers congregating together to talk or drink coffee or gravitating to "where the action is."

Districts and posts should be clearly described in the manual and by means of a graphic display (map or chart) so that each officer will know exactly his district or post. Strict rules should be enforced so that no officer leaves his district or post unless so directed or approved by the supervisor. The only exception would be during an emergency situation such as when the officer is pursuing a suspect; even then, the supervisor should be informed and the information should be made part of the record.

Minimum Staffing Requirements. Another weakness in scheduling may occur when a union has imposed minimum staffing requirements so that each shift must be staffed to cover all districts and posts. This weakness results in off-duty officers having to work extra shifts on overtime pay scales when their fellow officers are sick or absent for other reasons. Abuses of sick-leave privileges occur as officers learn to design an unpublicized plan of their own so that all personnel enjoy these overtime benefits. This "schedule" calls for officers to take sick leave on certain days so that others will be assigned extra overtime duty. No such inflexible staffing requirements should ever be entered into with a union or otherwise become a part of the security operation.

Two-Officer Patrols. Another staffing problem involves two-officer patrols. Unions and the officers themselves have sometimes argued successfully that they should always patrol in pairs to insure the safety of personnel. This concept probably evolved from large, urban police departments where the personal safety of officers in high-crime areas was in jeopardy. However, this safety aspect is not true on most campuses. Although isolated instances may justify two-officer patrols, in most cases single-officer patrols should continue to suffice. With today's excellent two-way FM radio communications, aid can be summoned immediately by any officer whose safety is threatened. Certainly, no agreement should be entered into requiring two-officer patrols at all times.

Two-officer patrols often result in the "buddy system," which can have some beneficial effects when two officers learn to work well as a team, but which more often creates disadvantages. In some departments in which the buddy system operates, cliques develop and some officers refuse to team up with certain others. When one-half of a team takes sick or other leave, the other half may also find a reason to be absent rather than work alone or with another officer. When two officers work together, one may cover while the other sleeps or otherwise "goofs off." Officers patrolling together in a car may observe very little because they are too busy talking to each other.

"Four-and-Two." Some departments have experimented with the so-called four-and-two scheduling—an officer works four days and then has two days off. This type of schedule has some merit because it automatically changes the days off each week and provides a fairer allotment of weekends and holidays off. However, it also provides two extra days off every six-week period.

Full Use of Capabilities

Scheduling and deployment of personnel should be programmed to insure full utilization of their rank, capabilities, and experience. For example, a waste of money and inefficient practice is to have the only supervisor on duty assigned to the office to take complaints, phone calls, and act as a dispatcher. These functions can be performed by regularly assigned office clerical personnel rather than supervisors or security officers. Supervisors should spend most of their time in a flexible patrol responding to nonroutine problems and exercising close supervision and support of their subordinates. In many departments, clerical personnel and responsible students have done an excellent job as complaint-takers and clerk dispatchers, thereby freeing higher-paid security personnel to provide better coverage.

ROTATING VERSUS FIXED SHIFTS

A definite difference of opinion exists regarding the value of fixed and rotating shifts. The majority of campus departments still utilize the fixed, nonrotating shift. In some cases this type of shift is continued merely because changing to a rotating shift would cause an upheaval among most personnel.

When the Yale University Police Department inaugurated rotating shifts and district assignments, for example, a hue and cry arose. Officers who objected the most were not the newer officers, most of whom were assigned to night or less desirable shifts, but the officers who had been working one shift and district for many years. Some of those objecting the loudest were officers who had rather flourishing outside businesses or steady employment that had caused their university security position to become somewhat secondary.

Dangers of Moonlighting

A major reason why some officers like a fixed shift is that it permits them to have a steady moonlighting job on the outside. Moonlighting usually results in one job becoming secondary so that both jobs suffer. When an officer prefers to work the "graveyard" or midnight shift, it can mean he is getting his rest at the college's expense, or he may be hiding an alcohol problem.

When the campus salary is too low to provide the officer and his family with a decent living, of course, moonlighting is understandable. A good salary must be provided to officers of any department with a rotating shift, because holding a regular outside job then becomes difficult. In any case, a well-paid officer who does not have to depend on outside employment usually provides a much higher level of performance.

Disadvantages of Fixed Shifts

Although arguments can be made that an officer working one district and one shift should become more effective because he becomes more familiar with his area and gets to know the people in it, there are also many disadvantages. The most prominent is that it limits the officer's performance and prevents him from becoming well rounded, knowing the entire campus, and being able to assume security responsibilities anywhere at any time. Another weakness is that a person working one district and shift becomes so familiar with it that he becomes complacent and stale and may even take shortcuts and otherwise reduce efficiency.

Rotating Shifts and Recruitment

A frequent reason for instituting rotating shifts is that qualified younger officers can be recruited and kept more easily than if they had to wait their turn to get on a desirable shift. Many fine officers have been lost because they and their families grew tired of the constant night, swing shift, and weekend assignments, with no change in hours to look forward to for years to come.

When shift rotation is adopted, it is recommended that shifts be rotated at intervals of approximately one month. Shorter intervals impose greater adjustment problems on security personnel and their families.

Rotating Supervision

If rotating shifts is not possible, supervision at least should be rotated so the same group of officers will not always be working under the same supervisor. Exposing the officers to different supervisors keeps them on their toes and prevents the abuses that can occur if they always work for the same individual—particularly if that supervisor is weak.

Some very unfortunate situations can develop when the supervisor becomes "one of the boys." For example, in one case the officers were systematically looting the food lockers at night with the full knowledge of their supervisor. A night custodian eventually notified this shift supervisor of his suspicions, but the supervisor promptly buried the complaint. Only when the custodian asked a university official what had happened to his complaint did the situation come to light.

When officers work under several supervisors they may also receive better training, because some supervisors have the knack of being able to train, motivate, and properly indoctrinate employees.

The fact that officers work under several supervisors also becomes important when efficiency reports are prepared and a cross section of supervisory opinions regarding the officers' performance can be acquired.

Scheduling Top Supervisors

Another trend related to the question of rotating or fixed shifts is that of assigning all top-security administrators to the day shift from Monday to Friday. In other words, the director and assistant director (or directors) all work this shift, and supervision at other times is delegated to a shift supervisor.

This type of scheduling is sometimes ineffective because it does not utilize top supervision when it is usually needed most—during the evening and night shifts and on weekends at some institutions. Top administrators can be used to better advantage by having the director work from about 8:00 A.M. to 5:00 P.M. each weekday and spending a great deal of time on campus over and above their regular hours. An assistant director, captain, or other high-echelon administrator would then assume command of the important and busy evening shift on a regular schedule but take over the director's shift during his absence. There should be at least an hour's overlap when both directors will be working at the same time and can confer on problems and management matters.

An exception to this procedure would be in large departments in which the director of public safety administers various security functions such as security, safety, parking, transportation, and so forth. In these cases, assistant directors directly administer each branch and naturally have to work normal hours as in other university departments.

MOBILE VERSUS WALKING PATROLS

Another controversial subject is the value of mobile compared to walking patrols. There is no hard-and-fast way of deciding which is of greater value in furnishing protection and response on a campus. Many factors have to be considered to determine the proper proportion of foot and mobile patrols. A happy medium should exist between the two types of patrols, depending on the size and composition of the campus, the number and location of buildings and other facilities, the type and number of security problems and crime, and the number of security personnel.

Police Use of Vehicles

Before the advent of the automobile, municipal police officers walked a beat or were assigned a fixed post. The only vehicles were horse drawn. These foot patrols continued until not too many years ago, when they were mostly replaced by mobile patrols for two main reasons: (1) increasing crime demanded fast and often multiple response, and (2) the growth of cities and the necessity for increased coverage in virtually all areas made it economically impossible to staff walking beats or districts.

In the past two or three years the old walking-beat concept has returned somewhat on the part of the local police departments in the larger cities. These patrols are designed primarily to detect and deal with street crimes such as muggings and armed robberies. Some of these street-crime units patrol areas for which statistics indicate a need. The officers are usually not in uniform but assume an appearance that will blend with the people who frequent the area.

Campus Needs Differ from City Needs

The average campus, although experiencing the same crime problems as a city, does not cover anywhere near the area of a city or approach its population. In some campus communities, however, the local police department has fewer or only a few officers more than the campus department, even though the city covers a wider area and a much larger population. It is no wonder, then, that the police must rely entirely on mobile patrols.

Campus security departments, however, can use foot patrols to good advantage. The more self-contained and closely integrated the campus, the more it lends itself to walking patrols. At Yale, for example, the majority of the academic buildings, resident colleges, and other facilities are located in a multiblock area in the city of New Haven. These blocks are covered by district foot patrols. The rather isolated facilities on the perimeter are patrolled by vehicle. At least one vehicle is also assigned to patrol all walking districts—not only to furnish additional coverage but also to respond to problems needing a vehicle and to lend immediate assistance to the walking-patrol officer. Supervisors also patrol in vehicles in all districts.

Where the walking patrol is used, officers should be assigned a specific district to cover and respond to problems. Sometimes a single-mobile unit can be used to patrol isolated areas such as athletic facilities and to furnish backup for the foot-patrol officers. In smaller departments, this mobile unit can be driven by the supervisor, who should respond to any problem of consequence.

Shortcomings of Mobile Patrols

On some campuses mobile patrols do furnish the best coverage because of an inadequate number of personnel. Practically no alternative exists but to patrol a fairly large campus by vehicle if only one or two officers are patrolling.

On other campuses, mobile patrols are used exclusively and excessively. On one large campus all foot patrols had been abolished, mainly because the police in that city used only mobile patrols. Campus officers thought they should follow the same policy and simply refused to walk. On the same campus, a security officer was asked to direct a visitor to the dean's office. He took the visitor to his patrol car and drove several blocks to reach a building that was only a hundred feet away by foot. Obviously officers just did not walk on that campus.

Mobile patrol is impersonal and often does not enable the officer to really get to know the campus or people. Mobile officers' contact with students and others is usually limited to when they have to see these people on business. A foot-patrol officer can foster excellent public relations because of his demeanor and the fact that he personally gets to know and talks to students and others in his district. This officer can build an excellent rapport with people. A good foot-patrol officer also gets to know every nook and cranny of the buildings and facilities in that district.

One other hazard of the mobile officer is that sometimes he becomes lazy and complacent. Sitting in a car for eight hours is not easy, but it certainly beats walking—particularly during hot weather if the car is air conditioned. Some mobile officers are reluctant to leave their cars to answer calls or to patrol buildings simply because they are too comfortable and have grown lazy. Other officers patrol but see very little other than the streets, grounds, and the outside of buildings. Sitting in a car alone, particularly at night, also makes it easy to doze off.

On some campuses mobile patrols have led to other abuses such as leaving the campus area for coffee or some other reason. Occasionally, particularly in smaller communities, campus mobile-patrol officers monitor the local police radio and respond when something appears to be of interest. Coverage on campus then suffers accordingly.

Foot Patrol Recommended

Sufficient personnel should be provided to cover at least the main campus and populated areas by foot patrols. They will not only provide superior coverage but also will enable the security department to better relate to and gain the confidence of the community. If a campus community has confidence in and respect for its security operation and personnel, it will also feel safer.

Chapter 8

IS POLICE AUTHORITY NECESSARY ?

The question of whether to provide police authority to campus officers cannot be answered with an unqualified yes or no. Many factors have to be weighed before this authority, which provides the power of arrest, is obtained.

First of all, the need for such arrest powers must be demonstrated by the problems faced on campus. Of even more importance is the caliber of the officer: does he posses good judgment regarding the use of these police powers? Other factors that must be considered are training, the quality and degree of supervision, and departmental policies and procedures to insure fair, clearly defined, and regulated use of these powers.

CITIZEN'S ARREST

Many campus administrators, faculty, and students are of the opinion that police authority is not necessary or desirable and that the so-called citizen's arrest power is equally effective. Citizen's arrest, however, provides only narrow and well-defined authority; in fact, it provides the campus officer only with the same arrest powers as a private citizen. If misused, it can result in the officer and institution being sued for false arrest and imprisonment, battery, assault, or other actions.

Crimes Not Committed in Officer's Presence

One of the most significant weaknesses of citizen's arrest authority applies to crimes not committed in the presence of the arresting officer. In most jurisdictions the sworn officer can also arrest, upon probable cause, for a misdemeanor not committed in his presence.

Usually, the campus officer who has no police power other than that of any private citizen can make an arrest only for misdemeanors that are actually committed in his presence. Any mistake may bring on a lawsuit. In several states where the common law applies, the misdemeanor must also involve a "breach of peace."

Under the common law a campus officer having only citizen's arrest powers can arrest for a felony not committed in his presence upon reasonable cause, but *the felony must actually have been committed.* The possibilities of a civil suit for false arrest and imprisonment here are unlimited. If physical force was used to detain or arrest the suspect, the threat of legal action against the officer and institution becomes even greater.

Question of Unreasonable Delay

Another factor that must be recognized by persons espousing citizen's arrest powers is that this type of arrest is only for the purpose of *holding* the arrested person until he or she is turned over to the proper police agency. It does not provide for detention to question the suspect or obtain a confession. If unreasonable delay occurs in turning over the suspect, the possibility of a civil suit is again very much in the picture.

Use of Force

Civil actions against the college or university and the individual officer can also arise in cases of search and seizure incidental to a citizen's arrest or performed by a security officer with no police authority. Still another critical area is the use of force either in making a citizen's arrest or in protecting the campus and its population. The officer without any arrest power can usually employ force only to an extent that is "reasonably necessary" to make the on-sight citizen's arrest. The question then arises of what constitutes "reasonably necessary" force?

A question can also arise as to what constitutes legally acceptable force by an officer in the performance of his duty. For example, what force can an officer use legally in ejecting a gatecrasher from a dance or athletic event or in breaking up a fight between two students? The answer will usually depend upon the laws of the jurisdiction under which the officer works and possibly the interpretation of the court, in the event of a civil action.

Complexity of the Laws

These weaknesses and areas of concern illustrate the fact that, contrary to the beliefs of some people on campus, citizen's arrest is a complex issue, and the campus officer had better be well versed in the laws of the jurisdiction under which he works. Otherwise (and sometimes in spite of it), the officer may expose himself and his institution to serious and costly civil actions.

In most cases where the citizen's arrest theory prevails, the security operation is very low level and often little more than a watchman-type department. Any campus security department today must have police powers to meet the challenges of crime effectively and legally; however, this authority should only be given to intelligent, well-trained, and supervised officers, and its use must be clearly delineated both from the legal and policy aspects.

OBTAINING POLICE AUTHORITY

Fifteen or twenty years ago very few departments had the power of arrest, and many campuses had little need for such authority. The level of campus security was quite low, making it unwise and impractical to provide police authority.

Members of departments who had police authority were usually sworn in as special police officers, constables, or deputy sheriffs by the local law enforcement head under a local ordinance. For example, Yale University police officers have for many years been sworn in as special officers by the chief of police in New Haven, Connecticut. By mutual agreement, however, their police authority is confined largely to campus property. (They do patrol the city streets that serve the campus and make a number of arrests that are sometimes unrelated to the university — for example, a subject breaking into a parked vehicle.)

State Legislation

Increasing crime and other problems on campus have contributed to the need for professionalizing campus security. These trends have, in turn, focused on the need for arrest and other police powers. As a result, over forty states have passed legislation to provide police authority to campus security personnel.

The legislation has differed substantially from state to state. Many states have passed laws providing for police authority for members of *state* universities and colleges but have not extended this authority to private institutions, which simply means that private institutions must turn to local law enforcement agencies to swear in their officers. The weaknesses and hazards of this type of police authority provided by local ordinance or statute will be discussed later in this chapter.

Fortunately, many states now provide for this authority for campus officers at private institutions as well as at state universities and colleges. Some states extend such authority not only to any institution of higher education but also to secondary schools and other institutions of learning. This authority is usually derived by the governing body or president of the educational institution petitioning the superintendent or commissioner of the state police.

Authority is usually granted in a routine manner after a background investigation, which frequently involves little more than a criminal record check based on the officer's fingerprints or sometimes merely his name, date of birth, and addresses.

Model State Law

The state of New Jersey in 1970 passed an act authorizing the appointment of special police. However, unlike many states, New Jersey extended the act to include not only public and private colleges and universities but also academies, schools (at any level), and "other institutions of learning."

Another unique feature of the New Jersey act was that application was made directly to the chief of police of the municipality in which the institution was located. However, a provision was included that if the educational institution was located in two municipalities, or in a municipality not having an organized police department, application would then be made to the superintendent of the New Jersey State Police.

Inasmuch as this New Jersey act is comprehensive and describes the type of police authority needed for most campus officers, pertinent sections are quoted here as a potential model.

Be it enacted by the Senate and General Assembly of the State of New Jersey:*

1. The governing body of any institution of higher education, academy, school, or other institution of learning may appoint such persons as the governing body may designate to act as policemen for the institution.
2. All applications shall, in the first instance, be made to the chief of police of the municipality in which the institution is located, except that where the municipality does not have an organized full-time police department or where the institution is located within more than one municipality, application shall be made to the superintendent of State Police. The chief of police or the superintendent, as the case may be, shall investigate

---

*New Jersey Acts (L–1970 C. 211 effective 10/8/70)
    18A: 6–4.2 Policemen; Appointment by Governing Body of Institution of Learning
    18A: 6–4.3 Application by Policeman; Approval; Issuance of Commission
    18A: 6–4.4 Police Training Course
    18A: 6–4.5 Powers
    18A: 6–4.6 Name Plate and Shield
    18A: 6–4.7 Traffic and Parking Violations; Authority; Procedure on Issuance of Tickets

and determine the character, competency, integrity, and fitness of the person or persons designated in the application. If the application is approved by the chief of police or the superintendent, the approved application shall be returned to the institution which shall issue a commission to the person appointed, a copy of which shall be filed in the office of the superintendent and with the chief of police of the municipality or municipalities in which such institution is located.

3. Every person so appointed and commissioned shall, within one year of the date of his commission, successfully complete a police training course at a school approved and authorized by the Police Training Commission; provided, however, that the Police Training Commission may, in its discretion, exempt from the requirements of this section any person who demonstrates to the commission's satisfaction that he has successfully completed a police training course conducted by any federal, state, or other public or private agency, the requirements of which are substantially equivalent to the requirements of that at a school approved by the commission.

4. Every person so appointed and commissioned shall, while on duty, within the limits of the property under the control of the respective institutions and on contiguous streets and highways, possess all the powers of policemen and constables in criminal cases and offenses against the law.

5. Each policeman, when on duty, except when employed as a detective, shall wear in plain view a nameplate and metallic shield or device with the word *police* and the name or style of the institution for which he is appointed inscribed thereon.

6. In connection with traffic and parking violations, the policemen appointed pursuant to this act shall, while on duty and within the territorial limits of the municipalities in which the respective institutions are located, and with the concurrence of the chiefs of police of such municipalities, have the power to enforce the laws regulating traffic and the operation of motor vehicles. Such policemen shall have the authority to issue and use traffic tickets and summonses of the type now used by the New Jersey State Police with such changes as are necessitated by reason of this act. Upon the issuance of any traffic or parking ticket or summons, the same procedure shall be followed as now prevails in connection with the use of traffic and parking violation tickets by the municipalities of this State.

7. Nothing in this act shall be construed to limit or impair the rights of any state, county, or municipal law enforcement officer in the performance of his duties.

Training Requirements

The New Jersey act, like others in many states, provides for mandatory training for campus officers who are to be commissioned. Although the New Jersey act is quite general, legislation in some states is specific in regard to the type and duration of training. Often these training requirements are the same as for municipal police officers.

Mandatory training should be part of any legislation granting police authority to campus officers, but some latitude should be provided in the type of training and who provides it. If campus officers are merely thrown into the same training sessions as municipal officers, they sometimes emerge with little sensitivity for the campus community they will serve. They may also have been exposed to a great deal of training they will never use. Therefore, the most productive and meaningful type of training must be tailored exclusively for the campus officer through specialized training for campus officers only or in-house training that will satisfy state standards.

Another element common to most legislation is limitation of the campus officers' authority to the premises owned or controlled by the college or university. Some acts also provide for this authority to extend to contiguous streets, highways, and other areas. Other acts provide that any off-campus authority applies only in a "hot pursuit" situation.

Establishing a Special Police Force

At least one university solved the problem of where to derive effective police authority by having special state legislation passed to establish a police force on that campus. The state of Connecticut has no legislation providing for police authority for campus officers. However, David P. Driscoll, former director of public safety at the University of Connecticut, in 1972 was able to convince Connecticut legislators to pass an act establishing a special police force. This act, in effect, made the university department a "duly organized police department" with the same powers and privileges as any municipal police department. The University of Connecticut is now virtually self-sufficient as far as security is concerned, with its own university police department providing protection and service superior to many municipal departments.

HAZARDS OF POLICE AUTHORITY ON CAMPUS

First of all, we must recognize that a sworn police officer must operate entirely within tight and often confusing legal requirements. The officer must be aware of what police authority entails and, particularly, what he legally can and cannot do under it. He must be fully conversant with the laws of arrest, search and seizure, and particularly, the rights of the individual or suspect. For example, the campus officer with police authority must advise any individual who could be a suspect of his right to remain silent, that anything he says may be used against him, and that he has a right to an attorney.

Ambiguities of Local Laws

Police authority is often obtained through the swearing in of campus officers by the local chief or police or sheriff under some local ordinance or act. Because these ordinances vary greatly, campus administrators should read local ordinances carefully and obtain a legal opinion as to what the ordinances really provide within the law. For example, on one campus the authority was provided under an ancient and ambiguous New England town ordinance* that did not specify what police authority it granted. The age and weakness of this type of so-called authority can be easily seen in its language, which provided that the mayor could appoint "two or more fence viewers, one or more measurers of wood or bark, a pound keeper, and one or more special officers."

Possible Police-Campus Conflicts

We must also recognize that swearing in campus officers under the local chief of police places them somewhat under his supervision. Conceivably, he could call on them for help in an emergency situation off campus. Sometimes politics can also be interjected into the picture, with the local police head or administration seeking to pawn off as campus officers political favorites who could not make the local department. At times, a chief or sheriff who is not friendly to the college or university can also have a disastrous effect on the campus department. In one instance, the chief of police rescinded the police authority of the head of the campus department after a personality clash and stated, "I am now running the campus department."

Police authority derived locally usually will only be as effective as the ordinance itself and the type of relations with the local police department and municipality that is granting the police powers.

One of the greatest hazards of swearing in campus officers under a state or local law enforcement head as provided by legislation is that the officers sometimes tend to believe they are in fact officers of the agency that commissions them. On several campuses, officers have practically delivered ultimatums to their college administrations by stating they had sworn an oath to the state police commissioner and owed their allegiance only to him.

Sometimes these problems arise when college administrators seek to curtail some "bust-happy" campus officers. On one campus an officer even lodged a complaint and tried to have a vice president arrested because he had suggested to the officer that one of the officer's arrests was not warranted and that the person involved should not be prosecuted. (Incidentally, the vice president was right—the arrest should never have been made.)

---

*Article II, Section 2-5 of Waltham, Mass. City Ordinance.

Officers must understand perfectly clearly that, even though they may be sworn in under a state act or local ordinance, they are still employees of the institution they serve and must perform their duties under the policies and procedures prescribed by their superiors. The fact that they derive their police authority from an off-campus source does not mean that they do not take orders or owe allegiance to the college or university that employs them.

Jurisdiction Only on Campus

A final problem concerns the campus officer's jurisdiction, which almost always applies only to when he is on *campus property*. In spite of this, officers on some campuses believe their jurisdiction extends off campus as well. On one campus in an urban area, a few campus officers took delight in chasing and harassing motor vehicle violators on streets removed from the campus and ordering drivers and passengers out of the car—often at gunpoint. On another campus, officers became tired of the relative calm on campus and assisted buddy officers in a nearby town in making arrests and other police functions.

Many campus officers are not well acquainted with the provisions of the act providing police authority and believe that they are "policemen" with arrest powers anywhere. On one campus after several false arrest suits and other incidents involving the activities of officers off campus, the commissioner of state police threatened to rescind the police authority of the entire department unless it confined its arrests and functions to campus property and the officers were more strictly supervised and disciplined.

THE ROLE OF THE CAMPUS INVESTIGATOR

Any discussion regarding police authority also focuses on the organization of the department and the capabilities of its personnel. One of the main factors that has to be considered is the ability of the campus department to properly conduct investigations of crimes on campus and also to research and survey areas and procedures to bring about safer conditions.

In the past many campus security departments had very little, if any, meaningful investigative ability. Security officers were merely recorders of complaints regarding thefts and other crimes, but no actual investigation or follow-up was conducted. Usually this meant that a short report was written to the effect that a crime had been committed. The report was filed and the incident forgotten. The only possible exception was when the crime reached the proportions where the local police were called in to investigate, which often just resulted in a repetition of the campus officer's action with a local police officer compiling another report but conducting no actual investigation.

In fairness to campus security administrators, let me hasten to add that in the past two factors contributed to a lack of investigative capability in campus departments. One factor was the reluctance on the part of campus administrators to recognize the need for a trained investigative unit. In fact, some administrators and even more faculty members felt strongly that a campus security operation should confine itself to routine duties and patrol and should not get involved in investigations. The second factor involved the institution's relationship with the local law enforcement agency that had jurisdiction of the campus. Many local police departments were inclined to look down on campus security operations and question the qualifications of personnel. Therefore, these departments demanded that all investigations involving possible violations of the law be referred to them.

This picture has changed drastically during the past few years and will continue to improve during the 1980s and 1990s. Practically every campus security department today has some type of investigative unit patterned somewhat after local police detective bureaus or similar investigative operations. The reason for this change again has to be attributed mainly to the crime problem. The campus population was no longer satisfied with having a campus officer merely take down the who, when, and where of the crime and say they were sorry it happened. They wanted something done about it, which usually meant a follow-up investigation.

The other reason for the growth of investigative operations and the training and assigning of personnel to these duties is a change of attitude on the part of municipal law enforcement agencies toward campus departments. This change has been prompted by the fact that local police departments are so busy (and usually understaffed) that they are most willing to have campus investigators assume the responsibility for investigations of the majority of incidents and crimes on their campus.

Every campus department should have this investigative ability that usually entails having one or more experienced, trained investigators assigned to a special unit or division. These individuals should have already proved themselves as officers and should possess the ability to conduct interviews, report factually, and think logically. They will have to know thoroughly the laws governing the interrogation of witnesses, suspects, and subjects as well as the rules of evidence, search, seizure, and arrest.

These investigators should be selected with great care not only because of the importance of their duties in solving and preventing crime but also because they will be dealing with and interviewing various segments of the campus population. The department's image will be enhanced or weakened by the way they handle themselves.

It is usually better to have these investigators work in neat, conservative business suits or, possibly, blazer-slacks outfits, rather than uniform. Because of the sensitivity of educational institutions it is also preferable on most campuses to avoid the title *detective*. Some institutions have adopted the title of *security specialist* for its investigators.

There should be a clear understanding with local police in regard to investigations on campus. This understanding should involve setting policy in regard to when the outside police would be called in to handle an investigation from its inception. At most institutions that have experienced investigators, there will be no need to call on the local police unless a major crime such as a murder or very serious theft or embezzlement is involved. If the local police covering the campus have respect for the ability of campus investigators, they also realize that the campus investigator is not only more familiar with the institution and its population but also will probably have more time to conduct a thorough investigation.

Establishing open communication with outside law enforcement agencies is vitally important so that they will be kept currently advised regarding investigations in which they might have an interest, especially those that might draw media attention. This communication should, in most instances, involve an exchange of investigative reports regarding matters with which either department might be concerned. Usually a good policy is to have a representative of the local police department's detective bureau and the campus investigative unit designated to handle these matters to insure a discreet, orderly, and controlled flow of information and good cooperation.

The first part of the chapter dealt with police authority. For campus investigators to have this police authority so that they can proceed through the investigation, collect evidence, and make arrests on campus is most desirable. However, if arrests are to take place off campus they will usually have to be made by the local police, preferably accompanied by the campus investigator. The booking procedure will undoubtedly take place off campus and follow the same pattern as that of outside law enforcement agencies.

Some local law enforcement agencies are content to let the campus investigators solve a case and build evidence, but they insist that local officers make the arrests. This type of policy should be avoided, if possible, if for no other reason than it is bad for the morale of the campus investigator. However, in certain cases involving arrests of students, faculty, or staff members, having the outside police make the arrest may be preferable. Arrest policies will have to be clearly delineated between the campus and local police.

This section has purposely avoided the nuts-and-bolts perusal of conducting investigations and interviews, search, seizure of evidence, and making an arrest because these aspects have been the topics of multiple good books, articles, seminars, workshops, and conferences. Needless to say, the campus investigator must abide by all the legal technicalities and laws regarding such activities. He must be extremely sensitive to avoiding even the slightest criticism of possible coercion; using force, threats, or trickery in conducting interviews; seizing evidence illegally, or making a false arrest.

In looking back on my over twenty years associated with campus security and law enforcement it is encouraging to see campus security departments becoming ever more professional and self-sufficient. Nowhere is this better exemplified than in the formation of capable, innovative, and effective investigative units that have produced excellent results in not only solving but also preventing campus crimes. The formation of these investigative units also creates another step in the promotion process that results in motivating and keeping young, ambitious campus officers.

CONCLUSION

The answer to whether police authority is necessary on campus would have to be yes, but only if the following qualifications and requirements can be met:

- Intelligent, high-caliber personnel;
- Policies and procedures clearly defined (preferably in a manual);
- Constant and effective supervision;
- Training, particularly in the laws of arrest, search, and so on;
- Constant use of good judgment and common sense in utilizing police powers.

Finally, the elements that make for effective legislation to furnish campus officers with this police authority are:

- Statewide legislation to cover private and public educational institutions at all levels (rather than by local ordinance);
- Mandatory training oriented toward a campus department;
- Provision for a criminal record check and a thorough background investigation;
- Full police powers, but confined to campus property and the areas immediately adjacent (including streets and highways servicing the campus).

Chapter 9

TO ARM OR NOT TO ARM ?

In many respects the question of arming officers is similar to the question of police authority; both are controversial issues on campus and cannot be answered with a simple yes or no.

Many of the same conditions that should be met before granting police authority also apply to arming a campus department. These factors include the location of the campus, the crime rate on campus and in the surrounding community, and the confidence in and respect for security personnel that the campus population has. The most important factors involve the qualifications, recruiting, screening, training, supervision, and particularly, the caliber, intelligence, and good judgment of the individual who will carry the weapon.

The arming of campus security or police forces is an extremely sensitive issue and must be treated with the utmost care. Any campus department whose officers have police authority and arrest powers certainly meets one of the principal requirements for carrying weapons. No security officer should be armed unless he is a sworn officer with full police authority. On occasion, however, some campus officers have been armed although they have no police powers.

TREND TOWARD ACCEPTING ARMED OFFICERS

Some campuses resist the carrying of weapons, arguing that firearms have no place in an educational atmosphere. The 1970 Kent State shooting of students by National Guardsmen is still fresh in the minds of many people. To my knowledge, however, no documented instance of a campus security officer's shooting of a student or other member of a campus community has ever occurred.

Although it is agreed that weapons are not part of the educational scene, criminals, unfortunately, do not look upon a college campus as being off limits. More and more they are invading the campus. The fact that a campus officer is armed in itself acts as a deterrent, because to the criminal it signifies the presence of a bona fide law enforcement officer.

During the past few years a marked softening of the attitude regarding weapons on campus has occurred, undoubtedly because of increasing crime — particularly crimes against the person. Still, a small but vocal group of faculty members, student affairs personnel, and administrators are often able to keep guns off campus. However, the students who, unlike faculty and administrators, reside on campus usually have little objection to weapons. As one student stated, "How can we expect our officers to protect us if they can't even protect themselves?"

Today the great majority of students not only *accept* the fact that their campus officers are armed, they *expect* them to be armed. A recent survey at a campus security workshop ascertained that, out of 125 colleges and universities represented, 86 armed their campus police or security officers. Of the 39 institutions not carrying weapons, the majority were two-year community colleges with no residence halls or those that had low-level contract or watchman-guard-type security.

OVERCOMING OBJECTIONS TO WEAPONS

In a campus department that does not carry weapons, the director usually has a difficult time convincing the campus community that officers need to be armed. He must really sell the community on the need for officers to be armed in order to protect students and others on campus.

The aversion of a minority on campus to the appearance of a side arm is not sufficient reason to deprive the rest of the community of the protection to which it is entitled. It certainly is not justification to deprive a police or security officer of the right to protect his own life while protecting the lives of others. Many heads of campus departments have waged lengthy, hard, and time-consuming campaigns to arm their officers. These security directors can assist in providing valuable advice and information to directors who are seeking to convince their administrators of the need for weapons. Two such men who have waged long but successful campaigns are Lawrence J. Slamons, Jr., Director of Public Safety, University of Arkansas, Fayetteville, Arkansas; and the dynamic Robert F. Ochs, Assistant Vice President for Public Safety, Rutgers, The State University of New Jersey, New Brunswick, New Jersey.

STANDARDS AND POLICIES FOR ARMING

A number of important policies and strict standards should be met if campus officers are to be armed.

First of all, salaries and qualifications (particularly, educational) should be high enough to insure that the officers are high-caliber personnel.

Every applicant for a campus security position must be thoroughly screened, as described in Chapter 6. This screening should involve some psychological testing to determine the applicant's stability and qualifications to carry and use a weapon.

Intensive and thorough firearms indoctrination should be afforded each officer before the weapon is issued. Although this training would include marksmanship, safety rules and, particularly, *when not to draw the weapon* should be stressed even more. Officers should understand clearly that the weapon should never be used for firing warning or disabling shots, drawn as a threat, or used as a club or similar weapon. At no time should it be drawn for "horseplay" or for display to students or others. It should be drawn only to protect the officer's life or that of another.

Two cardinal rules of gun safety must be constantly stressed:

1. Never point a gun at any person unless you would be willing to kill that person.
2. Treat every gun as if it were loaded.

FIREARMS TRAINING

Firearms training should be given by qualified instructors on a regular firearms range. This training should be a continuing involvement, with all officers having to qualify at least four times each year. One officer or supervisor who has been trained and has demonstrated an interest and proficiency with firearms may be named as a firearms training or range officer to supervise an in-house program. If firearms training cannot be obtained locally, the Smith and Wesson Academy in Springfield, Massachusetts offers an excellent training program under its director, Charles L. Smith, who has over forty years of experience in weaponry and related training.

Training for campus officers should emphasize all aspects of using a revolver such as those covered in the practical pistol course. Having an officer shoot at a bull's-eye target is not enough. The practical pistol course will stress the importance of drawing quickly and shooting at a silhouette target at close range, where most encounters take place. It will also enable the officer to become proficient while shooting from various positions — sitting, lying down, and from behind a barricade.

A record of the officers' firearms training and scores should be maintained. This record should be considered in making assignments and as part of the promotion process.

SIGNED STATEMENTS

The director should personally give the new officer his weapon after successful completion of training and emphasize the safety rules and necessity to maintain the revolver in good condition. A signed statement embodying these safety regulations should be obtained by the director at the time the officer is given the weapon. This signed statement should be kept in the officer's personnel file and should clearly indicate that any violation of the regulations would be reason for serious disciplinary action. The statement could read as follows:

USE OF FIREARMS

I realize that I am never to draw my firearm unless it is a dire emergency calling for the protection of my own life or that of another individual. I am fully aware that *under no circumstances* will I use my revolver to threaten anyone or as a club or similar weapon. I also understand that under no circumstances am I ever to fire a warning shot or a shot designed to disable.

I have read this statement and am fully aware of its contents. I am also aware that violation of these regulations may be reason for serious administrative action up to and including dismissal.

_____   _____
Signature   Witness

APPROVED WEAPONS AND AMMUNITION

Campus officers should be issued .38-caliber revolvers that should be carried in a snap-type or breakaway holster on the belt, permitting quick draw while still preventing the weapon from falling from the holster accidentally if the officer is running or otherwise active. Officers should be required to carry only these college- or university-issued revolvers and holsters and not their own weapons unless approved. Approval should only be granted for .38-caliber revolvers.

Many abuses take place in regard to personally owned weapons and holsters. On one campus several officers sported two pearl-handled revolvers, which they carried in low-slung western-style holsters reminiscent of Wyatt Earp. Nonapproved holsters may range from shoulder and cross-draw holsters to holsters containing small weapons strapped to the lower leg. Officers should also never carry weapons tucked under their belt or in their pockets.

High-powered guns and hollow-nosed, high-velocity bullets have no place on a campus. There is very little reason, for example, for a campus officer to carry a .357 magnum, which when loaded with supercharged ammunition, is extremely powerful and dangerous. It can penetrate substantial barriers and possibly injure or kill innocent persons, particularly if used in a closely populated campus setting. These high-powered handguns produce more recoil and require an experienced officer to use them properly and accurately.

A longer barrel (four inch) .38-caliber revolver is also not necessary for a campus officer. Although it is true that these longer barreled weapons are more accurate, it must be recognized that invariably a revolver is needed to deal with an emergency at close range, where a .38-caliber short-nosed revolver will be almost as effective. These shorter length–barrel weapons are also much lighter, less cumbersome, and easier to carry in a belt holster. They are also much less obtrusive on a campus and are particularly adapted to carrying under a blazer-type uniform.

Although conceivably some departments might make a bona fide case for carrying shotguns in patrol cars and having high-powered gas guns, carbines, and rifles, these weapons are not recommended for the majority of campuses. Normally, situations calling for such weapons require the use of well-trained SWAT or similar teams from outside police agencies.

Hollow-nosed, dumdum, or higher velocity bullets should never be used by a campus security department. The hollow-nosed bullet flattens out immediately after impact and, therefore, usually does not penetrate the target cleanly. It does indescribable damage to human tissue, and for this reason the so-called dumdum bullet was outlawed for military use by the Geneva Convention. Regulation, round-nosed, lead .38 special bullets should be the only ammunition allowed and issued.

WHEN SHOULD THE WEAPON BE WORN?

Considerable difference of opinion exists as to whether campus officers should always wear a revolver while on duty. Many departments have followed police procedures that call for officers being armed at all times while on duty. There are occasions, however, when the need for a weapon would be extremely remote and displaying it might be abrasive to those in attendance. Examples of such occasions would be alumni luncheons, memorial services, and various noncontroversial meetings or lectures.

Weapons should never be worn in handling any mass student demonstration. At Yale, for example, the freshmen used to customarily "riot" one night every spring, usually on the first warm night preceding exams. All Yale freshmen resided on the Old Campus that consisted of dormitory buildings clustered around a park-like quadrangle with city streets on the outside and the campus on the other side. During these occasions, University police officers concentrated on confining the hijinks to the Old Campus so that students did not flow out into the city streets. The campus officers were unarmed; most did not carry radios (to prevent breakage), and those wearing glasses were advised to take them off.

The carrying of revolvers may be left entirely up to the officer's judgment. This policy can be successful if officers are intelligent, possess good judgment, and are well trained and closely supervised.

Some campuses have a policy restricting the wearing of weapons to night hours. Such a restriction is inadvisable. Crimes requiring the officer to use a weapon can occur at any hour.

NEED FOR IMMEDIATE RESPONSE

Several campuses do not arm their officers but do allow a loaded revolver to be carried in the glove compartment of a single patrol car to be used in "an emergency." This arrangement is unsatisfactory for two reasons. First, experience has clearly demonstrated that a side arm is invariably used in a situation calling for immediate and unexpected action and response. There is usually not time to obtain a weapon stored in the glove compartment of a patrol car or, worse still, in the departmental office.

The type of incident calling for the immediate use of the weapon was illustrated on one occasion at Yale. An officer came upon three young men sniffing glue in the darkness in a university parking lot. As he approached them he was suddenly attacked and fell to the ground. His assailants kicked him in the face and head as they screamed, "Kill him." Only when he was able to roll over and draw his weapon did the three subjects run away. (All three were arrested a few hours later.) The case was given maximum coverage in campus and local papers to illustrate to the community why it was necessary for Yale police officers to carry weapons.

The other reason for not keeping a weapon in a glove compartment, even if it is locked, is that the revolver can easily be stolen when the officer is away from the vehicle. The first place a thief looks when breaking into a car is the glove compartment, even though it must be pried open.

SHOULD WEAPONS BE TAKEN HOME?

The practice of allowing officers to take their weapons home and wear them when not on duty is one that is followed by most local law enforcement agencies. The argument presented by campus officers is the same as for local police officers — namely, that they may encounter an emergency situation (robbery, assault, and so on) while off duty that would require use of the weapon. Although this argument may be valid for local police, it does not apply equally to campus officers.

A campus must weigh the advantages of having its officers armed while off campus against the disadvantages. The hazards of allowing officers to take campus-issued weapons home with them far outweigh the benefits.

In the first place, campus officers have no legally prescribed authority to wear or use weapons off campus. Their arrest power is almost always only applicable when on campus property. Therefore, in the eyes of the law they are just like any other citizen and come under the same laws requiring permits to carry weapons.

The chance for a civil suit against the officer and his institution looms large if the weapon is used. The institution becomes even more vulnerable if it owns the weapon, has issued it, and has sanctioned the officer to carry it off campus.

Police officers and, particularly, private security and contract guard personnel have too often discharged their weapons through carelessness, poor judgment, or accident, causing injury, death, or at the least, embarrassment to their departments. In a number of cases children have found dad's revolver at home, and the results have been disastrous. Occasionally the officer wearing the weapon has stopped for one or two drinks on the way home and used the weapon indiscriminately.

Another very real threat is that an officer's service revolver may be stolen from his home and used in a crime of violence. At one campus where officers were allowed to take their weapons home, an officer's house was burglarized while he was away and his university-issued revolver stolen. This weapon later was used in a series of violent crimes. When the gun was finally traced by the local police, the institution received unfavorable publicity.

If an officer desires to have his own weapon when off duty and away from the campus, that should be his personal choice. The college or university should not assume any responsibility. The institution should make clear to the officer the risks involved and that he must meet the same legal requirements (gun permit, and so on) as any other private citizen. Privately owned weapons should not be allowed on campus whether the office is on or off duty—except, as previously stated, by prior approval.

University-owned revolvers should be issued by the shift supervisor at the start of the shift and collected at the end of the shift. When not in use, guns should be stored in a supervised, secure metal gun cabinet that would be locked at all times. If officers are provided with individual, secure lockers, an alternative to using a gun-storage cabinet would be to have officers store their revolvers in their lockers. However, this should be done only if the lockers are secure and closely supervised to prevent theft.

MAINTENANCE OF WEAPONS

Officers should be held strictly accountable for cleaning and maintaining their weapons. Cleaning supplies and tools should be provided for this purpose. Supervisors should inspect these weapons regularly at shift changes to make sure the guns are well maintained and are functioning properly.

On some campuses, weapon inspections reveal many cases in which the weapon, if used, could be dangerous to the community and particularly to the officer using it. For example, the bullets may be rusted in the chambers, which would cause the weapon to malfunction or perhaps not fire at all in an emergency, or the ammunition may not have been changed in ten years or more.

Frequent and thorough inspection of weapons is vital. The best time for inspection is at the time the officer takes firearms training (at least four times each year), at which time the officer should use his service revolver rather than a target pistol or other weapon. Use of his own weapon will increase his familiarity and proficiency with it.

Revolvers should be unloaded when not being carried on duty. For increased safety it is advisable not to load the chamber under the hammer or firing pin.

NIGHTSTICKS AND BILLY CLUBS

The carrying of nightsticks, riot batons, or billy clubs is also a sensitive issue. In most cases, it would probably be better not to carry these protective weapons routinely. If a clear need for them is established, however, the campus should be fully informed of the reason for carrying them. Many departments maintain a supply of police batons to be used in certain emergency situations. Others confine their use to the night hours.

The sight of a nightstick carried by a campus officer usually results in some members of the campus population associating its use with so-called police brutality. The media have too often used photos or films of the police officer striking a seemingly defenseless individual on the head. Some segments of the campus community regard the nightstick with the same enthusiasm afforded to attack dogs and feel nightsticks have no place on a campus. Therefore, they should be carried and used only when absolutely necessary—preferably during the late-night and early-morning hours.

If police batons are to be carried, the shorter (ten to sixteen inch) billy-club type with a palm grip should be used rather than nightsticks, which are considerably longer (twenty to twenty-six inches). Riot batons that measure over thirty inches should never be carried routinely, and the twirling of batons by officers on patrol should also be ruled out. The shorter, plastic billy clubs are also much lighter (nine to fourteen ounces). They should be carried in a special ring attached to the belt and not drawn unless an emergency occurs requiring their use.

Police billy clubs or nightsticks must also be regarded as potentially lethal weapons, particularly if used by an untrained officer. If they are to be used by a campus department, officers should be thoroughly trained in their use. Contrary to popular opinion, the nightstick should never be used to strike someone on the head. It can then easily turn into a deadly weapon.

USE OF CHEMICAL MACE

Chemical Mace has sometimes been advocated as a humane alternative to a revolver, nightstick, sap, or physical force. During the days of mass student dissent and violence, Mace and pepper fog were used quite extensively on some campuses, usually by outside law enforcement agencies. As a result, any type of tear gas came to be looked upon in the same light as attack dogs, riot batons, riot-guard helmets, riot shields, shock batons, and other equipment used to quell mob action. Therefore, the carrying of Mace by officers as part of their uniform equipment should be closely evaluated before being instituted. Again, it is imperative to convince the campus of the need for Mace, emphasizing its humane and nonlethal aspects.

On most campuses there is probably not sufficient justification for the routine carrying of Mace by all officers. However, consideration might be given to carrying MK-V or MK-IV hand-held containers of Chemical Mace in at least one patrol vehicle or having them available in the department office for use as a last resort in certain cases.

Recognize that campus officers require training in the use of Chemical Mace the same as firearms. This training should stress the utmost discretion and good judgment. With proper use the dangers of serious or permanent damage are minimal, but with improper use (too close to the person, victim without normal reflexes, use in a closed space, or delay in exposure treatment) the hazard is increased. Mace, although certainly more humane than nightsticks and other weapons, is still a weapon and must be carefully regulated and used only by thoroughly trained, properly supervised personnel.

CONCLUSION

In order to perform their function and protect the campus community, campus officers must be given the tools to do the job. The revolver is as much a tool to the officer as the hammer is to a carpenter. It has also become the symbol of the professional police or security officer, in contrast to a watchman-guard type operation. Badges are worn or carried by many officers, but only the professional carries a weapon. However, as described in this chapter the campus officer works in an academic atmosphere in which weapons are not compatible with the aims of an educational institution. Therefore, the campus security or law enforcement agency must have a high level of sensitivity to the use of weapons, recognizing the following requirements:

- Selection of well-qualified and thoroughly screened personnel;
- Complete, thorough, and continuing training with emphasis on safety precautions;

- Well-defined and strict policies limiting the drawing and use of weapons to the protection of life;
- Close and effective supervision;
- Weapons to be .38-caliber, college-issued types and not allowed to be taken off campus;
- Use of standard .38-caliber ammunition only;
- Immediate reports in writing (verbal, if necessary) by the officer and supervisor regarding the reason for drawing or firing a service revolver;
- Constant inspection of weapons and ammunition to make sure regulations are being observed and weapons are in good working order;
- A continuing public relations type program to convince the campus of the need for weapons in order to better serve and protect.

Chapter 10

CAMPUS SECURITY EQUIPMENT

The campus security department requires proper equipment in order to perform efficiently, and the security director is largely responsible for selecting equipment best suited to do the job in a cost-effective manner. Major types of equipment of concern include patrol vehicles, mobile communications systems, and uniforms.

PATROL VEHICLES

Choosing the Right Vehicle

Unless proper consideration is given to selecting the appropriate vehicle for a campus security department, money may be spent unnecessarily for equipment with unneeded capabilities.

One campus, for example, purchased a large, high-powered station wagon as a patrol car. The campus was small and compact with a limited number of narrow, winding roads to patrol. The security department could give only a few weak reasons for purchasing such a large vehicle, and it had no valid reason for specifying the high-powered pursuit-type motor.

On most campuses, more economical vehicles would be more effective as patrol cars. Since campus police do not ordinarily get involved in high-speed chases, they do not need to drive high-pursuit vehicles that are expensive and use more gasoline.

The type of vehicle used by a campus security department should fit the needs of the campus. If officers must patrol narrow roads and tight places, then a compact or even a jeep-type vehicle might be considered. In some cases, economical three-wheeled electric or gasoline-powered scooters similar to golf carts are used on patrol. However, officers are usually unhappy with these vehicles, claiming they are unsafe, too cold in winter, and that they do not project a professional image. On campus after campus, vehicles of this type have been discarded or turned over to the physical plant operation. They do seem to work well in enforcing parking regulations, when the parking department is separate from the regular police or security operation and utilizes a different level of personnel.

Generally speaking, vehicles purchased for patrol should be four-door, low-horsepower, medium or compact models that can be maneuvered easily. A "police package" type vehicle should be specified to insure more rugged construction of upholstery, springs, shock absorbers, brakes, transmission, battery, and generator or alternator. In the long run ordering this heavy duty equipment is more economical because campus patrol vehicles receive hard usage with the constant turnover of drivers, slow speeds, and too often a general disregard for upkeep and maintenance.

At some smaller colleges, the security department shares a car or truck with the physical plant or buildings and grounds department. This arrangement is never satisfactory for either department, particularly for security. Any security operation should have its own vehicle.

Records of Operating Costs

A separate file should be maintained on each vehicle, giving a complete history of the initial cost, miles traveled, and cost of maintenance, gas, and oil. In this way the cost per mile of operating the vehicle can be computed and compared against other vehicles. These operating expenses can provide some indication of the make and model that is most economical to operate. However, security departments must recognize that a make and model that may be very satisfactory this year can change next year and prove to be just the opposite.

A schedule should be worked out so that one or more cars are replaced when maintenance costs indicate it is no longer practical to keep them running. Usually this means replacing a vehicle after two or three years of service.

Maintenance

Patrol car officers should be held accountable for the general upkeep and maintenance of the car. They should report deficiencies immediately and give the vehicle the same care as if it were their own. They should be held strictly accountable for the cleanliness and condition of the vehicle's interior (whisk broom and cleaning cloth should be provided), but they should not be responsible for washing or cleaning the exterior. Arrangements should be made for the periodic washing of vehicles.

Too often, patrol cars are sadly neglected and convey a bad image of the department. The cars may be dusty and coffee stained, with dirt on the floor, magazines jammed under the front seat, and an assortment of obviously unused equipment occupying the rear seat. Such an appearance gives the impression of a sloppily run department.

Patrol cars are often used to transport guests, visitors, VIPs, members of the board, and other people whose only contact with the security department is confined to that trip in the car. The department should look upon these occasions as an opportunity to show its best side by having an alert, personable, neat, and clean officer and an equally clean and neat patrol car.

A vehicle maintenance log (see Figure 10-1) should be utilized to keep a running account of the condition of the car and to fix responsibility for delinquencies. This log should be filled out by the driver on each shift and maintained and reviewed periodically by a supervisor who is assigned responsibility for the maintenance and upkeep of patrol cars. This supervisor should regularly inspect and drive each vehicle to insure that it is mechanically sound and safe, the tires have sufficient tread, and the exterior and interior are clean. A preventive maintenance program should be set up to insure regular motor tune-ups, oil changes, and inspection.

Finding an efficient automotive repair service that will provide prompt service is often difficult. Some large universities have their own automotive maintenance shops, but too often directors of security complain that patrol cars are still laid up for repairs for entirely too long. Sometimes with good reason, however, auto repair shops claim that as fast as they repair them, these vehicles are abused and returned for more repairs.

Patrol Car Equipment

How a campus patrol vehicle should be equipped will depend somewhat on the security program on that campus and the problems encountered.

Lights and Sirens. The need for flashing lights atop the vehicle, sirens, and public address systems will vary from campus to campus. Since crime is the major problem today, a high degree of visibility is desirable, and therefore in most cases this type of equipment is recommended. However, the use of sirens and flashing lights should not be left to the officer's whim but should be subject to strict rules. Their use should be confined to real emergencies—preferably after permission is obtained from the supervisor. Any use of sirens or flashing lights should be reported in

LICENSE: _____

PATROL CAR NO.: _____   GAS NO.: _____

DATE	SHIFT OR TRIP	OFFICER	MILEAGE AT START OF SHIFT	MILEAGE AT END OF SHIFT	TOTAL MILES TRAVELED	GAS & OIL PURCHASES	CONDITION OF CAR

Figure 10–1.   Vehicle maintenance log.

writing to the director, with reasons given to justify their use. The use and color of flashing lights will be governed by state and local laws.

Some campuses have used a single, distinctively colored, smaller light on the roof, usually between the flashing lights, to create more visibility and assure members of the community (especially at night) that they are being protected. This light is wired to go on as soon as the ignition is turned on. It can also act as a supervisory tool because it draws attention to the car and the officers' actions.

A powerful spotlight mounted on the driver's side is also an excellent tool for patrol after dark.

Radio. Every patrol vehicle should be equipped with a mobile two-way radio. In some cases, a fixed mobile is not used but a special receptacle is attached to the dashboard to hold the portable unit and to act as a charger. The officer can then take this hand-held unit with him when he leaves the vehicle. If any degree of mobile patrol is involved, however, the fixed mobile unit is recommended. It is more convenient to use and has proved more dependable.

Marked and Unmarked Cars. All patrol vehicles should be clearly marked, either by the department's logo on the front doors or some similar, easily visible method. In larger department in which cars are required to leave the campus or must be used in investigations requiring unmarked vehicles, at least one car should be without flashing lights or other means of identifying it as a police vehicle (other than a two-way radio).

The head of a campus security department of any size should be assigned an unmarked vehicle for his personal use. A campus director is literally on duty twenty-four hours a day and must be reached immediately in emergency situations. A high-powered mobile radio in his vehicle not only makes him accessible instantly when he is away from home but also acts as an excellent supervisory tool when he is off duty and in the car. By monitoring radio activities in the evening, for example, he may be able to give direction in certain matters. A good investment for any college or university is to provide a radio equipped car for the head of its security operation.

Emergency Box. Each patrol car should have in the trunk an emergency box containing, among other things, a fire extinguisher, disposable emergency oxygen kit, first aid equipment, disposable blankets and sheets, pillows, a pry bar, flares, rope, wire cutters, and a high-powered hand-held searchlight.

Unneeded Police Gear. On one campus, a small but vocal group of officers patterned their activities after the numerous television police programs and movies. One of their demands was to equip the back seat of a patrol vehicle with a prisoner conveyance cage. This campus was nonresidential and in a suburban area with very few problems. The only arrests made for months were for traffic violations. Although conceivably a violent person or prisoner might have to be transported, the history of the campus made this possibility very remote.

Number of Vehicles Necessary

The number of patrol vehicles necessary will vary from department to department. Enough cars should be available so that vehicles do not have to be used twenty-four hours each day. Around-the-clock use usually results in frequent maintenance problems and greatly reduces the vehicle's life. Ideally, a patrol car should work the same eight-hour shifts as an officer, except that the vehicle can work seven days a week. Backup vehicles are also needed to replace those being repaired or for emergency situations requiring more patrol cars.

COMMUNICATIONS

Good communications are the backbone of an effective security operation. The ability to provide prompt and efficient service should be one of the major considerations in selecting any communications system.

A number of years ago, flashing red lights were used on some campuses at strategic points to signal officers to call the office. At one woman's college with only two guards on duty at night, emergencies were called in to the dean of students, who resided on campus. She pressed the button in her bedroom to cause a blue revolving light in the center of the campus to signal the guards to call her.

Today, much more sophisticated, reliable equipment is available to provide officers with efficient communications. Unfortunately, however, some institutions have not recognized the need for a good two-way FM radio system. Even more schools have allowed their purchasing departments to buy cheap, inferior, inefficient equipment. On a number of campuses the head of security has requested and specified good quality radio equipment but has been overruled by purchasing personnel who felt that lower priced equipment from a local radio appliance chain would do the job. The results were that the radio signal did not reach all parts of the campus (such as tunnels and inside buildings), hand-held radios did not stand up, parts and services were not available, and the equipment was soon discarded.

One-Way Pagers

A too common procedure has been to equip officers with one-way communications devices only. These pocket size pagers signal the officer to phone the office and sometimes transmit verbal instructions. The officer has no ability to respond. One-way communications are fine for physical plant and similar personnel but are not adequate for officers who must be able to respond immediately to a variety of situations. Of even more importance is the officer's inability to call for assistance when his own life is in danger or when he comes upon a situation calling for additional manpower. Certain investigations also require officers to be able to communicate with each other.

Hazards of Shared Frequencies

Another common but inadvisable procedure is to have the security department on the same radio frequency as the buildings and grounds operation. In some cases, the base station and transmitter are even located in the buildings and grounds department, and security is added as a remote control console or desk set.

Having a buildings and grounds operation on the same frequency as the security operation can be compared to having a department of public works sharing the same radio as the police department. A security or police operation deals in emergencies and sometimes highly confidential matters. On several campuses officers complained that they did not receive dispatches or could not respond because maintenance employees were clogging the air with personal talk and inconsequential matters. Because people outside the security department could listen in on their radio messages, confidential internal investigations involving employees were greatly hampered.

Any campus security or police operation should have its own self-controlled radio communications system. It deals in emergencies in which a few seconds' delay in responding could possibly result in death to the victim.

Pager System for Service Personnel

Some smaller colleges cannot justify the expense of two separate radio systems for maintenance functions and security. Therefore, the security dispatcher may also have to act as the dispatcher for service personnel. In this case, a separate tone-and-voice-pager system is recommended, permitting the dispatcher to signal service employees by individual pagers and relate instructions. The service employees cannot respond. This type of system does not interfere with regular two-way transmissions to security personnel.

A less expensive alternative is a tone-only pager, which requires the service employee to telephone for instructions when he is paged. This type should be avoided if possible because it can result in the dispatcher having to devote excessive time to talking to the employees when they call in for messages.

These pocket-size paging units are powered by rechargeable nickel-cadmium batteries and require approximately the same maintenance as portable two-way FM radio units.

High-Band Frequencies

Only municipal police departments (or in a few instances, security departments) are granted high-band (150.8–174 Mhz) private frequencies. If maintenance functions are incorporated on the same frequency as campus police, the Federal Communications Commission (FCC) will not assign these frequencies.

Although state universities will usually be able to obtain these desirable police or local government frequencies, private institutions will be assigned business-type channels. Therefore, a private-line feature should be specified.

A digital, private-line squelch system is recommended. This solid-state system is coded to eliminate annoying cochannel message reception. Only those calls with the proper individual system code will be heard, thereby reducing dispatcher fatigue and missed or misunderstood messages.

Dispatcher on Duty

Any campus that has a residential community should have a radio dispatcher on duty at all times. In some smaller institutions, after-hours emergencies and requests for assistance are routed by telephone to an off-campus answering service that can reach patrolling officers by radio. This arrangement is most unsatisfactory because it places an untrained, sometimes unmotivated person, who knows little about the campus or about security, in a dispatcher's position.

On some campuses the radio dispatching is done by the telephone switchboard operator who handles all calls to the department. This arrangement is almost as unsatisfactory as the outside telephone answering service for most of the same reasons, and because the switchboard operator is sometimes extremely busy with other calls and does not respond promptly.

Basic FM Two-Way System

Let us examine a basic FM two-way-radio communications system for the average campus. The main objective at the outset should be to provide an FM transmission that is powerful enough to permit communication between the dispatcher at the base station and portable and mobile units throughout the entire campus.

The equipment would consist of a solid-state transistorized FM two-way-radio base station of sufficient power to effectively communicate to any location on campus and the area contiguous to it. These base stations are varied in design, size, and cost, depending somewhat on the wattage needed. The average campus will require about 30–50 watts RF power. Some very attractive, compact desk-type consolettes are available, equipped with digital clock and other accessories that are ideal for medium-range use.

As noted previously, the frequency assigned by the FCC will depend on several factors. The initial application is quite detailed and needs to be executed properly to receive the best possible frequency. Reputable and knowledgeable suppliers can provide assistance in obtaining a high-band frequency that will insure a maximum amount of private communication. These companies can also be of assistance when the application must be renewed (usually every three years).

The type of antenna will depend on a variety of factors, and the supplier should offer guidance in selecting it. Usually, a high-gain antenna is desirable. Most campuses have high buildings on which the antenna can be mounted, so a tower is not necessary.

Handie-talkie radio units vary in size, construction, wattage, and cost. Many features or options can be purchased, but the main objective should be to acquire units with sufficient power that are rugged enough to withstand constant, hard usage. The usual campus unit will range from three to five watts. Usually a basic model weighing from 20–26 ounces will suffice.

Accessories

Any number of accessories can be added to these communications units. Usually they should be kept as simple as possible unless a clear need for other features is demonstrated. Too frequently, these accessories are purchased at considerable cost and discarded after short usage. An example is the remote speaker microphone that can be clipped to the officer's uniform so he can converse without handling the unit itself. Most campuses have little need for this type of option. The department should experiment with one unit prior to ordering many for the entire operation.

A recommended accessory would be a leather carrying case to enable the unit to be carried easily on the belt when not in use. A variety of carrying cases are available, and one should be selected to meet the needs of the department. An alternative is to have a carrying clip backplate on the unit so that it can be clipped to the belt. If neither a carrying case nor clip is used, experience has shown that the units receive very hard use and prove inconvenient and cumbersome for the carrier.

Batteries and Chargers

Mobile radio units are powered by nickel-cadmium batteries that work for an eight-hour shift without charging. Mercury batteries are more expensive, slightly heavier, and last for up to thirty hours. For most purposes the nickel-cadmium battery will be adequate.

In order to insure that the units are always working at peak capacity, the batteries should be used in the same scheduling pattern as the officers—eight hours on duty and sixteen hours off. Therefore, three batteries should be ordered for each unit and labeled by small, color-coded stickers to signify the shift they work (e.g., 1, 2, 3 or A, B, C).

The supervisor in charge of the shift will have responsibility for seeing that the batteries are changed prior to the shift leaving headquarters, and he will insert the outgoing shift batteries in the charger.

A rapid-charge nickel-cadmium battery is also available that can be recharged in an hour. In most cases in which sufficient batteries are available, this type of quick-charging battery is not needed. However, one or two might be kept available for emergency use.

Battery chargers range from single chargers to multiple unit models that accept the nickel-cadmium batteries alone or the entire unit. For most departments the multiple unit will prove most economical and effective. If rapid charge batteries are used, a rapid-charge charger (single or multiple unit) must be specified. Rapid-charge equipment has the advantage of signaling by means of a green light when the battery is fully charged. Regular units have "charge" and "trickle" positions. Normally, when enough replacement batteries are available, the "trickle" position is used.

Monitoring Police Channels

Two-way FM radio equipment can usually be adapted to receive and send on two or more channels. In most cases, a single channel should serve a campus department effectively. Occasionally campus departments also utilize another channel on the same frequency as the local police department, making it possible for foot and car patrol officers to monitor the local police dispatcher and communicate with local police officers.

Although there may be a legitimate reason for being on a local channel in some instances, hazards are involved. One of the most common is the tendency of some campus officers to pay more attention to local police calls than to their own business. On several campuses, particularly during night hours, officers would leave their quiet campus unattended upon hearing local police dispatched to an accident or some other incident and go where the action was—where they usually had absolutely no jurisdiction. Instant and easy communication like this can also lead to a buddy system between local and campus officers that can create personnel problems such as officers converging on an off-campus diner for coffee or gathering at local nightspots.

Thus, the campus police should not share a local police channel. However, a good recommendation is for the dispatcher to have an inexpensive monitor to enable him to listen to local police dispatchers. The dispatcher should be furnished a list of the local police radio code signals so he will know the nature of the incident. The purpose of this monitoring is to be aware of any activity that is nearby or that might affect the campus community, so that campus officers can be alerted.

In larger departments a direct "hot line" to the police and fire communications center is usually advisable. This line would be open for emergency use only and would require simply picking up the phone and talking, thereby gaining valuable time and assuring continuing communication during emergencies when all normal lines might be clogged with incoming and outgoing calls.

Log of Radio Activity

Dispatchers should be required to maintain a running log of all radio activity. FCC requirements regarding these radio logs should be studied and complied with (see Figure 10-2).

One of the major problems with radio communications is the tendency of some personnel to use them too much, sometimes on strictly personal matters. Too much talk can tie up communications and should be discouraged. Messages should be short, businesslike, and to the point. Personal names should not be used, and at times locations should not be given. Code signals and badge or patrol car numbers should be used instead. Profanity, small talk, and departmental gossip should also be taboo. The FCC may be monitoring any communication at any time. Of even more concern is the fact that CB (citizens' band) radio is very popular today, and a growing segment of any community (including criminals) monitors police calls. Several campus departments have been embarrassed when students monitoring radio communications spotlight them in the campus newspaper.

Maintenance and Service

The most important topic regarding FM radio communication systems is maintenance and service. One of the long standing and frequent complaints by many campus security administrators is that service is poor and units are sometimes kept for weeks by a repair service. A number of campus directors have replaced their entire radio system with another manufacturer's system because of this lack of prompt, efficient service.

The problem appears to be that these systems are purchased from salespeople whose main objective is to sell and not to service. Once the sale is made, many salespeople tend to be disinterested or to refer the buyer to someone else.

Service Quality Varies. Service and maintenance for the same make of radio equipment varies greatly from area to area. In part this variance is because most manufacturers have so-called authorized service representatives, which are in-

DISPATCHER'S LOG SHEET

Dispatcher _____ Date _____ Shift _____ Hours _____ to _____

UNIT	NAME	RADIO	UNIT	NAME	RADIO	UNIT	NAME	RADIO

CODE	TIME REC'D	TIME ARR'V	TIME CLEAR	D	UNIT	COMPL/REP	TEL NO.	LOCATION/DESCRIPTION

Figure 10-2. Dispatcher's log sheet.

dependent companies that had nothing to do with the initial sale and which sometimes put their own business first. Not all of these service representatives are unsatisfactory, however. Some campus departments, particularly in smaller communities, have established excellent rapport with their service company and receive prompt and efficient service. Others, however, are treated as just another account and the service company is slow in responding, keeps equipment for long periods, and performs unsatisfactorily. This type of service company does not realize that a campus security or police operation deals in emergency situations that depend on good communications to insure effective handling. Therefore, servicing for a campus should receive top priority and not merely be scheduled in order with other accounts.

To insure good service, the campus department should first of all make service one of the top priorities with salespeople before placing the order. Unfortunately, failure to emphasize this priority is a shortcoming for some purchasing departments because they are looking for price and not performance or service.

Maintenance Agreements. Practically all reputable radio manufacturers have a maintenance agreement that goes into effect after the guarantee expires. This agreement should be read closely and some guarantee of prompt service should be insisted upon.

The security director may inquire of other security and police departments in the area that use the same make of radio system regarding the quality of service they are getting. He should find out exactly what company will be doing the service, where it is located, the extent of its parts inventory, its capabilities, what response time he can expect, how long shop repairs will take, and whom he will be dealing with.

Maintenance agreements are expensive, and the security department has every right to expect and receive prompt, efficient service. The usual excuse for delays—"I am waiting for a part"—should not be accepted. Most parts can be acquired from the manufacturer within two days anywhere in the United States or Canada. Some manufacturers even provide a toll-free number for their service representatives to facilitate parts deliveries.

Log of Service History. Campus departments that are experiencing service problems should build a case and go to the "top." A simple log (see Figure 10-3) will provide a history of service, giving the date the department called for service, the date the equipment was serviced or taken for shop servicing, equipment serviced (serial number, and so on), reason for repair, and date returned. Unsatisfactory performance should be called first to the supplier's attention. If service remains unsatisfactory, a letter should be sent to a corporate official of the company, with a copy to the supplier. In most cases this procedure will bring improved performance.

SERVICE RECORD

DATE CALLED FOR SERVICE	DATE SERVICED OR TAKEN FOR SERVICING	EQUIPMENT TO BE SERVICED (SERIAL NO.)	REASON FOR REPAIR	DATE RETURNED	CONDITION OF EQUIPMENT

Figure 10–3. Communication equipment service log.

UNIFORMS

Personal appearance is important in practically every professional endeavor but is particularly significant in the field of security and law enforcement. Many people come in contact with security or police personnel by sight only, which is how their impression of the entire department is formed. If an organization permits its security personnel to work in ragtag uniforms, the impression is conveyed that their performance will be sloppy and inferior. The morale, self-respect, and initiative of personnel are also affected adversely if they have to wear ill-fitting, incomplete, and dirty uniforms.

Trend Back to Police-Type Uniforms

The blazer-type uniform became popular during the student dissent era when it was considered prudent to soften the police image to enable campus officers to deal more effectively with student problems. However, the tendency in campus security today is to leave most student rule enforcement to student affairs personnel and to enforce only those laws and parking regulations that apply equally to all persons on campus.

Unlike the late 1960s and early 1970s, campus security today faces few problems with students. The emphasis now is on providing protection to the campus community from outsiders. Security should be as visible as possible in order to create a protective, police-oriented image and to act as a deterrent to persons intent on criminal activity on campus. For this reason uniforms are more acceptable on campus than they were a few years ago.

A uniformed officer is also more reassuring and helpful to visitors, students, and staff because he is readily recognized as a representative of the institution who is there to protect and assist. In most cases, however, it is recommended that certain supervisory and investigative personnel continue to wear neat, conservative, well-pressed blazer-and-slacks outfits with the department's seal and a nameplate displayed on the breast pocket. Sometimes the institution's official colors can be used in the blazer uniform or at least incorporated into the colors of the tie.

Many colleges and universities are replacing blazers or other civilian-type apparel with uniforms. The crime problem is the main reason for this trend. One of the best examples is at Yale University, where the traditional business suits and snap-brimmed hats of campus police officers were replaced in 1976 by police-type uniforms. Reflecting the magnitude of this change, local newspapers gave it front-page coverage and emphasized that it was another move to cope with the increase of crime invading the campus.

Specifications

Uniforms should be furnished by the college or university and should be high-quality, conservative police style. In many regions, different weight materials and clothing will be needed for summer and winter use. All uniform blouses, shirts, or jackets should carry a shoulder patch depicting the department's seal on each arm. A nameplate and badge should also be worn. If a hat is to be worn, a conservative eight-point or similar cap matching the uniform is usually preferable to the "smoky-bear" or sheriff-style hat.

Jackets and outerwear should be purchased according to weather requirements and the preferences of the officers who will wear them. Most officers prefer the lightweight but warm, windproof, nylon Eisenhower or police car duty jacket to the longer reefer coat. Every officer should be equipped with a lightweight, completely waterproof raincoat and rainhat. Airweave raingear that "breathes" through microscopic pores is usually preferred because it permits perspiration to evaporate and is very light and durable.

A minimum uniform allowance should include the following:

- 3 short-sleeved and 3 long-sleeved shirts;
- 3 pairs of trousers (different weights for summer and winter, if necessary);
- 1 cap (a lightweight summer cap is more desirable in some regions);
- 1 blouse or jacket;
- 1 patrol car or reefer coat;
- 1 raincoat and hat;
- 1 pair of white gloves for special occasions.

Shoes are usually purchased by the officer, although in some departments a shoe allowance is paid. Shoes are usually black and plain-toe oxford style.

Uniforms should be kept as simple as possible, avoiding too much brass and braid. Sam Browne shoulder and chest belts should also be avoided, not only because of their appearance but also because they provide a handle for an assailant and can be dangerous to the officer's safety unless a breakaway model is specified. For similar reasons, safety ties that hook onto the collar and easily pull away are recommended rather than a conventional tie, which can act as a noose.

In a recent campus study, female officers complained about having to wear the same uniforms as male officers. Obviously these uniforms had been tailored for men only. Attractive and practical policewomen uniforms are available that can match male officers' attire while tailored to fit women. These women's uniforms consist of skirt and pants outfits, women's blouses, shirts, and marine or military style headwear.

Cleaning Allowances

Officers are sometimes paid a cleaning allowance to insure that uniforms are kept clean and pressed. Caution is suggested in granting any cleaning allowances, because these payments become merely another fringe benefit and are not used for their intended purpose. Experience has revealed that, once such an allowance is granted, it will have to be increased continually and the chances of ever rescinding it are practically nonexistent. Campus officers can be held responsible for maintaining a neat appearance without the payment of an allowance. Businesspeople and other professionals, after all, have the responsibility of looking neat, clean, and well pressed.

If a uniform cleaning and maintenance allowance is decided upon, it should be strictly controlled to insure that this money is actually spent for cleaning, pressing, and repairing uniforms. This control can be accomplished by having a contract with a reputable cleaning establishment that will bill the department for its services. In this manner a direct payment to the officer is avoided and a certain number of cleanings per year can be specified and repairs authorized.

Renting Uniforms

Some departments rent their uniforms from uniform rental companies. The obvious advantages of this approach are that the department avoids accumulating unused uniforms when officers leave, and any item can be replaced quickly upon request. What department has not faced the problem of a collection of uniforms, yellowing shirts, and other items that just never seem to fit newly hired officers? Tailoring used uniforms to fit incoming personnel is expensive.

Although renting uniforms eliminates the problems of supply, repair, and usually cleaning and pressing, there are some disadvantages. The rental plan is more costly in the long run. The cost may run from $8.00 to $15.00 per week per officer, which usually includes a weekly change, cleaning, pressing, alterations, and repairs. The price will vary depending on the quality of the uniform, number of items issued, service, and the location of the department. An annual rental charge per officer would be roughly equivalent to purchasing a new wardrobe for that officer every year. However, no large capital investment or administrative costs are involved.

The choice of rental uniforms may be limited to stock items that, although satisfactory for guards and watchmen, may not be appropriate for professional campus security or police officers. A rental uniform usually will not fit as well as a high-quality uniform tailored especially for an individual officer.

If a uniform rental company is selected, care should be taken to insure that the company provides efficient service and individually fitted uniforms of good quality.

Distinction from Police Uniforms

A final caution about campus uniforms is necessary. One of the most common mistakes made some years ago by campus departments was to use exactly the same uniform as the outside local police department. This trend was part of the pattern of hiring retiring local police officers to head campus departments; these officers, in turn, fashioned the department in the same image as the one they had left. Unfortunately, most local police departments in college towns are not looked upon with favor by students, and dressing campus officers in the same uniform does not improve their image.

The mistake of having campus officers wear the same uniform as local police was clearly illustrated during the days of mass student demonstrations, sit-ins, and other protests. When students could not differentiate between local and campus police, they directed their abuse and wrath at both.

Campus officers should be attired in a uniform distinctively different than outside law enforcement agencies. They should be easily recognized as members of the campus community in order to maintain rapport with students to cool crowd situations before they escalate.

Uniforms and Upgraded Image

Sometimes a feeling exists on the part of a campus population that their security personnel are "Keystone Kops" types who are unable to provide professional service. When asked, "What is your assessment of the security operation on this campus?" students may respond with laughter, followed by remarks indicating a complete lack of confidence in security personnel and their ability. In such a case, the image of that department must change if it is to be effective.

This type of situation usually requires hiring a professional director and younger, better educated, and trained personnel. If these newly hired officers wear the same uniforms as the existing older, lower level guard-type personnel, the effect on the community will be largely wasted. The community will be inclined to place the new officers in the same category as security personnel existing prior to the new director. Even adopting new titles will not assist in improving their image unless their uniforms are also changed.

Present personnel who cannot meet the new, higher standards for security officers should remain in the same uniform as before but be classified as "guards" or "watchmen" to carry out routine security duties until replaced by natural attrition. The new class of knowledgeable, trained professionals should carry a different title (security officer, security specialist, police officer, and so on) and wear a distinctively different uniform. On some campuses, attiring new officers in blazer-type uniforms has been well received, particularly when these new officers will be used primarily for investigative assignments in which they will be responding to complaints and dealing with people.

MISCELLANEOUS EQUIPMENT

In addition to the emergency equipment that should be carried in patrol cars, a number of other items should be available to the campus security department.

Flashlights. Heavy-duty flashlights and battery-powered floodlights should be maintained.

Portable P.A. A portable, lightweight, self-powered public address system (bullhorn) should be considered for use in crowd control and certain emergency situations.

Fingerprint Equipment. Fingerprint equipment is also necessary for professional departments that conduct their own investigations and have at least a few personnel who are knowledgeable in the use of such equipment. Equipment to be considered would be a fingerprint-taking kit (holder, roller, and ink) and an all-purpose fingerprint kit for dusting, photographing, and lifting prints.

Cameras. Camera equipment and the ability to process film will vary from department to department. Usually, one or more members of a department are involved in photography as a hobby. They should be designated to handle most photography and possibly the processing of film. However, all officers and, particularly, supervisors should be trained to perform routine photography functions such as taking photos at the scene of an accident.

Every department should have available at least one camera that is relatively simple to operate. An instant camera is sometimes desirable because it produces a picture immediately, and the officer can asses the results to determine if additional photos need to be taken.

Reflective Clothing. If the department is involved in night traffic operations, a supply of high visibility clothing such as traffic vests, belts, and gloves is recommended.

Medical Emergency Equipment. At least one resuscitator should be available to campus departments whose officers have been trained in its use.

A serious question needs to be asked as to whether campus security or police operations should be involved in transporting persons who require emergency medical care, other than routine cases, to hospitals or the infirmary. If the department does undertake this responsibility, an ambulance or similar vehicle should be available, equipped with stretchers and other equipment. Persons attending to and transporting victims *must* be well trained in first aid and medical matters.

Chapter 11

DEPARTMENTAL OFFICE SPACE

One of the most common shortcomings of campus security departments has been inadequate, poorly located, and often poorly maintained office space.

Some departments have been housed with the buildings and grounds operation in a maintenance building in which both security and buildings personnel share lockers, time cards, and office space. Other departments are buried in basement space unacceptable to other campus departments. Some departments work out of boiler rooms and so-called guard houses. Of various departments surveyed by myself, one used a construction shack left over from a recent building site. Another occupied what was formerly an airport control tower — the campus had been built on a former airport. Still another used a discarded Quonset hut. One department was housed in what had been a small store, behind plate-glass windows that provided little privacy and security and was similar to working in a goldfish bowl.

On a number of campuses, nearby private homes have been acquired and turned over to the security departments for their exclusive use. Although some of these homes were in deplorable condition when acquired, they were renovated and refurbished to provide sufficient working space for the security operation.

PLANNING A BUSINESSLIKE FACILITY

An encouraging development during the past few years has been the advent of specially constructed, one-story buildings on campus to house the security operation. Hopefully, more campus administrators will recognize the need for providing this type of facility, which certainly promotes the image of the department and improves morale and efficiency.

If such a security building is contemplated, the director or chief of the department should be involved from the outset in planning the layout rather than trusting entirely to architects and others. Visits should be made to colleges and universities having similar new facilities in order to profit by their experience.

A campus security operation should be administered like an efficient business and create a businesslike office atmosphere. Space should be large enough and designed to promote efficiency. Office space should be well lighted, attractive, functional, well maintained, and furnished.

Layout of a Typical Small Department

Minimum space for the typical small department (fifteen to thirty personnel) should consist of a general operations area which would house most files; the dispatcher's desk or console; various supplies; and a counter over which the public would transact business.

On the other side of this counter would be a relatively small public area with possibly several chairs or a bench and a table on which some reading material might be displayed. The general public would be restricted to this area unless authorized to enter through a door or doors controlled by the dispatcher-clerk, who can take routine complaints in addition to other duties. Often the secretary for the department can act as dispatcher and deal with the public during regular campus working hours. The secretary can also administer the files and perform other clerical and secretarial functions.

Access to this area must be limited to the dispatcher, secretary, supervisor, or other personnel who are actually working there. Unless strict rules are imposed, these areas can easily become gathering places for officers and other personnel, a practice that can greatly reduce the efficiency of employees trying to carry out their duties. A businesslike image is certainly not conveyed when an outsider walks in and observes several officers in back of the counter talking, drinking coffee, and reading newspapers or magazines, rather than attending to their duties.

A clean, well-lighted, and uncluttered locker room of adequate size should be provided, including full-length, individually lockable lockers of sufficient width and depth and with slanted tops to prevent articles from accumulating and to facilitate dusting. The locker room should also include a full-length mirror, a good-sized bulletin board, table and chairs, benches, and possibly a refrigerator. Nearby toilet, sink, and shower facilities are also desirable. Most directors agree, however, that officers rarely use department showers because they prefer using those at home or in the gym after exercising. If squad rooms are large enough they can also serve as classrooms, although it is usually preferable to use regular classrooms for training purposes. A small library of law enforcement and security magazines, books, and periodicals is also desirable.

The remainder of the space should include a private office for the director that should be well furnished and large enough to include a small conference table and confidential file cabinets. That the director's office be located here rather than elsewhere on campus is important so that he will not be isolated from many of the day-to-day activities. Surprisingly enough, on some campuses the head of the department and his secretary occupy office space in buildings far removed from the security office and its operation.

Most departments will also need secure space to maintain supplies and lost-and-found articles.

A small office for supervisors that can sometimes double as an interview room is also desirable.

Figures 11-1 and 11-2 depict floor plans of typical office space for the smaller department.

Figure 11-1. Typical layout of office space for a small security department, sample 1.

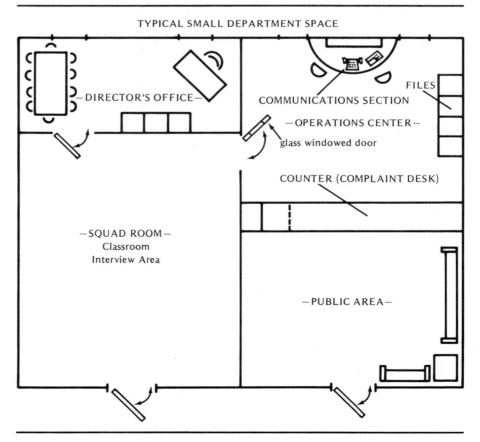

TYPICAL SMALL DEPARTMENT SPACE

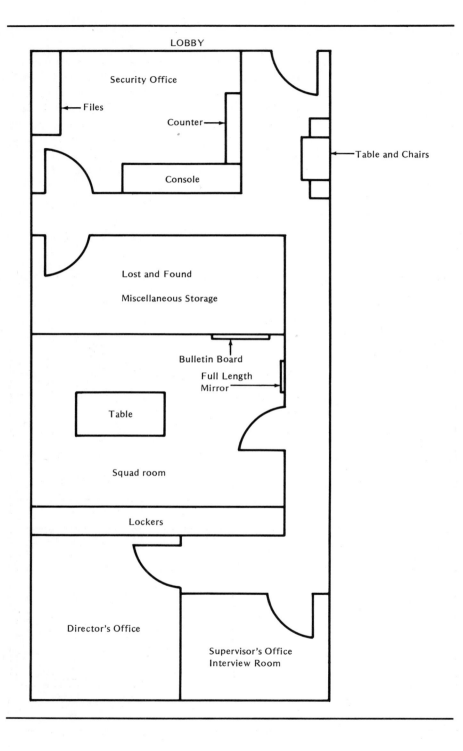

Layout of Larger Departments

The larger campus department will naturally need more space. Such space might include an office for the director's secretary that would also house files, an office for an assistant director, and possibly private offices for other supervisors and investigators. At least one private interview room should also be available. Larger space for equipment and supplies may have to be provided, as well as a separate secure storage area for lost-and-found articles.

Figure 11-3 is a floor plan of a larger department.

Security of Office Space

The security of any campus police or security department should be considered during the layout and construction of space. Although the days of student take-overs of campus security facilities appear to be over, these offices still house a vital part of the campus operations and must be afforded a higher level of security than other administrative offices. The fact that the offices have personnel on duty at all times is a big plus as far as security is concerned, but physical aspects should also be considered in planning for space. For example, expansive glass windows on ground-floor space should be avoided or breakage resistant glazing should be utilized.

Also some sort of access-control system should be considered to control persons entering, particularly at night and during periods of emergency. For example, the dispatcher or other employee assigned to the lobby reception area can observe and communicate with those persons desiring entry by intercom prior to activating an electric strike to permit entry.

Location on Campus

At the start of this chapter some examples were given of where the security department should *not* be located. However, some campus administrators and, particularly, faculty and student affairs personnel are still inclined to hide the security office as though it were a necessary evil.

A few years ago an architectural firm was designing a very large multipurpose facility for an urban university that had inadequate security space in the buildings and grounds department. Although all agreed that new space should be planned for and allotted to security in this new building, consultants failed in their efforts to locate the office on the main floor where it would be visible and accessible. In addition to the library, a theatre, offices, and other activity rooms, the building

Figure 11-2 (opposite). Typical layout of office space for a small security department, sample 2.

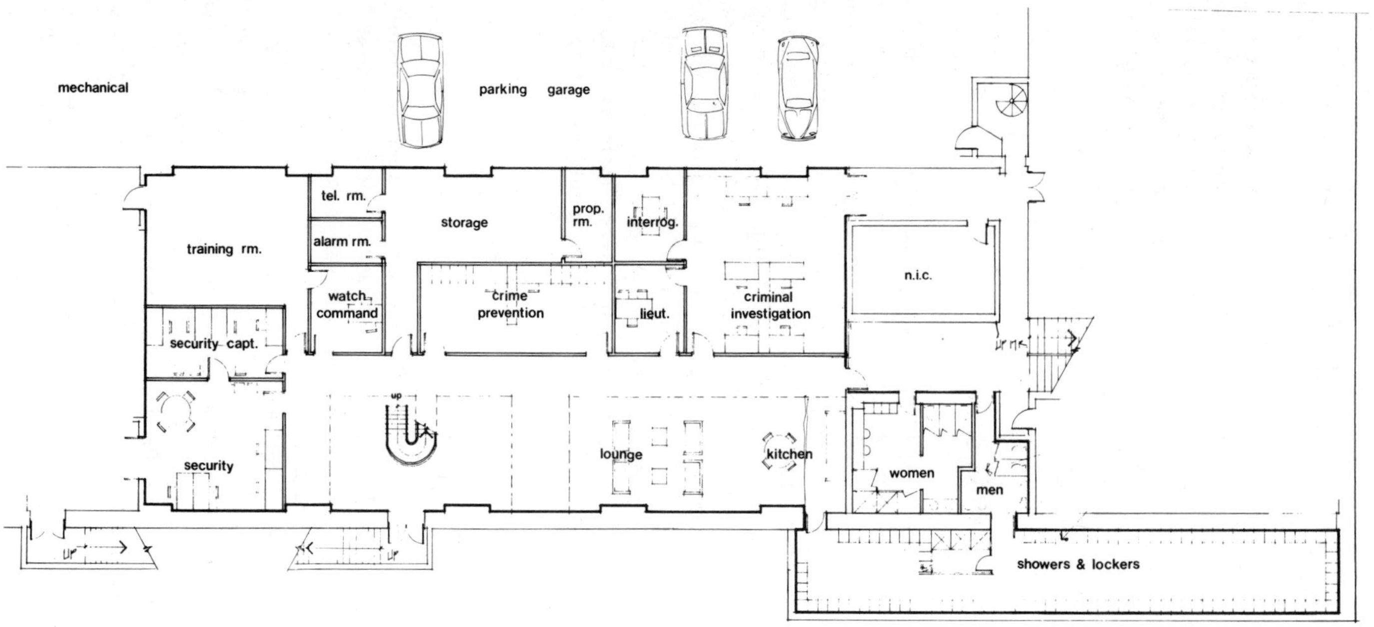

lower level

mechanical

parking   garage

training rm.

tel. rm.

alarm rm.

watch command

security capt.

storage

crime prevention

prop. rm.

interrog.

lieut.

criminal investigation

n.i.c.

up

security

kitchen

lounge

women

men

showers & lockers

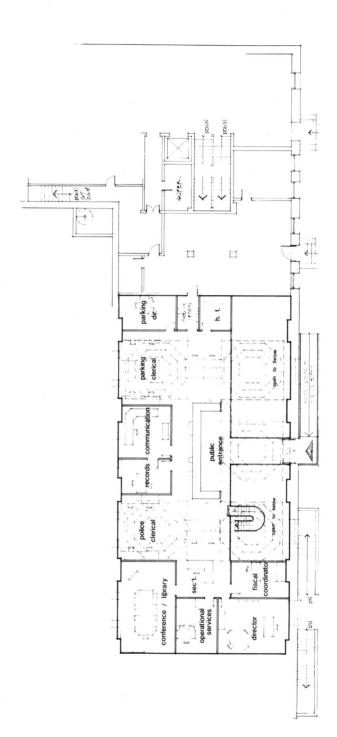

upper level

Figure 11-3. Typical layout of office space for a large security department. Courtesy of Harvard University Police Department, Cambridge, Massachusetts.

housed student affairs and the student union. The dean of students and members of student affairs successfully argued that locating the security department in such a prominent place would be "abrasive and harassing to students" and that it should be buried out of sight in the basement. This kind of thinking does a disservice to both security and the campus community it serves.

Another trend, which fortunately is disappearing, was to equate security with the maintenance operations and house it in the same area, removed from the mainstream of student and campus life. This trend was undoubtedly the result of the fact that security started with a watchman operation in buildings and grounds.

One of the best illustrations of this type of thinking was encountered in the late 1960s during a security evaluation and reorganization at a large state university system. This state was engaged in building a number of entirely new campuses, following the same pattern of a loop access road, parking on the perimeter, and academic and administrative buildings clustered in the center. The only buildings not following this pattern were the buildings housing the maintenance operations. These buildings were located on the opposite side of the loop road from all other buildings, usually in an area completely removed and sometimes out of sight. You have probably guessed already where architects and planners had allotted security space—in the basement of these maintenance buildings.

A campus security department should be located in the core of the campus, preferably on a ground floor where it will be visible and easily accessible to students and the campus community. The space should be functional and aesthetically pleasing. Good housekeeping should prevail and equipment and extraneous matter unnecessary to the operations of the office space should be stored elsewhere. Various forms and other printed material that are used frequently or handed out to visitors can be stored out of sight on shelves under the counter separating the work space from the public reception area.

ANALYZING SPACE ALLOTMENTS

A security director who is not satisfied with the department's present space, or who is planning to build new office facilities, should look around the campus and do an analysis of present space allotments. Invariably, some desirable space will be available in a building in the center of the campus that meets all or most of the requirements outlined in the preceding paragraph. Renovations may be needed, but once administrators are convinced of the need for such space, the security director should also be able to convince them that renovating present space is more economical than constructing a building to house security. However, I am not saying that a separate building for security would not still be preferable, providing it is located near the focal point of campus activity.

If the security director can make his case and get administrative support for new space, including it in the architectural drawings of a new building is possible.

This provides the opportunity for the director to have a voice in the layout and guarantees a fresh, new, well-lighted, and functional office. Directors should be cognizant of all planning for new construction, not only for possible relocation of the security department but also so they will have a voice in security design and equipment.

MAKING A CASE FOR NEW SPACE

A frequent complaint of heads of security is that their department's working space is entirely inadequate and not functional. However, in some cases these directors have not really tried to convince their superiors and the administration of the need for better space, other than to complain about their present location.

Usually more than a "I need new space" is required for the administrator to grant a director's request. It means furnishing facts and statistics on why new space is needed, such as the effect on the performance and morale of the department, how new space would improve efficiency and the department's image on campus, how inferior their office space is compared to other campus departments, and similar factual information.

The director should also select several possible sites if a new building is planned and present at least a rough drawing and floor plan with some idea of costs. If use of a present building is to be proposed, some idea of the renovations necessary, floor plan, and approximate costs should be presented. Naturally, the director should also build his case by pointing out the space problems and inefficiencies of the present location: how the department has outgrown it, the poor picture it presents to the community, the lack of privacy, the increased flow of disrupting traffic, and other faults.

Most of the director's campaign for new space should be carried on in writing directed to the proper decision-making administrators. This proposal should be supplemented with meetings at which the director would present his case using visual displays, statistics, factual reports regarding the increase in personnel and their duties, the ever-growing problem of crime, and similar convincing arguments.

In a recent visit to Harvard University I was afforded an excellent example of "convincing" an administration when it was learned that, after prolonged efforts, Director of Police and Security Saul L. Chafin had been given approval for new departmental space. How did he do it? He came up with facts, figures, floor plans, and a selling campaign that proved to his superiors that new space was badly needed and that the security program on campus would be enhanced by providing adequate, functional, pleasing, businesslike space to work in.

Director Chafin, upon discovering that one of his personnel had a BA degree in environmental psychology, had her perform a study and submit a report regarding the effects of the physical and spacial environments of Grays Hall (long-time location for the department) and what moving to a new space would mean to the

department. In her excellent report, she examined the working conditions in the
depressing Grays Hall basement office and the effects of working in such an environment upon the performance and psychological attitudes of members of the Harvard
University Police Department. The following are some pertinent excerpts from this
study that might apply and be used by other departments endeavoring to acquire
new space.

> Located one step below most other departments on campus, the visibility
> of our services important to efficient performance is cut short.

> Police headquarters should be readily seen and accessible.

> The noise level rises — the result is a greater expenditure of energy in order
> to narrow the focus of attention required to block out excess stimuli.

> The criminal investigation unit suffers from a shortage of flexible space
> required to perform its duties well. . . .The image which such a department
> portrays is inefficiency, because too many activities are going on simul-
> taneously without clear distinct spaces for interviewing, consulting, plan-
> ning, and fingerprinting. As a result, down time is often instituted in order
> to accomplish an assignment. One item is worked on at the cost of another,
> and the entire criminal investigation unit rate of success becomes slower,
> slower, and slower.

> Proper ventilation is not available — resulting symptoms such as dizziness,
> nauseousness, and eye irritation are the immediate effects.

> Several members of the staff have tried to grow plants in the basement
> department. All have died, even though careful care was provided.

> The lack of windows, natural sunlight, fresh air, space conducive to group
> and individual work, separate areas requiring voluntary and involuntary
> attention mechanisms have created an environment in Grays Hall basement
> which is unhealthy both physically and psychologically to those who must
> work within its perimeter. The environment is one of inflexibility which is
> reinforced by the hard and immovable architecture and furnishings which
> it presents. As a result, the first impression which we give to those who use
> our facilities is one of disorganization and rigidity. The personnel who work
> here find themselves functioning actively in an environment which is con-
> ducive to passivity. They are trained to respond here, not to react, and
> this setting is definitely not conducive to the former. A hard environment
> will breed inflexible people with insensitive attitudes towards their work.
> Choice in the arrangement of the space, air, light, and other accessories
> already mentioned are advisable. Control of the environment by the indi-
> viduals so as to enhance their productivity would benefit the entire univer-
> sity if this were to take place with HUPD. Improved physical conditions
> will enhance a positive psychological attitude upon the individual, thus
> yielding a higher rate of efficiency and productivity.

> In summary, poor and inadequate working conditions make this office
> expend an incredible amount of energy to maintain an adequate working

situation. This same amount of work, if put in the proper environment could be accomplished using only half the energy, and attitudes would be more positive than they are right now.

It should be noted, that the only reason that everyone is surviving down here is because people get along with other people. Tempers, however, can only withstand so much before they cannot take it any longer. The camel has just received another straw. . . .This time it just might break its back.*

The result of all these efforts culminated in a sympathetic administration relocating the department to an existing building that had to be almost completely gutted prior to extensive renovations being made. Figure 11-3 contains the floor plan for this two-level, modern, functional space in which Director Chafin had a major voice in formulating.

PLANNING FOR RELOCATING OFFICE

If an existing department is to relocate to other space, it is best to plan for this move early so that appropriate renovations and modifications can be made to accommodate existing office furniture, file cabinets, and equipment. One easy way of planning for a move is to make a furniture and equipment floor plan drawn to scale. Another simple technique is to measure all larger pieces of furniture (desks, tables, cabinets, and so on) and use a removable tape to outline them on the floor of the new space.

CONCLUSION

What has been most encouraging in the past few years is to see campus security and police departments emerging from dark and often damp basements and boiler houses into bright, new, well-furnished, well-equipped, and businesslike offices. Also encouraging has been the observation that these offices are located in the heart of the campus where they are visible and easily accessible to the communities they serve. However, some colleges and universities still are inclined to treat security as a second-class citizen. Hopefully this chapter may assist in convincing administrators that any campus security operation deserves to be housed in decent, respectable space.

---

* Courtesy of Harvard University Police Department, Cambridge, Mass.

Chapter 12

REPORTS, RECORDS, AND FILES

An effective reporting and records system is essential to any efficient campus security or law enforcement operation.

A variety of reporting and filing systems exist at colleges and universities. This chapter does not recommend any particular system over others, but it does suggest certain forms and procedures that might be of assistance to campus security departments. (See Appendix for complete display of forms.)

The test of any reporting and record-keeping system is whether information can be easily and quickly located and whether meaningful, accurate statistics and factual reports are being maintained.

Records are particularly sensitive on college campuses, and care should be exercised to insure the confidentiality of all communications and reports. This confidentiality entails fixing responsibility for the administration and filing records on as few personnel as possible and not allowing access to the files to outsiders. Procedures should also be established to channel and limit departmental personnel's access to files. In other words, access to records should be strictly on a need-to-know basis.

Although an efficient record keeping system is a basic requirement for any law enforcement or security agency, some campus administrators and others still refuse to recognize this need. The main reason for this attitude is often that the administrators do not want to focus on the crime problem on campus and want to "sweep it under the rug." They are also afraid that confidential, sensitive information on members of the community might be explosive and embarrass the institution if publicized. This attitude was common during the early years of campus security, but higher standards of performance and professionalism have gradually resulted in administrators recognizing the need for factual and complete reports and records.

A record keeping system should be kept as simple as possible. Usually large departments with diversified activities will require more extensive and complicated record-keeping systems than smaller, less active departments. However, any system should be tailored to the individual departmental needs.

NEED FOR CENTRALIZED STATISTICS

Many state university systems have set up effective reporting procedures that are usually patterned after other state law enforcement units. Most of these universities furnish crime statistics to the FBI to be included in its *Uniform Crime Reports*. At present, this is the only centralized record keeping system for campus crime statistics. However, only a relatively few campus departments execute these reports for the FBI.

A definite need exists for a central depository of campus crime statistics to which all campus departments, both private and public, would contribute. At present, no meaningful statistics exist on a nationwide basis. The creation of such a depository should bring about more uniformity in record keeping, which now varies greatly from campus to campus.

FACTUAL REPORTING SYSTEM

The starting point for good record keeping is the reporting system. To be meaningful, reports must contain complete, factual, and accurate information. Statistical data such as the value of property stolen or recovered should also be included. Because it has been one of the most prominent weaknesses of the law enforcement officer, report writing requires concentrated training and constant supervision.

Strict policies should be established to insure that officers submit factual reports on practically any action they take. These reports should be submitted before the officer leaves the department after completing his tour of duty. The decision of whether a report is necessary should not be left to the officer's discretion and reports submitted a day or two late should not be acceptable.

Report Form

A report form should be used that carries the title (name of subject, suspect, or brief description of incident) and usually some simple "reminders" to officers that certain information should be reported. These reminders will increase or decrease with the caliber and training of the officers making out the reports. For example, most contract guard agencies use a long check sheet of duties to be performed or matters to be reported as reminders to guard personnel. In contrast, a well trained officer should be able to execute a complete and accurate report without these reminders. Therefore, a simple report form is suggested that will fix responsibility on the officer to act or investigate and report his findings.

Figure 12-1 is a simple combination complaint and report form that provides spaces for the identity and address of the complainant, the date and time received, and the name of the clerk-dispatcher or officer taking the complaint and filling out the report. Other spaces are provided for the title of the report, the character (type) of case or incident, and for the signature of the supervisor who approves the report.

"Character of Case" refers to a classification of the incident to determine its number and the file category it will be filed in. Each of these characters of cases carries its own distinctive category file number preceding the chronological case number. For example, in a theft of personal property, the character of the case would be "Theft of Personal Property"; if the identifying classification file number was 10, the first case would read 10-1, the second 10-2, the third 10-3, and so on. Under this system all "Theft of Personal Property" cases would be filed by date in the same file where they could be easily located and statistics readily computed regarding one type of crime or service rendered.

Bound Filing

Bound serialized files of these reports are recommended rather than loose filing. Bound filing protects the confidentiality and orderliness of the reports. If a report or case has to be removed, a charge-out slip should be inserted in the file to indicate the file number, date, and identity of the person using it. A short time limit such as two or three days should be required for the return of reports. Multiple case reports may be filed in a single bound file volume with the outside cover indicating the first and last file numbers in that volume.

Index System

The next important phase of any reporting system is a good card index system to act as a ready reference and to facilitate in locating any case or incident report. These index cards are usually filed alphabetically by the subject or suspect's name or a brief title of the incident (e.g., "Unknown subject—theft of $35 from desk of John Jones '80, room 42, Smith Hall, 9/7/77"). In most cases the victim's name should also be indexed as well as names of any other individuals who might appear in the body of the report and to whom it might be necessary to refer in the future.

COMPLAINT AND INVESTIGATIVE REPORT FORM

Title _____   Name of Complainant _____

_____   Address & Tel. No. _____

_____   _____

Character of Case _____   Complaint Received

_____   Personal _____   Tel. _____

File Number _____   Date _____   Time _____

DETAILS _____

_____

_____

_____

_____

_____

_____

_____

_____

_____

_____

_____

ACTION RECOMMENDED OR REMARKS _____

_____

Clerk's or Officer's Name _____

Date _____

APPROVED _____

SUPERVISOR IN CHARGE

Figure 12-1.   Combination complaint and report form.

The assigning of the file number, the making of the index card reflecting this file number and identifying data, and the actual filing of the report may be assigned to the director's secretary in smaller departments and to a clerical employee or file clerk in larger departments that can justify additional clerical or secretarial personnel.

Fixed Responsibility

It is important that shift supervisors or persons directly responsible for the officer's work read and sign each report to indicate he has read them and approves of their content and the action taken. This procedure fixes responsibility and results in the supervisor returning reports for corrections—in effect, training officers under him to write better reports.

STUDENT RECORDS AND REPORTS

Sometimes a decided difference of opinion exists between the dean of students and others in student affairs versus the director of security in regard to reports and records involving students. Persons in student affairs often believe that any information regarding students, particularly of a derogatory nature, should be confined entirely to their office and that the security or campus police department should not retain such records.

The retention of these reports by the security department after the student graduates or withdraws is another issue, with some people arguing that these records should be destroyed.

Policies regarding student records will vary from campus to campus. Any report involving an arrest of a student or a serious offense, however, should be treated exactly the same as a similar report involving a nonstudent. The only difference might be that index cards on students could be filed alphabetically by class, and each year the entire set of cards pertaining to the graduating class could be placed in an inactive file.

One of the reasons student records should be maintained is that sometimes these matters, particularly arrests, arise in connection with employment applications, and the student may need the facts of the incident to verify his own statement of what occurred. Many times these offenses sound worse than they really are, and verification of the student's account of what happened by means of a report can assist him or her in obtaining a position.

Inconsequential reports involving minor incidents or violations of college rules can be purged from the records after the student graduates, and all records can be destroyed after a few years.

The release of records to other law enforcement agencies and government investigators is another sensitive area. In the case of arrest records, the same state laws pertaining to disclosure of records by public police departments should apply. Inquiries regarding violations of student rules and similar matters that had been initially referred to the dean's office for handling should be directed to that office.

DISSEMINATION OF INFORMATION ON CAMPUS

Who should get security reports? Some departments disseminate copies of reports widely, while others drastically restrict distribution. On some campuses almost any employee can acquire a copy of a report simply by asking for it. At other institutions reports are severely restricted, and the dean's office, director of residence halls, and others complain that they are not kept informed of matters within their scope of responsibilities.

Persons who should receive copies of reports are persons who have a need to know. This means that each report must be carefully reviewed and copies sent to those administrators who would have a pertinent interest or responsibility. For example, copies of most reports involving students should be directed to the dean of students. Reports concerning incidents in a residence hall (theft, vandalism, and so forth) should go to the head of residence halls.

The vice president or other administrator to whom the director answers should also receive copies of those reports involving more serious incidents. Some administrators may even want to review all reports daily.

The director's responsibility is to keep other administrators advised regarding matters in their area of responsibility. Occasionally it may even be necessary to phone the administrator to inform him of some pertinent information that will not wait for the preparation and delivery of a report. A preferable method may be to submit a memorandum to other department heads rather than merely sending a copy of the officer's rough report, particularly when several reports have been submitted by officers working on one case. The memorandum should include only pertinent information and provide a succinct and clear account of what transpired.

UTILIZATION OF STATISTICS

Periodic statistical reports should be submitted to appropriate campus administrators to indicate crime trends and incidents. Many campuses already follow this policy and submit them on a daily, weekly, or monthly basis. This information can be filled in on a form that reflects statistics and trends. The form can be tailored to suit the needs of a particular campus but should reflect a comparison with recent months and possibly give the general location of incidents (residence halls, college union, and so on). Among other things, the form should reflect the number of thefts, assaults, rapes, and other crimes reported as well as those solved, value of property stolen and recovered, arrests and charges; and it should give a brief account of any serious incident or investigation.

The Importance of an Annual Report

Another use for statistics and trends is in an annual report. Every campus security department should prepare an annual report indicating to the community the problems faced by the department, progress and achievements made during the year, and an accounting of services rendered. The annual report should be widely distributed throughout the campus community and, if possible, be spotlighted in the campus newspaper and other publications.

The report should not be merely a dry listing of statistics but should employ graphics to depict yearly trends, contain photos, and give some account of services performed such as medical emergencies transported, money escorts, lost-and-found activity, and so on. These annual reports can prove to be the "convincer" at budget time and are excellent for promoting better communications and relations with the campus community. Too often, members of the community, particularly students, have little idea of the activities of a campus security department and are prone to look upon officers as dispensers of parking tickets with few other responsibilities.

SECTION III.
SPECIFIC PROTECTION
AREAS

Chapter 13

ELECTRONIC PROTECTION
OF CAMPUS BUILDINGS

College and university campuses contain millions of dollars' worth of buildings and other facilities that, in turn, house millions of dollars' worth of property. Often these facilities house valuable works of art, rare books and manuscripts, and similar collections that call for a high level of protection. An important responsibility of any campus security operation is to provide around-the-clock protection, not only by patrol but also by the use of various types of security equipment. This chapter deals with security planning for new buildings and how these facilities and property can best be protected.

THE INCREASING USE OF ELECTRONICS

The ever-growing crime problem on campus has focused attention on the need for electronic security systems to supplement and strengthen coverage provided by security personnel. The advent of the open campus, although excellent from a community relations standpoint, has contributed to the problem of making campuses easily accessible to thieves, burglars, rapists, and other undesirables.

Campus administrators must face the fact that the days of controlling access to a campus by fencing and guard posts at entrance roads are over. They must think in terms of *anyone's* being able to enter the campus, and they must establish security systems and procedures that will protect buildings and the valuable property they contain. The question must also be asked, "Do the people working and studying here feel safe, and is their property afforded at least a reasonable degree of protection?"

Any campus that is not considering a proprietary electronic intrusion and detection system is overlooking what is rapidly becoming a necessary part of an effective security program. Remember, however, that a university campus, with a unique, residential community, is unlike a shopping center or large office complex that can close and lock all facilities at a certain time each night or at other times when the facility is not functioning and occupied.

Most campus facilities have to be accessible to the people working and studying there at all hours. Even though buildings are locked, faculty members and other people have keys. The work habits of some people using certain facilities such as laboratories require these people to be on campus during the night and early morning hours. This virtually "open house" approach means that a basic perimeter alarm system will be ineffective. A more sophisticated type of access-control and protection system is needed.

Care in Choosing Equipment

Utmost thought and care should be exercised in purchasing any security device to protect campus buildings and certain critical areas. Many campuses have purchased security devices that were incompatible with other devices or not suited to that particular application. Many times various alarms and other electronic devices installed on campus are not even used because they are not effective. Often they were purchased by a nonprofessional from a convincing salesperson. The proper electronic detection and intrusion system, however, will increasingly replace the old watchman-guard concept of performing clock rounds and similar routine security functions.

Many times when proprietary security systems are recommended, campus administrators immediately reject the proposal because of the initial high cost of equipment and installations. It is sometimes difficult to convince them that such systems not only provide more reliable protection and better coverage, but also in the long run they are more economical than watchmen or similar patrols. The ever-progressing state of the art in the electronic security industry provides devices and systems to cope with practically any security situation. The time is rapidly approaching when the primary responsibility of security personnel will be to respond to problems detected by electronics. Electronic coverage has already drastically reduced the need for certain lower level security personnel, and this trend will undoubtedly continue.

Do Devices Replace Security Personnel?

Although various types of alarms, access control systems, closed-circuit television (CCTV), and other devices provide excellent tools and backup for security personnel, they do not entirely eliminate the need for security officers. Personnel are still needed to respond to problems reported by the electronic systems. An expensive proprietary security system is a waste of money unless alert, trained security personnel respond to problems immediately and knowledgeably. For example, an extensive and rather sophisticated proprietary system was designed for a large, new civic center. This system, which involved various types of fire and intrusion alarms, emergency signaling devices, CCTV, electric door strikes, and similar equipment, was monitored at a central console in the security department's office. Although an in-house professional security staff had been recommended, the owners decided to save money by hiring low-level contract guards who could not respond efficiently to anything but the most routine problems and who could not even monitor the console and dispatch properly.

Director's Responsibility

The head of any campus security or law enforcement operation today needs to know what electronic devices are available, and he must keep up with new equipment as it comes on the market. The head of the department should be able to recommend the best and most reliable equipment that can be purchased at the lowest price to be used in a particular situation. He should be deeply involved in planning for such equipment and should have the final say regarding what equipment is to be purchased and installed. Too often alarm devices and similar equipment are purchased by various campus facilities with very little input from the security department, even though that department will have the responsibility of monitoring and responding to these alarms.

A number of sources are available for the campus security director to utilize to acquire information about electronic security systems and keep pace with the ever-changing state of the art. Magazines such as *Security Management,* published by the American Society for Industrial Security, and *Security World* often carry excellent articles. Several basic books on alarm systems also can be consulted.

A wealth of information can be obtained by attending conferences, workshops, and seminars such as those sponsored by the International Association of Campus Law Enforcement Administrators, the American Society for Industrial Security, the International Security Conference and Exposition, and the National Crime Prevention Institute.

Conferences of the International Security Conference and Exposition, which are usually held three times each year in Anaheim, California, Chicago, Illinois, and New York City, have the largest group of exhibitors of electronic security systems anywhere in the world. Spend a day in the exhibit area viewing displays, talking to exhibitors, picking up literature, and keeping up with the state of the art.

The American Society for Industrial Security and the International Association of Campus Law Enforcement Administrators also have numerous exhibitors of electronic security devices at their annual conferences.

PROPRIETARY SECURITY SYSTEMS

Central Monitoring Console

The heart of any security system is the central console at which all electronic intrusion alarms, access control systems, output of CCTV cameras, remote door controls, watchmen tour stations, fire detectors, and other components are monitored. The radio base station is also located here and the console operator acts as dispatcher. Emergency phones are also answered here and hot lines exist to outside police and fire agencies. Many central consoles also are equipped with weather alert monitoring capabilities and monitor outside local police and fire radio systems.

Since the advent of the transistor and by use of microprocessor-based computer central processing units, the size of these central stations has been drastically reduced. In fact, the advances have been so dramatic that the console of ten years ago is practically obsolete today.

The central processing unit should tie together all security alarms and devices; alert the operator to a problem audibly and visually; graphically display the date, time, location, and source of the problem; and provide instructions for responding to emergencies and other problems. A printout should furnish a complete record of alarms and other activities. This printout provides an excellent management tool for the director and other supervisors because it relates a twenty-four-hour-per-day history of events monitored that can be cross checked against officers' incident reports and other records.

Any central processing unit purchased should be capable of accepting future alarm points and other electronic sensing devices.

CCTV cameras will also be monitored at this console. The old concept of monitoring numerous cameras with the operator staring at ten or twelve individual monitoring screens has now been replaced by more effective sequential viewing where outputs of cameras hold for a few seconds on a single screen before producing the next picture. The ability to pull out and hold any picture on a larger holding screen, while other pictures continue to revolve, should be present.

Purchasing the Proprietary System

I would caution readers that when purchasing a proprietary security system it is better to secure bids from several reputable companies that can supply the console and the entire system—various types of alarms, access-control system, CCTV, and so on. Problems can result when a number of suppliers are contracted to supply various devices and components making up the system. At times some of these devices may not be compatible with others, the installation schedule can become confused resulting in delays, and when malfunctions occur one supplier may be inclined to blame the product and installation of other suppliers.

Complete responsibility for the installation and servicing of the system can be clearly fixed when the entire package, with the possible exception of the radio system, is contracted with a single company.

One of the most important factors in purchasing any electronic security system is to make sure that the supplier can supply *prompt and efficient service.* Usually this service is furnished under a maintenance contract after the installing company guarantees the system for the first year. Check with other security directors utilizing similar systems purchased from the same supplier to determine their reactions to the system and, particularly, the company's track record for service.

Should Building Functions Be Monitored by Security?

Some difference of opinion exists regarding whether building equipment control and monitoring functions should be monitored by the security department at its central console. These functions include monitoring and, in some instances, stopping, starting, and controlling building equipment such as boilers, turbines, chillers, condensers, pumps, fans, compressors, refrigerators and freezers, elevators, lighting, air flow equipment, generators, and various types of environmental controls to save energy.

Although in smaller institutions the budget may dictate that both security and mechanical functions be monitored at security's central processing console, I would recommend that all building-related functions having nothing to do with security be monitored exclusively by the physical plant department that has responsibility for them. This will entail having a separate monitoring console.

The reason I strongly recommend that building and security functions be divorced from each other is because security personnel are not building maintenance oriented or trained and vice versa. Clogging up a security function with plant-related matters can also seriously affect the efficiency of the security department, particularly when an emergency occurs. To my way of thinking, a security department should only be directly responsible for monitoring equipment dealing with the safety of the campus community and its property, including all security alarms, access control systems, CCTV, and similar components that would normally be associated with security and frequently require response by a security officer. All smoke, rate of rise, and other fire-detection devices and alarms should be the responsibility of the security department and, possibly, the monitoring of sprinklers could also be included.

One of the common faults I have found on many campuses is a complete lack of maintenance personnel on duty during at least some of the night hours and on weekends and holidays. Therefore, security is faced with the problem of trying to get maintenance people to respond when a problem occurs. (It is often surprising to find so many maintenance personnel not home or sick when called during off hours.)

The ideal situation is to have at least one maintenance employee on duty at all times who would monitor the building related functions and equipment and be responsible for calling in the proper personnel or, in some instances, correcting the problem himself. The participation of security should be limited to having a single trouble alarm from the physical plant console so that when the physical plant console is not staffed, security will get a signal, an officer will check the physical plant monitoring unit to determine the nature of the problem, and follow instructions regarding what action to take.

Commercial Central Stations

This section does not discuss at length commercial, outside central station monitoring of campus alarms and other devices because on virtually all campuses a twenty-four-hour security office is in operation where the central console would be located and staffed by security personnel. However, in some small institutions with minimal staffing, an outside central station may have to be used with signals being transmitted from campus via telephone lines and the central station operators notifying the local police or campus patrol of problems. If an outside central station is used, make sure it is a bona fide, reputable central station (not a telephone answering service) and that operators are properly trained regarding what action to take when alarms are activated.

ALARM SYSTEMS

UL Standards

In discussing alarm systems we first must recognize that practically the only standards existing at present are those set by the Underwriters Laboratories (UL). Many misconceptions have occurred over the role of UL and "UL Approval" of products. Insurance companies will always require that burglar or intrusion alarms of all types be "UL Approved." These UL standards were written primarily for commercial security devices.

UL standards represent only the *minimum* acceptable requirements for the design and performance of alarm equipment for a particular application. Therefore, one system may be vastly better than another but each may be rated equal by UL standards. Also, some equipment not listed by UL may be equal or even superior to UL standards but because of some technicality (i.e., type of installation) may not have been approved. Therefore, in purchasing security systems, UL approval is only one of the factors to be considered.

Local versus Central Station Alarms

A local alarm system relies on someone's hearing the alarm bell or siren and reporting it to the security department. Many times these alarms are ignored and their main value, hopefully, is to scare the intruder away. Sometimes they also annoy the intruder who then vandalizes the property before leaving.

A local alarm on a campus will only be effective if responsibility is delegated to someone within hearing distance who will report it immediately. Obviously, such coverage is difficult, and therefore, monitoring intrusion alarms at a central console is considerably more effective and desirable. A silent alarm to the console also enhances the chances of catching the intruder.

The use of local alarms on fire doors is fairly common at many institutions. For the most part they are also ineffective because students ignore the signs indicating "emergency exit only—alarmed" and proceed to use and prop open these exists, causing the alarm to ring until its battery is exhausted or someone resets the alarm. At many institutions these local alarms have been so ineffective that they are either no longer operative or no one pays any attention to them. These local door alarms are also subject to vandalism.

Premise Alarms

A wide variety of alarm triggering or sensing devices are used that are broadly known as *detectors* and *sensors*. These devices vary from the basic door sensor to ultrasophisticated motion detectors employing ultrasonics, infrared, radar, microwave, laser beams, and other advanced concepts.

A highly sophisticated premise security system is usually not necessary on a campus—except, possibly, to protect valuable art collections. Therefore, I confine my description of premise alarms to the simpler, proven applications that in the long run may be more effective and economical.

Premise alarms can be broadly classified into "peripheral" and "internal" or "space trapping." These alarms are often used in conjunction with each other.

Peripheral Alarms. *Door and window (button type) switches* are similar to those used in car door frames that cause interior lights to go on when the doors are opened. They are easily defeated by taping or holding down the button but are easily installed, neat, inexpensive, and relatively trouble free.

Magnetic switches are still the simplest and most trouble free system for low risk applications. These switches may be surface mounted on doors and windows, and when opened the contact is broken and a signal is activated. When planning for new construction, doors and frames should be precut so that these switches will be recessed, thereby improving security and making the switches more pleasing aesthetically. Switches can also be purchased as part of the door hinge, which disguises them even more.

Magnetic switches can be rather easily compromised (i.e., using another magnet so contact will be maintained) but still provide better coverage than the door and window switches previously mentioned.

Metallic foil tape can be used to signal the breaking of a window. It carries a constant electrical current that, when interrupted by breaking, signals an alarm. The experience with foil tape has been rather poor because tape is not only unsightly but also is easily broken during window cleaning, and it dries out and deteriorates. Foil does not lend itself to most campus applications.

Internal Traps. *Infrared photoelectric* alarms are activated by the breaking of an invisible infrared beam between a projector and a sensitive receiver. Since they produce a narrow cross section, they can be located and avoided by a careful, more sophisticated intruder.

Infrared beams are somewhat expensive but are relatively trouble free and effective for certain inside applications. They can also be used to activate concealed surveillance cameras, to open doors and parking gates, and so on.

Passive infrared detectors are also available that are activated by the body heat of the intruder. These are fairly new devices, but they have been successful in providing coverage in certain relatively quiet areas.

Capacitance alarms, in which the protected object acts as part of the capacitance of a tuned circuit, demonstrate one of the most successful applications of electronic techniques. If a person approaches or touches the protected object, usually a safe or file cabinet, a change in the capacitance occurs that upsets the balance of the system and triggers an alarm.

This type of coverage is excellent for the protection of a safe in the cashier's office or elsewhere, but I would recommend tuning it to activate at touch rather than when a person approaches it. Therefore, cleaners and other people near it will not cause false alarms. Be sure to warn cleaners and employees not to touch the safe when the alarm is activated.

Ultrasonic alarms work just within the limits of the audio frequency spectrum and generate high frequency sound waves that fill an enclosed area with a pattern of sound. A sensitive receiver, connected to an electronic amplifier, picks up the waves, and no alarm will be activated as long as they are the same frequency as the sound emitted by the transmitter. Any motion within the area will send back a reflected wave differing in frequency that will be detected and amplified causing an alarm signal.

The disadvantage of this type of alarm system is that it is susceptible to false alarms when any movement occurs in the room (i.e., air currents, moving machinery, loud and extended noises and vibrations). They can sometimes be defeated by an intruder moving very slowly. At times, a person with very sensitive hearing can hear the sound waves emitted, which can prove annoying. However, these ultrasonic alarms have been vastly improved in the last few years so they can be adjusted to the proper sensitivity to overcome disturbance factors.

Audio alarms (space alarms) differ from ultrasonic in that they "listen" to a protected area and do not "fill" it with sound waves. Unlike ultrasonic alarms, they can tolerate air currents and other forms of motion as long as the noise factor is low. Audio alarms can be defeated by wearing rubber-soled shoes and being very quiet. The sensitivity of these alarms has to be adjusted to compensate for normal noises, or else cancellation microphones may have to be installed near noise-producing equipment to nullify that sound and prevent false alarms. This type of alarm coverage can be used in large but normally quiet areas.

One type of audio system that employs listening microphones enables the console operator to not only receive an alarm but also to actually listen and record what is transpiring in the protected area. This factor is particularly valuable to police and security personnel because it has the advantage of advising them what is transpiring (i.e., how many burglars are present, their location, when they are leaving, and so forth).

Radar and microwave alarms are somewhat similar to ultrasonic except that they work on the principle of flooding an area with radio or microwaves that are reflected back to an antenna or similar detector. An intruder breaks the normal pattern of waves, and a different frequency is created that trips an alarm relay.

This type of coverage is not affected by air currents, noise, light, or sound. However, radio waves are not easily confined to an enclosed area and alarms may be activated by moving people or vehicles outside the area.

Under the rug *switch mats* are simply thin vinyl mats containing a network of ribbonlike wire conductors. When an intruder walks on the carpeting some of these small wire conductors will be pressed together causing an alarm to be activated.

In certain internal areas such as carpeted stairs, these switch mats can be effective. However, installation under existing carpeting may be a problem and some mats do not wear too well under heavily traveled carpeting. They also have to be located in free areas where no furniture or similar objects are standing on the carpet. At times, these under carpet mats may cause bulges in the carpet itself.

ACCESS-CONTROL SYSTEMS

Access control systems on college campuses are only as effective as the people using them want them to be. Therefore, they must be acquired with caution and only after there is some assurance that students, faculty, and staff will use them properly. Educating the campus population regarding the need, performance, and use of these devices is a *must,* if they are to be utilized.

COLLEGE OF THE SEQUOIAS

LIBRARY

Remote Control of Entry Points

Certain entry points can be remotely controlled at the central console by the use of electric strikes. These systems usually involve the console operator's identifying the individual desiring entry prior to depressing a button that remotely unlocks the electric strike. Identification is usually made by a two-way intercom conversation and the display of an ID card. Split screen images that allow the console operator to view the ID card and the face of the person desiring entry are also used.

This sytem of entry is quite effective at doors where little traffic is involved —particularly during hours when buildings are secured. However, it does not prevent unauthorized people from following ID cardholders through the opened door, and if other access doors exist (i.e., fire doors) and are open or violated, the entire system breaks down.

Cipher Locking Systems

Access control at perimeter and interior doors can also be acquired by the use of cipher keying systems requiring that a certain memorized code of numbers or letters be pressed in the proper order to deactivate the lock.

Some of these systems are mechanical only but others are electronic and can be monitored at a central station. Their weakness is again piggybacking and the fact that the code can be given to others and is usually easily acquired by anyone desiring entry.

Card-Key Systems

These card-key access systems that use ID cards can be programmed to permit multiple levels of entry or can be very simple, providing for only the insertion of a card on a local reader that permits entry. Their use in residence halls will be more fully discussed later.

Card-key systems have been successfully used in business and industry where employees adhere to security procedures, but on college campuses their effectiveness has been somewhat questionable.

They do provide an excellent means of after-hours entry to certain buildings and internal locations. The card-key access system of today is computerized so that cards can be programmed to meet any requirement. Lost or stolen cards can be immediately voided and various levels of security programmed. For example, after-hours entry can be programmed so that the card reader will only accept designated cards for certain hours.

Card-key programming is peformed at the central console, and a printout may be provided to record the time, location, and identity (card number) of the

COLLEGE OF THE SEQUOIAS

LIBRARY

individual entering as well as cards rejected. This printout furnishes an excellent record, particularly for after-hours access, and above all places the security department in control when it issues and programs the cards. It certainly provides better control than when keys are freely issued and copies are made and distributed.

Another level of security is provided by combining the card-key entry system with the cipher lock. This combination is not needed on most campuses except for in critical areas such as audio/visual equipment rooms, art galleries, and similar locations.

LOCKS

Locking hardware for student dormitory rooms will be discussed later in Chapter 14.

This section does not attempt to discuss the construction and technical differences of locking hardware but briefly explores some of the difficulties in securing campus buildings and offices and suggests some measures that might assist in making them more secure.

I have emphasized previously the fact that a college and university campus is unlike any other facility, especially in regard to locks and keys. Over the years a tradition seems to have prevailed among faculty, staff, and students that there should be practically free access to every building at any hour of the day and night. Although crime problems are gradually changing this attitude and bringing about better security, every campus security operation faces a most difficult task in keeping buildings, offices, and rooms secured. One of the most common complaints of campus officers is "as fast as I lock that door they unlock it and prop it open."

Trying to "educate the educated" to lock doors is a most difficult task, but the security department must lead the way through a preventive education program. Faculty members and others have got to realize that they are part of the security team and that locking doors is everyone's responsibility.

The top administration of a college or university should also back the security department in its efforts to get the community to lock doors and close and lock windows. However, unlike the heads of business and industry, a campus president or administrator has little clout in enforcing any rules and regulations but usually has to sell the idea to the community before it is adopted.

There has always been and will continue to be a conflict between fire and security departments as far as locks are concerned—fire departments are trying to open doors and security departments are endeavoring to lock them. The greatest problem encountered by security in trying to secure buildings are fire doors that have to permit egress at all times and, therefore, severely weaken any access security measures.

I wish I had the answer on how to overcome this problem but again, the only answer seems to be in educating the community and hoping for its cooperation. Some other measures, which have worked with varying degrees of success, are alarming fire doors and prominently marking them as emergency exits only, alarming and covering them with CCTV cameras to identify violators and trespassers, equipping panic bars with breakable enclosures, posting security personnel at doors to prevent violators, and other measures.

A great deal of campus locking hardware, particularly in older buildings, can be easily compromised and needs to be replaced. However, merely replacing the hardware will not assure better security unless the door itself is properly fitted to the frame and the frame itself is well constructed. A common entry procedure for intruders is to give the door a solid kick, causing the frame to shatter.

A common fault in old buildings is a gap between the door and frame or between double doors, permitting the latch area to be attacked or manipulated. This gap also makes it easy to insert a crow bar or similar tool to pry the door open enough so the latch or dead bolt will be disengaged. The installation of tamper proof heavy gauge steel plates covering this gap improves security.

KEY CONTROL

Speaking about key control on most campuses prompts the inquiry, "What key control?" I can truly say that in my over twenty years of close association with campus security and law enforcement I never observed or knew of an effective key control program—although some institutions claim (and really believe) they have one.

The overriding problem is the wholesale careless dispersal of keys, including master keys, to practically anyone who wants them, even though a genuine need has not been established. The other major problem is the duplication of keys. In this connection some institutions believe that "Do not duplicate" stamped on the issued key will prevent duplication from happening, which is wishful thinking because if one key maker won't make the duplicate, the next one will.

The usual procedure on most campuses is for keys to be controlled and made by the physical plant department. However, keys are made by that department and furnished to anyone on campus upon written or verbal authority by practically anyone. For example, a faculty member may authorize all his students to have keys to his department and building.

How do you cope with this problem? First of all, I believe key control should be administered by the security department, not the physical plant. In large institutions this will mean that a full-time locksmith will have to work for security. However, even making key control the responsibility of security will not help the situation unless tighter standards are imposed regarding the distribution of keys, particularly master keys. Without the backing of the top administration and the effective application of tight key control measures the ball game will be lost. The difficulty in starting such a program is usually compounded by the existence already of so many unauthorized keys and master keys on campus. Therefore, a program of systematic rekeying will also have to be instituted.

Another measure that can be taken, as will be mentioned again in Chapter 14, is the use of keys at entrances that cannot be duplicated at usual key-making locations.

SECURING THE COMMUNITY COLLEGE

Electronic after-hours protection and access control can be used to even more advantage at a community college than at a resident college or university. A proprietary security system should be a part of every community college. Although many of these colleges have been constructed in the past few years, unfortunately a security system was not even considered for the majority of them.

The reason why electronics can be used so effectively by community colleges is because, in contrast to four-year institutions where student, faculty, and staff residing on campus require entry into numerous dormitories and other buildings at practically all hours, the community college can be completely secured during certain periods. The usual schedule for community colleges involves their being open on school days from about 7:00 A.M. to 11:00 P.M. and secured at other times. At most community colleges no one but security will be on campus from about midnight to 7:00 A.M.

Another reason why community colleges lend themselves more readily to electronic protection is the fact that many are single-facility structures made up of one large building or a series of interconnecting buildings or complexes. This insures better after-hours access control through a single entry.

Community colleges are relatively new in the past twenty-five years and are still being planned and constructed in various areas in the United States. I urgently recommend that preplanning considers security in design and includes electronic protection and access-control systems. In this regard the following section entitled "Security Planning for New Facilities" should prove helpful.

The recommended security design for community colleges, although tailored independently for each facility, should include as few ground-level windows as possible, particularly if the campus is located in a high-crime area. Windows should be fixed since most buildings today are environmentally equipped for the control of air and heat. If plans call for windows to be opened, they should be designed so as to not provide sufficient space for entry. Unbreakable glazing might also be considered.

All perimeter doors should be alarmed and monitored at the central console, which should record a printout of all activity. No hardware should be installed on the outside of fire doors.

Parking control and security in parking areas is especially important in community colleges because at most institutions the campus population comes and goes by automobile. Therefore, a top priority of community college security organizations has to be an effective parking control program and protection of vehicles, property in these vehicles, and the persons coming and going to parking areas.

Since community colleges have what amounts to a two-session day with the second session lasting well into the night hours, the security department must provide day and after-dark protection. Daytime protection can be accomplished by frequent walking or riding patrols and CCTV coverage. A three wheel enclosed-cab scooter or golf cart type vehicle can usually be used to advantage in patrolling parking lots.

CCTV can be used to scan parking areas, and officers can be dispatched when anything suspicious is observed on the central station console monitors. CCTV cameras can be mounted on high poles in the parking lots or on nearly buildings to cover parking and other exterior areas. Cameras that pan automatically should also be considered for these applications.

Good lighting that will flood parking lots and walkways servicing them is the best way to protect and reassure parkers after dark. This lighting should be backed up by increased patrol, especially during class breaks.

A community college, unlike a four year resident university, has a diversified student body that encompasses young undergraduates just out of high school, older youths who may be employed, still older men and women who are working full time, housewives, and even senior citizens. This student body arrives daily from various communities and its only reason for coming is to attend class.

Therefore, unlike the four-year college in which students make numerous acquaintances through sports, various organizations, social affairs, fraternities and sororities, and living and eating on campus together, close association or unity among community college students is rare and also very little college spirit or loyality to the institution exists. This highly impersonal atmosphere makes it difficult for a community college security department to communicate with students and secure their cooperation in regard to assuming some responsibility for preventing crime. This impersonal relationship in which students recognize only the people who are in class with them also makes community colleges more vulnerable to undesirables coming on campus without fear of detection.

After-Hours Access Control

If the facility is self-contained and entry permits access to the entire building or complex, options are available for after-hours access under the supervision of the security department. Entry should be channeled through one entry point and all other perimeter doors should be locked and alarmed. The person authorized to enter would have to enter by means of this single door. However, in some facilities in which entry does not permit access to the entire facility or where several buildings are involved, this plan will have to be adjusted accordingly.

Card-key access-control systems can be used for after-hours entry to a community college. A card-key reader or readers should be located at the entrance or entrances. If access to the entire building can be gained through one main access door this procedure should be adopted, even though it might involve additional walking for the after-hours visitor.

Card keys should be issued and under the control of the security department. A genuine need should be established before any card is issued. A printout at the security console should furnish a complete account of after-hours access and the capability of quickly voiding or programming cards should exist.

All other perimeter doors would be under alarm and monitored at the console. A security officer would be dispatched to investigage any alarm. Alarmed perimeter doors should not be violated after hours. If they are, flagrant violators' card keys should be voided so as to deny entry for a period. Patrolling security officers should also check on persons occupying buildings after hours to determine if they have been authorized. A check of their ID against the card-key entry printout will furnish this information.

The other means of access control would be by an electric strike under the control of the console operators, as previously described. A faculty member or administrator authorized for after-hours entry would then merely signal the operator by inserting his ID card in a split-screen CCTV viewer equipped with two-way intercom. The console operator would then activate the strike to permit entry.

Staffing

Staffing during the day (7:00 A.M.–3:00 P.M.) and evening (3:00 P.M.–11:00 P.M.) shifts should be approximately the same with possibly increased patrol of parking areas during the evening shift. Once the building or buildings are cleared (usually about 11:00 P.M.), everything should be tightly secured, the alarm system activated, and one of the access-control systems mentioned previously would go into operation. Staffing then can involve a minimum of personnel. In some instances this could mean as few as three officers with one operating the console, another patrolling and responding inside, and another responding and patrolling outside. In some cases in which sufficient low-light-level CCTV scans the outside areas an outside patrol would not be needed. In low-crime suburban or rural areas one officer may be able to patrol both the inside and outside, particularly at smaller colleges.

The use of electronic tour stations that record the patrolling officer's progress and coverage at the central console are also better suited to community colleges than multiple-building four-year institutions. They should be planned for prior to construction. One of the main reasons why they should be utilized in community colleges for after-hours patrol is because only a minimum of officers will be on duty with little supervision and electronic tour stations provide a good management and supervisory tool to insure proper after-hours patrol and coverage.

SECURITY PLANNING FOR NEW FACILITIES

Proper security planning prior to the start of construction of new buildings and other campus facilities has been sadly neglected. A frequent comment from security administrators after a building has been completed is, "Those architects never even considered security." This remark illustrates the fact that for too long a wide gulf and very little communication have existed between architects and security professionals. The security professional has been content to criticize the architect for not designing a secure facility and failing to recognize the need for security equipment to be specified and installed during construction. On the one hand, in many cases these security professionals have been content merely to criticize, without becoming involved in planning for new facilities. On the other hand, many architects have very little confidence in the capabilities of the security professional and are apprehensive about the possibility of their design being changed.

Architect-Security Cooperation

The crime problem has finally resulted in the professional security administrator and architect realizing that they need each other. The architect often encounters the question from owners, "How secure and safe will this building be?" The owner knows he will be asked this question by prospective tenants and buyers, and the success of the facility may depend on the security image it presents when completed.

Fortunately, the gulf between architects and security professionals is slowly narrowing. If ever two professionals needed each other, it is in this area. The crime problem must be met with new concepts of design and construction, electronics, secure locking hardware, access-control systems, unbreakable glazing, CCTV, and other protective security measures and equipment.

Security Consultant's Approach

Let us look now at the proper approach to any new facility from the security consultant's point of view. This approach can also be largely adopted by the director or head of a campus security department, providing he is knowledgeable about security equipment.

Security planning must start at the inception of the project rather than becoming an expensive afterthought when the building is completed. Time and time again, a security consulting firm is called in after the completion of a large facility because no thought was given to security prior to construction. Problems then arise concerning aesthetics when outside wiring and molding have to be used, and various alarms, CCTV cameras, and other electronic intrusion devices have to be surface mounted rather than recessed.

When the world-renowned Beinecke Rare Book and Manuscript Library was under construction at Yale, for example, there was great concern for the preservation of the priceless collection of books and manuscripts by means of a sophisticated humidity and temperature-control system, fire devices that would not damage books, and book control procedures. Very little attention was given, however, to after-hours protection. Consequently, a basic magnetic-type door alarm system was the only protection included in construction. Only after a student, testing the nighttime security, was able to gain access by using a bent coat hanger, was a demand for "better protection immediately" voiced. The problem then became one of aesthetics. The cost of installing a sophisticated, practically custom-made intrusion system was at least ten times what it would have been if it had been planned during construction, when hidden conduit and aesthetically pleasing recessed detection devices could have been installed.

It has been encouraging to see some architectural firms realizing the need for utilizing security consultants the same as mechanical, electrical, landscape, and other specialized consultants. Together the consultants and architects can produce a structurally sound, functional, aesthetically pleasing, safe, and secure facility. Architects are now increasingly hiring security consultants and listening to security directors to insure that the proper electronic intrusion and detection systems, locking hardware, and security aspects of construction are planned for and specified from the start.

In the past, architects and engineering firms have relied too much on manufacturers, dealers, and contractors to handle the security aspects of new facilities. Security today is big business, with many sophisticated electronic and other devices flooding the marketplace. Some of this equipment is excellent, while some is worthless. Even security consultants find it increasingly difficult to stay up with the state of the art and to recommend the best equipment to do the job at the lowest cost.

Selecting a Security Consultant

What are the criteria for selecting a security consultant? Some clients hire consultants without first acquiring any real knowledge of their capabilities and experience or inquiring from references where such consultants have performed past services. A consultant should be selected with the same care as an attorney, accountant, or other professional.

The most important criterion is that the consulting firm be completely impartial, objective, and capable of performing in a professional manner the same as consultants for the other building trades. A consultant cannot be objective or ethical if he sells equipment, makes installations or is obligated in any way to a supplier, manufacturer, or installer. His concern must be strictly for his client (the owner) and, eventually, the persons who will be using the facility.

Another factor that must be considered is the security consultant's ability to work with the owner, the architect, engineers, and all segments of the large team that will be involved in construction. Today the public and private owner of new facilities is increasingly becoming involved as a member of the building team rather than relying solely on the architect/engineer or the general contractor or both. More and more, owners are either strengthening their own building program staffs or hiring qualified construction managers to represent their interests. Security will probably be one of the main concerns of the owner, and the security consultant must work closely with the owner to design an effective and acceptable program.

Phases of Security Planning

What can the security consultant do to insure a safe and secure building and what is his approach? The architect and consultant should approach the project in phases. It is again emphasized that campus security administrators can adopt this same approach and, in effect, act as consultants to architects prior to and during the construction of new facilities.

Phase 1: Concept. The concept phase involves considerable research and communication with all concerned. The consultant will meet not only with the architects, engineers, and others directly concerned in the planning and building but also with the owner.

Consultants should meet with persons who will be directly concerned and who will have to "live with" the completed building and security system. These meetings will explore such matters as what security problems have been encountered in the past, security staffing, concerns and philosophy regarding security, and so forth. Basic information such as hours of operation, key control, present security procedures, and their effectiveness would also be discussed. This type of approach gives the owner and persons who will occupy the premises a voice in security planning from the outset and avoids the later complaint of "Nobody ever asked me about security."

A report is then submitted describing the proposed security system and program. This report should be nontechnical and describe clearly in layman's language the system, equipment, and possibly the personnel to be utilized. At least ballpark budget figures should also be included. If architectural drawings are available, the location of security equipment can be depicted on them by symbol. This report will be reviewed by all persons concerned with the project.

Phase 2: Specifications. After everyone has been given an opportunity to read the concept report, comments should be solicited. Eventually, meetings will be held to answer questions and sift down the security recommendations to those on which the majority agrees.

The next step would be to write specifications for the system (central-monitoring console, various alarms, CCTV, access-control systems, and so on). These specifications should be designed to insure the best possible system at the lowest cost. They should be directed at writing a complete package so that one supplier is responsible for the entire system. Otherwise, certain equipment may not be compatible and suppliers are inclined to blame some other suppliers' equipment for problems.

These specifications then go out to responsible, qualified security contractors for competitive bidding.

Phase 3: Review and Selection of the Contractor. The consultant should be involved in reviewing the bids and selecting the successful bidder. He should be particularly careful to insure that any "equivalent" equipment is of high quality and truly equivalent as far as the specifications are concerned.

A key factor to be considered in choosing the contractor should be the company's ability to provide prompt, efficient service after installation.

Phase 4: Inspection during Installation. The consultant should perform several inspections during installation to make sure the specified equipment is being utilized and that it is installed and wired correctly. In one large new facility, for example, consultants discovered that all television cameras had been installed upside down.

Phase 5: Final Check-Out. This final phase involves the consultant's checking out the entire system to make sure it meets specifications and is working properly.

EXTERNAL PROTECTION—PREVENTING CRIMES AGAINST THE PERSON

External protection deals mainly with measures to insure the personal safety of the campus population. Students and others should feel safe while walking and driving on campus at any hour of the day or night. The responsibility of the college or university is to do everything possible to make all areas of the campus free from personal attacks, robberies, rapes, muggings, and other crimes.

Campus Lighting

Lighting is still the least expensive security that can be purchased. Good exterior lighting is a rarity at many colleges and universities. At times it seems that the newer the campus or facility, the poorer the lighting. This problem is caused to a large extent by low-level, decorative lighting that is completely inadequate from a security standpoint.

The security approach to lighting will be at odds with the approach of lighting consultants and architects who are concerned with aesthetics. Because lighting is a deterrent to crime and a reassurance to the community, however, maximum lighting is recommended, particularly in certain areas.

When analyzing lighting on campus from a security point of view, measuring footcandles or conducting a scientifically oriented lighting study is not always necessary. Students and other members of the campus community may simply be asked where, in their opinion, they feel insecure after dark because of a lack of lighting. Almost always, the areas they mention do require better lighting.

Some of the areas that are of greatest concern in regard to lighting are described now.

Parking Lots. Although most faculty and staff cars are removed after dark, student cars remain, often in dead storage for long periods. Student parking areas are also usually the farthest removed from the campus, sometimes in rather isolated areas. One of the major problems on most campuses is the theft of stereo, CB radios, tires, batteries, and other equipment from student vehicles and an increasing number of thefts of the vehicles themselves from campus parking areas.

All parking areas should be saturated with light. High-mast, clustered reflector-type lighting has proved very effective. Some parking areas can be well illuminated by six 1,000-watt mercury or metal-halide reflectorized lamps mounted on a single mast 100 feet high. Such lighting is estimated to illuminate an area as large as four football fields.

This type of lighting cuts down on the need for many lamp posts or masts, and the lamps can be replaced and serviced easily by means of a secure control that allows them to be raised and lowered.

Walkways. Campus sidewalks and paths, particularly those that are heavily used by students, should be well illuminated. Students are often "night people" and more pedestrian traffic may occur after dark then during the day.

These walkways should also be afforded increased patrol, especially after dark. The value of walking patrols cannot be overstressed in this application. Officers in patrol cars cannot afford the coverage and reassurance generated by the sight of a nearby officer on foot. This walking officer can also relate better to students and other members of the community by a simple "good evening" or exchange of pleasantries.

Stadiums. Another often forgotten area where good lighting is necessary is the football stadium or other outdoor athletic facility. These can be the target of rival campus student hijinks and other vandalism. Some campuses, for example, have suffered expensive damage to artificial turf by fire or chemicals.

Conclusion

This chapter has endeavored to emphasize that college and universities should recognize that the age of electronics has arrived in the security field and should be an integral part of any security program. Any institution that is rejecting the central digital monitoring of electronic intrusion devices, keyless access control systems (card keys, coded combination, etc.) and other intrusion and security related devices is probably not facing up to the fact that, in the long run, security personnel used to provide similar coverage is more costly — and usually not as efficient.

This book has also emphasized that *crime prevention* should be one of the most important priorities for any campus law enforcement operation. The use of electronics such as various type alarms, CCTV, access control systems and other devices contributes immeasurably to preventing crime and acting as a deterrent.

However, in selecting any electronic security system or the components that are part of it, I cannot emphasize too strongly the need for *caution*. The professional campus security administrator of today usually has a good overall knowledge of security products and their suppliers. His expertise should be utilized to the utmost prior to buying this often expensive equipment rather than have the purchasing, building department, or others make the decision. If the head of security does not have this knowledge, a completely unbiased, objective and proven security consultant should be engaged to insure that money is not wasted on a wrong or inefficient system.

Chapter 14

RESIDENCE HALL SECURITY

The most critical buildings on campus today from a security standpoint are student residence halls and other housing facilities. The highest percentage of crime usually takes place in these areas. Since the personal safety of people is involved, the pressures on the security operation grow in proportion to problems encountered in residence halls.

The era of student demands and dissent, coupled with today's open campus, resulted in a drastic increase in security problems in residence halls. One of the major demands granted to students was complete freedom in the residence halls, with virtual abolition of parietal rules, curfews, and similar restrictions. The advent of twenty-four-hour visitation by either sex, as well as the end of restrictions on the coming and going of resident students, has contributed to thefts, attacks, rapes, armed robberies, and other crimes in residence halls that were infrequent or non-existent not too many years ago. No doubt undesirables have been attracted to college residence halls because of the ease of access and slight chance of being detected, particularly if these outsiders are young and blend with students.

Crime in the residence halls has caused the pendulum to swing somewhat away from the open-door policy. Some students, particularly women, are demanding a return to tight access-control systems, security personnel on the premises, and other security measures reminiscent of the past.

HIGH-RISE VERSUS LOW-RISE

Any campus security director in the country will state, and will usually prove his statement by statistics, that crime is considerably higher in high-rise residence halls than in low-rise buildings. At the University of Massachusetts at Amherst, for example, where excellent computerized crime statistics exist, crime was *at least 50 percent greater* during 1975 and 1976 in the four 22-story high-rise dormitories than in the thirty-five 4-story low-rise dormitories.

David L. Johnston, former director of public safety at the University of Massachusetts, stated that these four high-rise dormitories, each housing approximately 2,000 students, are "breeders of crime and other problems." Living in these large complexes becomes impersonal. Students do not even get to know their neighbors, which makes it easy for outsiders to trespass freely and commit crimes undetected.

Johnston also stated that studies by the university revealed that students do not like living in these high-rise buildings. They voice their unhappiness and displeasure by committing acts of vandalism, particularly on the elevators that have become the symbol of the high rise. Willful damage to elevators has been so high that the university now offers a $50 reward to anyone reporting a person committing these acts. Service employees are often harassed by students when they attempt to repair damage caused by students. On several occasions students forced open elevator shaft doors, threw objects, and even urinated on elevator servicemen as they worked at the bottom of the shaft to restore service.

The clustering of four high rises and approximately 8,000 students in one relatively small area caused, according to Johnston, a "horrendous parking and traffic problem." Because of limited vehicle access to the high-rise units, a public safety hazard was created when fire lanes became clogged with illegal parkers and traffic.

Some rather unusual problems have also occurred, such as students' shouting or playing stereos at full volume from upper-floor windows at all hours, annoying and keeping awake students occupying rooms at approximately the same level of a nearby high-rise. Another problem has been the throwing of beer cans, bottles, and other potentially dangerous missiles from upper-story windows. The throwing of these objects particularly at university police, fire, and service vehicles, appears to be another form of protest by students against their having to reside in the high-rise dormitories.

Still another unexpected problem has been the relatively high suicide rate of students and even outsiders jumping from the upper windows. In one case, a resident of a city many miles away was driving by. Seeing the high-rise towers emerging in the distance from the otherwise flat, rural terrain, he proceeded to one of the top floors and jumped to his death.

As a result of the experience at the University of Massachusetts and at other campuses, the conclusion has to be that high-rise buildings are hazardous from a security standpoint and, furthermore, are unacceptable to students.

Colleges and universities are now shying away from building these high-rise residence halls and recognizing the fact that, for the most part, students do not like them, and they produce security, maintenance, and other problems. However, those institutions that have such buildings must endeavor to point out to residents that, because high rises are more vulnerable to thefts and other crimes, they must be even more cautious and responsible in protecting themselves and their property.

Any semblence of tight access-control procedures is extremely difficult to achieve unless residents cooperate fully. If they do, channeling access through one or two entries by means of a card-key or other access system may be effective. A floor-by-floor patrol, particularly during the night hours, can also help. This patrol can be by student residents of the building under the supervision of the campus security department.

Other methods and equipment are also discussed in this chapter that can be utilized to produce better security in these high-rise buildings as well as in other dormitory areas.

ENTRANCES

One of the major problems in residence halls is how to provide ready access to students at all hours while still keeping out thieves, rapists, and other undesirables. Colleges and universities have tried various means of access control, such as card-key systems, remote-controlled locking devices, and simply issuing students keys to the main entrance. *These systems are only as good as the resident students desire them to be.* If they use and prop open fire doors, duplicate or loan keys to outsiders, and otherwise circumvent the system, it is of no value. This lack of cooperation is why so many campuses have given up and use an expensive guard or monitor to supposedly screen persons entering and to admit students when all doors are locked.

As few ground-floor doors as possible should be specified in the design of residence halls. If possible, one main entrance that can be controlled should be included rather than several. Fire doors should be alarmed, clearly marked as such, and have no hardware on the outside.

LOCKING HARDWARE

A cylinder requiring a key that can be duplicated only at the factory or by an authorized locksmith using specialized equipment should be utilized for entrance doors, particularly if students are issued keys. This same key can also be programmed to admit the students to their rooms.

Interchangeable-core locking cylinders have also been used successfully where tight key control procedures exist. These cylinders enable the keying system for an entire dormitory or certain floors to be changed periodically at very little expense.

Pickproof keyless door locks, which are operated by depressing buttons in the correct order, have also been used successfully for student rooms on some campuses. This system eliminates keys being lost, stolen, forgotten, or copied. The combination of the lock can be changed easily and more economically than a conventional lock.

These systems have been accepted and worked very well at some institutions, while at others they have been unsuccessful. Before such devices are ordered for an entire residence hall, they should be tried on the rooms of one floor to determine their usefulness.

A number of colleges and universities have also gone to the expense of installing wide-angle peephole viewers in dormitory room doors. These will be effective only if residents keep their doors locked and use the viewers prior to admitting anyone.

LANDSCAPING AND LIGHTING

Shrubs, bushy trees, and other plantings outside first-floor rooms and adjacent to entrance walks often contribute to crime by furnishing hiding places for Peeping Toms, muggers, rapists, and thieves. Such plantings should be avoided or low-growing bushes and shrubs selected.

The exterior of residence halls should be illuminated to produce a moat of light around the dormitory building. Naturally, lighting has to be positioned so it will not shine directly into bedroom windows and interfere with sleep. Lights should also be positioned so that security officers or others inside will not be blinded by the light when they observe the outside area and entrance walks.

RELATIONS BETWEEN SECURITY AND THE HOUSING OFFICE

A sensitive area in residence hall security involves the relations between the residence hall staff and the security department. Occasionally, a complete lack of understanding exists, which does not contribute to an effective security program to serve the resident community.

Many heads of campus security complain about policies that, in effect, bar security officers from entering other than public areas of the residence halls unless specifically requested. In some cases, resident directors and their staffs have assumed practically all security responsibilities and directed student residents to report matters to them so they can decide whether the security department will be notified. On some campuses this policy has been dictated because of the security department's inability to furnish any meaningful protection and response to problems. At several colleges the housing office, in desperation over the lack of protection and service provided by their own security department, has hired a contract guard service to provide security—an inadvisable procedure.

There must be close and workable liaison and cooperation between all segments of residence hall operations and the security department. Policies should be established that will neither restrict security in residence halls nor cause it to become overbearing and restrictive. The final say in security matters should be the responsibility of the director of security, although he should confer with and be guided by the thinking of the director of residence halls or housing. No security programs should be instituted independently by residence hall administrators under their exclusive direction.

A free flow of information should also exist between residence hall and housing offices and the security office. Workable procedures should be agreed on for the exchange of information so that it will be handled discreetly and acted upon properly.

RESPONSIBILITY OF RESIDENTS

Security in residence halls and other campus housing complexes will only be as effective as the people who are affected by it want it to be. If residents do not at least observe normal security procedures such as locking their doors and reporting thefts, trespassing, and other incidents, they cannot blame the security department for a lack of security.

The importance of a preventive education program to enlist the help of the residential community in protecting its property and its own safety has already been emphasized. However, also a good idea is to form a security committee in each residence hall as a means of focusing on the issue and emphasizing the fact that security is everybody's responsibility.

Students who reside in a dormitory can also be used to advantage in patrolling or providing a security presence. They may also influence their peers to be more security conscious. These students should be trained and under the supervision of the security department.

One of the most important aspects of any crime prevention program in a residence hall is to constantly remind students that a problem exists that they can help alleviate by personally observing various security practices and precautions. Florida State University utilizes two rather innovative methods to attract attention to crime in the residence halls and make residents more security conscious.

One of these methods is called "Stall Stories" and involves cartoons printed on eye-catching pieces of paper that are placed inside toilet cubicle doors. These cartoons convey a brief security message to a captive audience and the stall story program has proved quite popular with resident students. Figure 14-1 depicts some of these cartoons.

Figure 14-1. "Stall Cartoon" to impart a brief security message to students. Courtesy of Florida State Department of Public Safety, Tallahassee, Florida.

Figure 14-2. Security poster used in dormitory residences. Courtesy of Florida State Department of Public Safety, Tallahassee, Florida.

The other Florida State program utilizes "Don't Let a Thief Make Your Room a Shopping Center" posters that are posted in conspicuous locations in residence halls. These posters relate up-to-date monthly theft statistics of the value of property stolen in the residence hall. They serve as a graphic reminder to students to increase awareness of their own security responsibilities. One of these posters is shown in Figure 14-2.

Chapter 15

PROTECTION OF CAMPUS
AND PERSONAL PROPERTY

Thefts or so-called rip-offs of campus and personal property are problems faced by every campus security department today. The extent of the problem varies from campus to campus, depending on the location of the institution, its size, and numerous other factors. This chapter examines some measures that can be of assistance in combating property thefts on campus.

PROTECTION OF CAMPUS PROPERTY

A common target of both external and internal theft is valuable audio-visual equipment such as tape recorders, movie and slide projectors, and similar items that can be easily sold or fenced.

Also vulnerable to theft are electric typewriters, calculators, small copying machines, and similar office equipment. These items are sometimes even stolen to meet the specifications of the prospective buyer.

Microscopes and other valuable scientific instruments are also common targets, particularly of internal theft. Such equipment seems to "disappear" near the end of the academic year, when students or employees who have been using the items are leaving the university.

One of the most difficult tasks faced by any campus security operation is to prevent these thefts or recover stolen equipment. This task is made even more difficult because of the attitude prevailing at many institutions that seems to regard this expensive equipment as "expendable."

Poor Property Control on Campus

A marked difference is evident in the way in which private corporations and companies regard and care for equipment and the way colleges and universities treat their equipment. Private companies keep good records, conduct frequent inventories, fix responsibility for safekeeping and care, identify each item as company property, and are quick to notice and report anything missing. Many companies even take photos of valuable pieces of equipment and property. Most property of value is stored in a secure location when not in use.

In contrast, many colleges and universities maintain poor and incomplete records (some do not even record serial numbers), never conduct an inventory, do not fix responsibility, and fail to identify the equipment properly. Sometimes weeks or months pass before someone realizes that a piece of equipment is missing. On many campuses losses are never even reported to the security department—or are reported long after the loss has been noted. Too often a total disregard exists for proper storage of property in a secure place.

Most campus security administrators will agree that it is very difficult to "educate the educated" in regard to the protection of university property. It is not uncommon for a faculty member to borrow a 16mm projector to be used in a class and then walk away after using it, leaving it unattended in an unlocked classroom. Only when another faculty member seeks to use the projector—perhaps a week or two later—is the loss noted.

The attitude on the part of many people who use campus equipment is, "So what if it's missing? We will requisition another one." Only when their own personal property such as a radio or clock is missing is a cry heard for better security. If only people using university equipment would regard it as their own, the job would certainly be easier for security!

Several campuses have taken steps to fix responsibility and reduce this careless attitude toward campus property by not replacing stolen equipment immediately. At least one campus held each user of equipment strictly responsible for its safekeeping and, unless there were some extenuating circumstances, would charge the user if the equipment was lost.

A difficult responsibility of the director will be to set up tight security and property control procedures and, in some way, to convince the people using equipment that they should protect it as if it were their own.

Effective Property Control Programs

The State of Florida, recognizing the need for fixing responsibility in property control, has established the position of property custodian, who is responsible for the supervision and control of property. At Florida International University in Miami, the property control program is under the supervision of a property manager who works under the director of purchasing. This program delegates responsibility for all university property to the vice president for administrative affairs but fixes custodial responsibility squarely on the administrative head of the department to which the property is assigned.

Florida International University has also produced an excellent *Handbook on Property Control** that establishes procedures, safeguards, and areas of responsibility. For example, the campus security department's responsibility is enumerated as follows:

1. They [campus security] may request any person removing University property from the campus to show the authority for the removal. This approval must be in writing by the Accountable Officer.
2. They shall investigate all reports of lost or stolen property and submit a written report of findings to Property Control.
3. Bring to the attention of Property Control any recurring breach in security over property.
   Examples would include:
   a. Doors continually unlocked when room is not occupied;
   b. Unattended equipment left outdoors;
   c. Repeated losses within a department.
4. When accountable property that has been lost or stolen is recovered by Campus Security or other source, a report containing the circumstances and a description of the article should be sent to the Vice President for Administrative Affairs and Property Control. The recovered property should be turned in to Property Control for verification and reissue to the department sustaining the loss. The inventory record will then be corrected to reflect the return of the accountable property.

Inventory Records

A number of measures can be taken to protect campus property and aid in its recovery. These measures boil down to being able to answer three simple but important questions: What is it? Where is it? Who has it?

---

*From *Handbook of Property Control* by Harold Mann, Property Manager of Florida International University, Miami, Florida.

A trail or history of every piece of tangible, movable property of any value of a nonconsumable or expendable nature should exist from the time it is received until its ultimate disposal. This trail should start with a detailed inventory and distinctive marking of the property as soon as it is received.

The inventory of property, which can be recorded by computer, should include a complete description of the piece of property, with the following headings:

	Example
Name of Property	Bell & Howell Projector
Description	16mm-Model 50
Serial Number	2125400
Date Acquired	5/1/77
Vendor	XYZ Cameras
Purchase Order Number	30456
Cost	$401.50
Identification Number	5761
Department Assigned	Audio-Visual
Date Inventoried	5/4/77
Condition	Good
Action and Dates	

The identification number should be etched or otherwise imprinted or affixed to the property as proof of ownership and to provide positive and immediate identification. Prominently stamping property with "Property of _____ University" also sometimes acts as a deterrent and assists in identifying the item if recovered. No markings or means of identification are absolutely secure from being removed or obliterated, but a system should be used that is difficult to erase, remove, or paint over.

"Action and Dates" refers to any action in regard to the property, such as repairs, reassignment to another department, and eventual sale or disposal with reason and authorization.

It is important to inventory all property at least once each year and record its existence and condition.

Authorization Forms

No property should be transferred from one department to another without written authorization and a record of the move.

No property should be allowed to leave the campus except for official (not personal) use. This removal should be authorized by the department head or individual held accountable for property and should be recorded on a form used for keeping this kind of record. The original copy of this form would be designated for the property control manager and copies would remain with the department authorizing its removal and the individual removing it. Figure 15-1 is a sample of such a form.

A similar authorization form can be used for the in-house borrowing of equipment. For example, most audio-visual departments maintain property inventories and execute removal record forms when slide and movie projectors, tape

Figure 15-1. Authorization form for removal of campus property.

AUTHORITY FOR OFF-CAMPUS USE OF ACCOUNTABLE PROPERTY

Date _____

Department _____   Building _____
                                        Room _____
Person Requesting _____

University Address _____

Phone Extension _____

Property To Be Used At Following Location _____

For The Period From _____ To _____ .

Identification	Quantity	Article	Serial Number

Permission is hereby granted to_____ for removal of above listed article(s) from the university campus. It is understood that this property is to be used solely for the benefit of the university and will be returned to the campus as soon as the need has ended.

_____
PROPERTY OFFICER

Date Returned _____ Condition _____

_____
PROPERTY OFFICER

---

recorders, and similar equipment are borrowed for classroom use. However, the whole system of property control breaks down when the borrower fails to return the equipment after he is finished with it and no follow-up is made. Invariably, when this type of equipment is left in a classroom or office it can disappear with no one's noting its loss—until someone else has a need for it.

A successful investigation to locate lost property is very unlikely when not even the date the property was taken is known. A successful investigation is even more remote when the security department is not notified until weeks later when the insurance carrier or a campus official asks, "Were the police notified of the loss?"

Importance of Secure Storage Facilities

A major security weakness on many campuses is the lack of secure storage facilities for valuable equipment. Sometimes good property records are maintained, but the property itself is left in very insecure storage facilities. For example, on one campus all audio-visual equipment was stored in a walled, vaultlike area entered by means of one sturdy door fitted with good locking hardware keyed independently. However, as in many institutions, this building had hanging acoustic tile ceilings. It was a simple matter for thieves to remove several of these tiles, climb over the vault walls (which did not extend to the ceiling) and remove over $10,000 worth of projectors, cameras, tape recorders, and other valuable and easily disposable equipment. This type of easy access to valuable goods is possible in many colleges and universities because of acoustic tile ceilings and interior walls that stop some distance from the ceiling.

Audio-visual and similar equipment should be stored in secure walled-in areas, and these areas can also be protected by relatively simple alarm systems, such as magnetic contacts, infrared beams, or audio to signal unauthorized entry at the central console in the security office.

Metal cabinets and file cabinets can also be used to store audio-visual equipment as well as microscopes and other scientific instruments. However, these metal containers should not be keyed the same as similar containers throughout the facility. During an internal theft investigation in one corporate office, investigators found that the key for the metal cabinet housing the expensive liquor supply also fit the cleaning supply cabinets used by practically all cleaning personnel. It came as no surprise to learn that cleaning personnel were enjoying twelve-year-old Scotch and other fine liquors.

Office-Machine Locking Devices

Office machines that are in use daily, particularly typewriters, can be secured by means of specially manufactured locking devices. Some of these devices use a locking bar and permit the typewriter to swivel; others utilize a cable lock and permit the machine to be moved all over the desk. One device incorporates a thick rubberized mat that is attached permanently to a desk or table top by an adhesive. The typewriter, calculator, or other machine is then locked into the mat, thereby eliminating the need to drill holes in the desk or table.

These devices, although somewhat expensive, have proved effective in most offices in which thefts of office machines have been prevalent. They have drastically reduced thefts and certainly justified their expense. Installation is relatively simple and can be done by campus service personnel. If thefts of office machines appear to justify the expenditure, locking devices should be considered. Consideration might also be given to selective use of such protection devices—for example, all valuable executive-style typewriters might be secured. However, these devices will not prevent the nonprofessional thief from damaging the machine or desk in attempting to remove the secured item.

Support for Security Measures

Getting faculty members, students, employees, and others to follow security procedures is usually difficult. This problem appears to be particularly true in laboratories in which expensive microscopes and other instruments are often left unsecured and are literally "up for grabs." Colleges and universities are not managed like corporations, where authority stems from the top and where rules and procedures are closely supervised to insure they are followed. Colleges and universities seem to be made up of a number of departments that consider themselves autonomous. Security will probably only be as strong as the chief administrator of each department wants it to be. Without the support of the department head the security director's work is made difficult, because he cannot hope to impose successful, preventive programs to protect property.

PROTECTION OF PERSONAL PROPERTY

Thefts of personal property have increased drastically on campuses in recent years. Although fortunately these thefts have crested and actually declined at some colleges and universities, the problem is still prevalent and is one of the challenges security departments face.

Some institutions have made clear in student handbooks and other publications that they will accept no responsibility for the loss of personal property. My belief, however, is that when colleges accept students and rent them dormitory rooms, they have at least a moral responsibility to provide a reasonable amount of protection for students' possessions. In addition, even though the institution disclaims any responsibility for losses, a great hue and cry will go up and much community pressure will be applied on the administration when too many thefts occur and nothing is done to prevent them or recover stolen property.

Operation Identification

Most campus security departments today have instituted the so-called Operation Identification or similar theft-preventive programs that call for the student or employee to etch an identifying number (such as his Social Security number) on the property with an electric marking tool. This number, as well as the serial number and other identifying data and value, is then recorded. In the event the property is stolen, this information will be readily available to the investigator and can be used as a positive means of identification if the property is recovered. The security department supplies a decal that can be displayed to reflect that the property has been identified and registered. Figure 15-2 shows such a decal.

Figure 15-2. Operation Identification decal for property protection. Courtesy of Florida State Department of Public Safety, Tallahassee, Florida.

Operation Identification programs have been quite successful on some campuses, while at others they have been used mainly as a public relations gimmick to try to convince the community that something was being done. These programs will be only as effective as the community wants them to be. If students and others fail to respond, or if publicity and administration of the programs are weak, they will be ineffective and largely a waste of time.

Vacation Theft Vulnerabilities

Student property is usually most vulnerable to theft during vacation periods when residence halls or dormitories are unoccupied. On many campuses systematic looting of student rooms has taken place, involving thefts of stereo equipment, cameras, tape recorders, television sets, calculators, and similar property. Practically all rooms have been entered, apparently by a master key, which is not surprising in view of the weak key control procedures on many campuses. After vacation, returning students and their parents are understandably upset about their losses and the campus newspaper singles out the security department for its failure to protect these possessions.

Protecting dormitory rooms and student property during vacation periods is extremely difficult. Although residence halls are supposed to be locked and secure, service personnel still have access, usually a few students get permission to remain. And it is relatively simple for anyone to gain access through a window or other means.

Who steals property from student rooms over summer vacation periods? Students fail to realize that cleaning and maintenance crews really go to work over the summer. Often the regular service employees of the university or college are assisted during summer vacations on major projects by painters, carpenters, electricians, roofers, and other contracted service people from outside the school. These workers have no loyalty or regard for the institution and sometimes consider student property fair game. Just a few dishonest workers can perpetrate a number of room thefts. Many times during vacation periods student property is found in janitors' closets, basement areas, or under shrubs outside first-floor windows, waiting to be picked up after work.

Some colleges and universities hire students from other institutions to supplement their own work force on summer projects. Some of these students seem to make a game out of taking property from student rooms. Although much of this property may be of no great value, such as banners, stereo records and tapes, beer mugs, posters, and similar objects, it nevertheless is being stolen.

Checks by Patrolling Officers

Campus security departments have experimented with various procedures to protect student property during vacation periods. Many of them are not entirely effective. One procedure is to have the officer patrolling that particular dormitory check janitors' closets, supply storage rooms, basement areas, and similar locations where stolen property could be momentarily secreted. The officer also unlocks each student room periodically and notes the date and its condition on a special form. A looted room is usually apparent because drawers are pulled out, boxes broken open, and property dumped on the bed and strewn about.

Although officers can discover by this procedure that a room has been looted and the approximate date, they cannot determine what was taken until the student returns. The security department has the advantage, at least, of contacting students and asking them if they lost anything, rather than having them report it. In this way, students are made aware that security officers were checking their rooms while they were away and trying to do something about the theft problem.

Another technique that may prove fairly successful is to at least visually check departing workers when they finish work and challenge them if necessary. For example, one officer noted a worker leaving one hot summer day wearing what appeared to be a rather heavy sweater. Upon questioning, he found this worker wearing not one but four sweaters he had taken from student rooms.

Removal of All Property

Some colleges and universities require students to remove *all* property over the summer vacation and suggest the removal of more valuable property during shorter vacation periods as well. This requirement can impose a hardship on the students, however, particularly if they live a considerable distance from the campus.

Providing Secure Storage

The security department can take a positive measure and promote better relations with students by providing a secure storage space for property during vacation periods. This measure would involve advising students that valuables such as stereos and television sets can be stored by the security department.

Campus departments should not offer this service without careful planning. It involves tagging the stored property and issuing receipts to owners. The tag on the property should briefly identify it (in case the tag becomes separated from the article) and carry the name, address, and telephone number of the owner, the date left, and when it will be picked up. The condition of the article should also be noted so that the student cannot allege it was scratched or damaged.

Care should be given to the selection of the storage room to make sure it provides maximum protection. It should be a walled, vaultlike storage area with one secure entrance door keyed independently of the master system. This storage area should also be alarmed. The area should be in operation only during normal business hours. One employee, possibly the director's secretary, should have responsibility for the key and administration of the area. If a secure area or vault is used for lost-and-found articles, a section can be allocated for vacation property storage and the same administrative procedures and personnel used.

It is extremely important that the tightest security be maintained in the storage area. In accepting this property the institution also accepts responsibility for its safekeeping. Instances have occurred in which residence hall directors decided to provide vacant but insecure rooms for this storage purpose, only to find them practically empty when vacation was over.

Some directors of security and administrators will argue that the safekeeping of student property is entirely the student's own responsibility and should not be a function of the security department. Others feel the institution does have a responsibility to provide property protection and service. If students do not avail themselves of this service, and property left in their rooms is missing upon their return from vacation, criticism against the security department is largely nullified.

Individual Responsibility

We now come full circle to face the fact that the best protector of property has to be the owner of that property. An alert, responsible individual who takes at least normal security precautions and reports suspicious individuals and incidents immediately to the campus security department is still the strongest ally of a security operation.

Chapter 4 emphasized the role a campus security department should play in educating and influencing members of the community to protect themselves and their property. *Prevention* has to be the key word in any successful campus security program. Preventive measures and procedures have to be largely the responsibility of the individual, with the security officer playing a responsive and backup role. A campus can be saturated with officers, sophisticated electronic devices, the best of locking hardware, and other security equipment, but unless the faculty members, students, administrators, employees, and other members of the community become part of the team and face up to their security responsibilities, the game will be lost.

Chapter 16

PARKING CONTROL

Every campus faces the problem of parking control. Everyone wants to use the parking area closest to his or her office or classroom thus complicating the situation. Many institutions with sufficient parking space still have a major problem because members of the campus community simply will not walk a block or two from parking lots to their destination.

Parking space has become an important issue on campus. Before accepting a position, new employees and faculty members often ask where they will park. They want to be guaranteed that desirable space will be available. Many people no longer regard parking as a privilege but as a right.

LACK OF ENFORCEMENT PROGRAMS

Some campus security departments lack any effective enforcement of parking regulations. On a number of campuses, officers issue parking tickets that are meaningless because no workable procedures exist for the collection of fines or the denial of parking privileges. On some campuses students are assessed parking fines on their bursary bill or are not allowed to register for the next semester or to graduate unless they have paid their fines. At some of these same institutions, however, faculty and staff members tear up parking tickets because no mechanism exists for collecting the fines.

On many campuses general confusion exists in regard to parking, leading to a complete breakdown in enforcement. This confusion usually results from weak or vacillating parking policies on the part of the administration. Although the security department is directed to control parking, it does not have the all-important administrative support to be able to enforce regulations.

An effective parking enforcement program must have, first of all, the complete backing of the administration, and it must be enforced equally for all, from the president down to the newest student or employee. For some reason, certain faculty members absolutely refuse to abide by any parking regulations. High-level administrative support is crucial here. No parking program can be successful unless procedures are set up that allocate parking spaces fairly to all (students, faculty, and staff) and enforcement applies equally to everyone. No selective enforcement of parking regulations should occur.

Separate Parking Departments

Two important phases are involved in any campus parking program: (1) allotment of space and (2) enforcement. In the past, both of these responsibilities have largely been delegated to the security department. On some campuses, however, the registration of campus vehicles, allotment of space, and collection of parking fines have gradually been assigned to other departments, while enforcement still remains with the security department. A more recent trend, particularly for larger institutions, is the creation of an entirely separate department to administer and enforce parking. This department should still be one of the responsibilities of the director of public safety but should have its own manager and personnel. Preferably, it should be located in an office separate from the security operation.

Delegating full responsibility for the entire parking program to one central office and staff not only relieves security officers for more important duties but also promotes a more effective approach to parking. The parking and traffic office can register cars, issue yearly parking permits, allocate space by a system that is fair to everyone, enforce parking regulations, and process the collection of fines. Computerized systems are increasingly being used to administer these parking programs.

Most colleges and universities have a traffic and parking pamphlet that provides all information on the parking regulations, procedures, and policies that will be followed. These parking pamphlets should be made available to all persons registering vehicles and should be publicized throughout the campus community.

TRAFFIC AND PARKING COMMITTEES

Also desirable is to have a traffic and parking committee made up of representatives of students, faculty, and staff. The director of security should be included on the committee, although he will not vote on appeals and similar matters. The committee should act in at least an advisory capacity regarding parking policies and procedures. The committee should also hear appeals from fines.

Organization of a parking program should include formulating procedures for equitable allotment of space and enforcement. Arrangements are also needed for handling fines. Fines should be collected through approximately the same administrative procedures that are used for other campus invoices.

Appeal Procedures

Care is required in setting up an appeal procedure. On many campuses the entire enforcement process has broken down when appeals stacked up because the commitee did not meet often enough or was inefficient in handling appeals. Students were quick to realize that an appeal meant deferring their fine indefinitely (sometimes until graduation), and practically all took advantage of the appeal process.

PAID PARKING

Many colleges and universities absorb some of their parking costs by imposing a registration and parking fee. Others use coin parking meters or coin-operated gates. Some utilize commerical gate controls that issue a ticket with the time and date of entry; an attendant collects a fee when the vehicle departs.

If paid parking is to be instituted, the parking program should be administered efficiently and fairly, and enforcement should be effective.

Paid parking does create certain problems. One of the hazards of a paid-parking policy is that it ostensibly guarantees the parker a parking space. However, on most campuses the more desirable parking areas are usually oversubscribed, making guaranteed space impossible.

Paid parking also requires a high level of enforcement to insure that non-paying violators do not take spaces from paying parkers.

Paid-parking policies differ from campus to campus. Some campuses still follow the dubious practice of charging students for parking space but providing it free to faculty and staff. In addition to having to pay a parking fee, students are often allotted less desirable space some distance from the campus.

The amount charged for parking can vary from a token payment to cover decal and administrative costs to a substantial charge. Some institutions scale their parking charges according to the location of the lot, with the most-used and desirable lots commanding the higher fees.

MULTILEVEL GARAGES

Many colleges and universities have been forced to build multilevel parking garages. Entry to these structures can be controlled by card-key, or a pay-as-you-go policy can be in effect as in commercial parking areas. The pay-as-you-go policy is easier to administer. The driver obtains a mechanically dispensed time- and date-stamped ticket on entering and pays when departing. A three-wheel scooter or similar type of patrol is effective in providing control of parking and security.

Costs for these parking facilities have risen considerably, and most campuses find they must charge for parking to defray some of the costs of construction and maintenance.

PARKING ATTENDANTS

On some campuses, largely because of ineffective enforcement measures, the administration in desperation has stationed attendants, guards, or security officers at parking lot entrances to screen the persons entering. This is a very expensive way to control parking. It should be used only if there is an acute need.

GATE CONTROLS

Another method to control parking is the use of a card-key parking gate. A number of problems are associated with the use of these gates, however, as follows:

- The gates are often damaged by violators driving through them or vandalized by those who resent them.
- The equipment usually requires constant maintenance.
- Vehicles are sometimes damaged by gates closing before they have passed under them.
- Severe winter conditions can sometimes cause problems with treadles in the pavement and other mechanisms that actuate the gates.
- Students and others on campus are very ingenious in "beating the system" by devising means to open the gate.
- Card keys may be lost or loaned to others.
- Any parking area using a card-key control must be fenced or otherwise protected so that vehicles cannot enter by circumventing the gate.

PARKING METERS

Parking meters have been quite successful on many campuses, but only if a frequent and effective parking patrol exists. Some colleges have dispensed with the coin aspect of these meters and merely use them to time the vehicle's stay. The repeat violator becomes a problem in this case, as he or she returns to reset the meter as it is about to run out of time.

DESIGNATED PARKING FOR INDIVIDUALS

Parking spaces should not be allotted to individuals by name or number. This policy should pertain to everyone from the president on down; if one administrator or faculty member has a special space assigned by name, others will want the same treatment. Assigned parking is not only difficult to enforce but is a waste of space when an individual is away from campus or otherwise not using his space. (Special parking should be designated for the handicapped, however.)

TOWING—PROS AND CONS

The towing of violators is a very sensitive issue on campus, and many institutions shy away from it. In some instances, however, towing proves to be the only effective enforcement measure.

At one eastern university, for example, no effective mechanism existed for collecting parking fines, although thousands of parking violation tickets were issued each year. With the parking lots in a chaotic condition, and faced with an avalanche of complaints from authorized parkers, the director of security reluctantly started to tow flagrant violators. Although he expected the worst, his phone started to ring with faculty, administrators, and staff who were congratulating him on finally doing something to insure them their authorized parking spaces. Illegal parkers from nonuniversity offices and commercial establishments had been using campus parking lots for months. The threat of having to pay a $15 towing fee to retrieve their vehicles proved to be the most effective measure in deterring nonuniversity violators.

At many institutions, there are effective parking controls on registered vehicles, but unless the tow is used, there is no effective enforcement or control of parkers from the outside whose vehicles have not been registered. These vehicles do not carry a coded registration decal, and therefore, their owners cannot be easily identified. Collection of university-imposed fines and other penalties is virtually impossible. Students are sometimes quick to see that the unregistered vehicle is free from parking restrictions and penalties, and so they do not register their vehicles. Therefore, there must be a firm policy in regard to all students registering their vehicles. Unregistered vehicles should be towed away, and spot checks should be made of license plate numbers to determine if the vehicles are owned by students.

Avoiding Problems in Towing

A few recommendations can be of assistance in avoiding complaints and problems when towing is used.

First of all, the campus should make sure that it is on safe ground from a legal standpoint. Most municipalities have local ordinances that provide for towing. The fact that security officers are sworn personnel with police authority also usually helps because it provides the legal authority to tow.

A college or university does not usually need to have its own tow truck. A major reason is the expense of purchasing and maintaining a tow truck and hiring an operator. Also the important question of responsibility comes up when cars are damaged in towing (as often occurs). Safe storage of towed vehicles and the collection of towing charges before the vehicle is released (and sometimes receiving verbal abuse from the car's owner) are other concerns. Another problem is the violator with the second set of keys who simply drives his car away.

If tow trucks are to be used, the college should seek the most reliable tow truck operators(s) in the area. They should reach a definite understanding as to when vehicles will be towed, how they will be handled, and the charges. Part of the agreement should include a stipulation that the security department has the right to occasionally request that a towed vehicle be released without charge. This stipulation is important because, on occasion, a vehicle may be towed that belongs to a visitor, parent, or guest. If the one-time violation is excused, the vehicle's owner may forget the shock of the tow and have a favorable reaction toward the security department and the university.

Towing should only be employed as a last resort for flagrant violators who disregard tickets and warnings or who park in fire lanes or block other vehicles. In most instances, it is better not to leave the decision to tow entirely up to the officer's judgment. Usually, the decision should be made by a supervisor. A record should be kept of the tow, including among other information, the condition of the vehicle. Any damage should be recorded so that allegations cannot be made later that the damage occurred during towing. The dispatcher should be notified immediately so he can fill out a car-towing log (see page 245) and be ready to advise the owner that the vehicle has been towed. The average person, finding his vehicle missing, believes it has been stolen. Unless he is immediately advised that it has been towed, he can understandably become quite upset.

Every time a vehicle is towed, a security officer should be present to insure that it is not damaged. A violation citation should also be affixed to the vehicle.

FINES RETURNABLE TO LOCAL MUNICIPALITY

One parking control measure that can be effective is to issue parking violation tickets returnable to the local court or municipality. These citations usually have more teeth than campus-controlled tickets, unless the municipality has a weak collection process.

One campus had a policy that fines would be collected by the local court but the proceeds would revert to the university scholarship fund. This arrangement did not work, because the court took little interest in acting as the collector for the university. At least a portion of the fines collected by the university itself, however, could be diverted to scholarships or some other worthwhile purpose.

AMOUNT OF FINES

How much should parking violators be fined? If fines are too low ($1 or $2, for example), the violator will be more prone to take a chance. A minimum fine should be $3, with an escalating feature to increase the amount for subsequent violations (e.g., $3 for the first violation, $5 for the second, $10 for the third and thereafter).

A limit should be set on the number of violations a driver can accumulate in one semester or academic year before his right to park is rescinded. Rescinding the right to park will be difficult unless towing and/or other disciplinary measures are employed.

Excusing of fines should be limited and should be based on established standards. Only the parking committee or other specified individuals should have the power to excuse fines.

MARKING AND SIGNING PARKING AREAS

The marking and signing of parking facilities is important in controlling parking and maintaining an orderly lot.

In most parking areas a sign should be displayed at the vehicle entrance indicating that parking is for authorized vehicles only. If towing is utilized, the sign should state that violators will be towed at their own expense.

Parking areas should be paved. Spaces should be delineated by prominent, brightly colored markings carefully planned to insure maximum use while at the same time providing maneuverability.

Specially marked spaces for the handicapped should be allotted in certain areas accessible to the campus. Vehicles authorized to park in them should be issued an easily recognized means of identification, such as a registration decal of a different color. Because these areas are in prime locations, it is usually difficult to insure that only handicapped individuals use them. Constant patrol, larger fines, and towing are usually effective in preventing violations.

Severe winter weather can create problems at institutions when parking space is reduced (even after snow plowing) and pavement markings are obliterated. Parking during these periods can be chaotic. Plowing during the night hours when lots are largely unoccupied, or closing off lots to permit plowing, can ease the situation.

Chapter 17

CROWD CONTROL AT SPECIAL EVENTS

A campus security department is exposed almost daily to crowd control situations involving everything from athletic contests to rock concerts. If one word were selected to best describe a successful security approach to these events, it would have to be *preplanning*. The first and most important ingredient contributing to a smoothly running, trouble-free function is a well-thought-out plan designed first to prevent incidents and second to provide immediate, effective response to problems.

COOPERATION BETWEEN SPONSORS AND SECURITY

A problem frequently encountered at many colleges and universities is the failure of persons in charge of various events to notify the security department far enough in advance so proper plans can be made. This lack of communication occurs most often with student-sponsored events such as dances, rock concerts, beer parties, mixers, and similar affairs. Sometimes security is not notified at all or is asked for assistance at the last moment.

A clear-cut policy should be developed, backed by the administration, that the security department should be furnished on a regular basis a list of future events as soon as they are scheduled. Furthermore, those responsible for those events should be required to meet with the head of security or his designate to plan for security. This type of approach can be of great assistance to the people running the events, particularly students, because it furnishes them with excellent advice based on past experience.

Who should dictate the number of security personnel to be utilized at an event—those running it or the director of security? The people running the event are usually budget conscious and, although they may think nothing of spending high sums of money for a musical group or controversial speaker, they are reluctant to spend very much on security. However, the security department is charged with the responsibility of maintaining a peaceful and safe campus and will probably be blamed if incidents occur. The same policy should be followed as exists in many municipalities in which the chiefs of the police and fire departments are authorized by law to decide how many officers and fire marshals will be assigned to various events.

FACTORS IN SECURITY PLANNING

Security coverage for each event must be evaluated on an individual basis. Many factors have to be considered, such as the following:

- Type of event;
- Approximate number and general composition of those attending (students, outsiders, and so on);
- Location (ability to control entrances);
- Admission charge or free admission;
- Access-control procedures (ticket sales and collection);
- General rules regarding those participating and attending;
- History of similar events in the past;
- Policies in regard to arrest, ejection from premises, and so forth.

The director of security should have the final say in regard to the security aspects of any event. This say should include the right to recommend that a particular event not take place if evidence and circumstances clearly indicate that it could jeopardize personal safety, property, and the reputation of the institution. Calling off any event on a campus will surely bring cries of suppression of freedom of speech and similar accusations, but in isolated instances in which overwhelming evidence exists that staging an event would be hazardous, someone has to take a stand. Usually, that someone is the head of security. He should be backed in his decision by top administration.

This chapter discusses some of the types of events that are common to most educational institutions and offers suggestions in regard to security's role and effective crowd control procedures.

ATHLETIC EVENTS

The head of the campus security operation must work closely and harmoniously with the director of athletics and the athletic department. Security at athletic events should be chiefly the responsibility of the security department but will have to be closely coordinated at large events with the athletic department and its personnel.

Use of Outside Police Officers

Universities with large football stadiums present the greatest security challenge. No campus security department can staff and assume full responsibility for security at these contests attended by the general public, meaning that local and state law enforcement officers must be utilized to handle traffic and maintain order. Usually this hiring involves payment to outside officers for their services.

On some campuses, outside coverage for major athletic events is negotiated with local and state police departments by the director of athletics and his staff, without the director of security being involved. At a few institutions, local police officers are paid in cash for their services at athletic events. Neither of these practices is desirable.

The head of security at a university or college should be charged with the responsibility of representing the institution and carrying on liaison with all outside law enforcement agencies. This should include athletic events, which involve not only hiring outside police officers but also planning a coordinated security approach.

The practice of paying outside police officers in cash for their services is extremely sensitive from a tax standpoint and should be avoided. Payment should be made by check directly to the police department involved, upon receipt of a detailed invoice enumerating each officer's services.

Developing Written Plans

Planning for major events that will be attended by thousands of spectators must involve the athletic department, security department, outside law enforcement agencies, ambulance and medical personnel, and others. Plans for these should be in writing so that everyone involved knows exactly what his responsibility is and where he is assigned. Usually, these activities demand approximately the same coverage each year, with changes dictated largely by experience. Therefore, the same written instructions can usually be used from year to year with only minor changes. It may be possible to print a number of these detail-assignment plans for athletic and other yearly events (such as commencement and reunions) and, by leaving the names of persons assigned to various duties blank, use them year after year merely by inserting the names of individuals assigned.

Also a good idea, at the completion of an event, is to dictate a memo for that file regarding any problems encountered and changes that might be incorporated into future plans for the same event.

Prior to the start of the football season a meeting with all persons responsible for supervising the various activities should be held. This group would include representatives of outside law enforcement agencies, the campus security organization, the athletic department, medical and ambulance administrators, and other people who will be involved. Written plans should be distributed at this meeting and an overall briefing session should take place so that everyone thoroughly understands his or her responsibilities.

Role of Campus Officers

What part should campus security play at football games held in university-owned stadiums? My experience at the Yale Bowl (capacity 72,000) was that Yale police officers could best be utilized in controlling student activities. Since students were allocated tickets in certain sections, campus officers were stationed near the top of the bowl in these sections where they could observe student activities and take action if objects were thrown on the field or other incidents occurred involving students. The students were found to respond much more readily to Yale officers whom they recognized than to outside police officers. Potentially serious situations were "cooled" before they escalated.

The campus officers were also in radio communication with a control or communications center so that they could be dispatched to any area where student problems occurred. A central-control center is a necessary part of managing and controlling major athletic events effectively.

Campus investigators were also assigned to handle accident cases in which the university had an interest. An investigator obtained the facts of the accident, took pictures, if necessary, and rode in the ambulance to the hospital with the victim to acquire all possible information and ascertain the extent of the injury.

If the victim refused medical attention, he or she was asked to sign a form to the effect that, although a medical checkup had been offered and recommended, it had been refused. This waiver was witnessed and signed by the Yale officer and submitted with his report of the incident. These reports were made available to the university insurance carrier.

The accident reports were particularly valuable when the Yale Bowl was being used for professional football games. Professional games generated a different type of accident-prone fan than did college games, mostly because of excessive drinking and the age and physical condition of many people attending. From a security standpoint it is inadvisable for professional teams to use campus stadiums.

Security problems are increased as fans become more violent, and acts of vandalism may involve thousands of dollars in damage.

Another tactic that worked reasonably well in the Ivy League on football weekends was to have present the director of security from the opponent institution and one or more of his officers. Stationed in a position in which their own students could observe them, these individuals largely controlled their own people. They were also of assistance after the game, as they made themselves available to handle problems involving their own students and spent time with Yale officers patrolling and visiting social affairs.

Local police officers were used for crowd control and to respond to situations that ushers and other personnel could not handle. However, state and local officers were used mainly to handle traffic in and out of university parking areas and contiguous streets and highways.

The decision to arrest or eject an unruly spectator from the stadium has to be somewhat spelled out prior to the game. No firm policy can be established here, however, because so many factors are involved. The officer himself will have to make this decision based on the circumstances and what type of action he has to take. If physical force has to be used to restrain or otherwise deter the violator, an arrest will probably have to follow in order for the officer to protect himself from possible legal action.

DANCES AND OTHER SOCIAL EVENTS

Dances and similar social events are usually student sponsored and procedures should be in effect to make sure they are not disrupted. This usually means that the student affairs office, with input from security and other interested departments, should establish certain regulations and guidelines regarding such affairs. These guidelines should include applying for the campus hall or room to be used for the event far enough in advance for plans to be made. Information should also be acquired regarding the type of affair and estimated number of attendees, whether admission will be charged, whether it will be open to nonuniversity people, and access-control procedures to be utilized. The security department should be notified and furnished this information at least one week prior to the event so security coverage may be arranged and a meeting held with persons in charge of the activity. This meeting is important so that everyone will have a clear understanding regarding the role security officers will play and what security measures will be taken.

Importance of Entry Control

One of the keys to running a successful and trouble-free dance is tight control of persons who enter. Most trouble emanates from outsiders and "crashers." A security officer can be used at the door to furnish backup for the people taking tickets and controlling entry.

Other hazards, particularly at events held on a ground floor, are windows and fire doors that have to permit egress and are often opened to permit unauthorized people to enter. Guarding against this hazard is difficult, but one of the most successful measures is to utilize student personnel to watch these areas and insure that no one enters through fire doors.

Student Control

Students can be most effective in controlling and policing their own affairs. However, this should be done either under the direction of the security department or after clear-cut procedures and policies have been established. Students are particularly valuable in dealing with their peers and in "cooling" certain situations before they escalate into problems for security personnel.

ROCK CONCERTS

Most colleges and universities have auditoriums, stadiums, or similar facilities in which various events are held. Each of these events requires a certain level of crowd control and a security approach tailored to cope with situations that might occur. Rock concerts involving a variety of performers and groups often present a major challenge to any campus security operation. These concerts can sometimes erupt into nasty situations unless security planning and response are effective.

The head of security must be directly involved from the outset in planning for these rock concerts. He should have a definite voice in matters pertaining to the safety, health, and welfare of those attending, as well as the protection of campus and private property. Too often student organizations and members of student affairs schedule volatile performers who appeal to youthful nonstudents as well as students. The planners of these events are either naive or inclined to overlook security problems that can occur. Some rock concerts in the past have involved knife and fist fights; assaults utilizing chains, baseball bats, and other weapons; armed robberies; muggings; pocketbook snatchings; and expensive damage to property such as smashed or slashed chairs.

Problems with Outsiders

The history of problems at campus rock concerts clearly indicates that most trouble emanates from nonstudents who are attracted to the concert and over whom the college or university has very little control. If these concerts were restricted to students and campus-affiliated attendees, the chance of security problems erupting would be greatly reduced. Unfortunately, rock singers and musicians demand high fees, and the campus organization running the affair is interested in filling the hall. This factor usually means selling tickets to anyone.

The problem of outsiders increases when a campus is located in or near a city. For example, at Northwestern University in Evanston, Illinois, a suburb of Chicago, estimates at one sellout rock concert indicated that only 16 percent of those attending were students. The remainder were mostly young adults from the Chicago area who had no ties or responsibilities to the institution. Although numerous arrests for violent behavior and other criminal acts were made at this concert, not one of those arrested was a student.

Importance of Proper and Careful Planning

The key to handling rock concerts successfully from a security standpoint has to be proper and careful planning. Each concert has to be evaluated individually. A rubber-stamp approach should not be utilized.

Recently, I was engaged as an expert witness by attorneys for the plaintiff in a substantial civil suit against a public coliseum and the promoters of a hard-rock concert. This incident involved a fourteen-year-old girl who was assaulted by an older female without provocation. The incident occurred on the floor of the coliseum after ushers and a few police officers had made repeated but half-hearted attempts to control those crowding the aisles and the area in front of the stage. My report of findings clearly showed that the people running the affair had done no real security planning but had treated this volatile rock group, which had a past history of audience violence, the same as any other event. After receiving a copy of the findings, the attorneys for the defendants settled the case out of court.

Colleges and universities, as well as student organizations and people involved in the promotion of rock concerts, should be aware that they can be named in civil suits if trouble develops. In all probability, these lawsuits will be successful unless it can be shown that specific plans were made and a responsible and adequate security operation was in effect.

Insurance and Contract Requirements

The concert promoters should be required to obtain insurance as follows: at least $100,000 per person and $300,000 per occurrence for bodily injury and $25,000 per occurrence for property damage. The university should require certification of such insurance well ahead of the performance.

The first step in security planning must be concerned with negotiating with the producer and formulating a strong, all-inclusive contract to be signed by the parties involved. Although this contract will have to be drawn up by an attorney, the head of security should be consulted in regard to stipulations that can contribute to a trouble-free performance.

Some of the matters that must be considered and included in the contract, with suitable penalties (usually financial) if violated, are the following:

- All rehearsals and preperformance preparations must be completed at least two hours (or more, depending on size of crowd) prior to the start of the performance. Occasionally, performers insist on rehearsing or setting up too close to the time of the actual performance, which can create problems (particularly in bad weather) when several thousand ticketholders crowd entrances waiting to be admitted.
- The director of security should be authorized to assign as many security personnel as he feels necessary to control and police the event. Naturally, the number and type of security personnel assigned will vary depending on various factors that will be enumerated later. The producer will usually be responsible for paying these personnel and should be given at least an approximate budget figure for these services that, according to the contract, would be paid directly to the university with other charges.
- The contract should clearly state that the performance must start on time. Increasing financial penalties should be imposed for tardiness. For example, no penalty would be imposed for up to the first ten minutes, but an escalating penalty would be specified for each ten minutes' delay after that. Many problems can develop when performances do not start on time and audiences become impatient.
- The director of security or public safety should be authorized in the contract to terminate the concert at any time because of undue delay in starting or if danger of personal injury or property damage is imminent. Naturally, this action would only be taken as a last resort and care should be exercised not to precipitate a violent crowd reaction as a result of stopping or canceling the show.
- Policies should be formulated well in advance regarding complimentary admittance and persons who will be allowed backstage and in dressing rooms and similar areas.
- The sale of records, souvenirs, and similar items should be regulated in the contract, and policies should be formulated to prohibit taking pictures and recording the show.
- State clearly that, in case of a cancellation, the university should be notified well ahead of performance in order to prevent a sometimes ugly and violent crowd from gathering.

Number of Security Personnel Needed

The head of security will have the responsibility of assigning the proper number of security personnel to insure an orderly affair. This figure is very difficult to arrive at. The director can be embarrassed if he assigns too many officers to a problem-free concert or not enough to an event at which violence erupts.

Certain factors have to be considered well ahead of any rock concert in order to arrive at the number of personnel that should be assigned and their deployment. Let us examine some of these factors.

Previous History. Planning for a rock concert, which appeals to a young, excitable audience, requires some research regarding the history of audience reaction and behavior at similar appearances. This research can usually be accomplished merely by phoning directors at other colleges and universities where the group has performed. Usually, a list of past performances can be obtained from the producer, but problem concerts may have been purposely eliminated from it. If trouble has occurred on one campus, its director of security will probably be able to supply information about other locations where similar problems happened.

Some of the questions that should be asked deal with the type of crowd the performer or group attracts (e.g., drug users); the type of performance and cooperation of the performers and the producer (if the performers incite the crowd, know how and when to calm the fans, and so on); incidents and security precautions and procedures and their effectiveness; size of the audience and number of police and security personnel used (where and how deployed); and other problems likely to incite trouble (such as performers being late or not showing up, being under the influence of drugs, or smoking on stage in a no-smoking hall).

This research prior to the concert should be designed to furnish valuable information in tailoring an effective security operation for that particular event. It furnishes the track record of the particular performer or group so that a prevention-oriented security approach can be formulated.

Type of Event. The type of concert also must be considered in determining manpower needs and security measures to be taken. For example, a performance by an "acid rock" group that has the reputation of attracting drug users will require more security than a concert by a performer with a wholesome, more conventional image.

Time and Length. Events held in daylight hours usually result in fewer problems than events taking place after dark. The length of the concert is also important because some performers at times cut their performances short, which may result in a violent reaction from persons in the audience who have paid high prices to attend.

If traffic and parking are the responsibilities of the campus department, the time and length of the event become even more important to avoid rush-hour congestion.

Composition of Audience. Because outsiders are responsible for the majority of problems, more security personnel must be assigned and tighter security procedures utilized if outsiders are expected to attend than when the audience is composed mostly of students from the campus.

Remember also that some rock groups attract followers who trail them from campus to campus. Some of these followers may be drug users and can be difficult to control. They can also cause trouble and commit crimes on campus after the concert.

Location. The location of the concert is important in regard to security planning. If the auditorium has multiple ground-floor fire doors and windows, access control becomes more difficult. The size of the space is important because crowded conditions sometimes promote problems. Seating arrangements are also important. For example, if fire regulations permit, seating right up to the stage and solid seating across the auditorium floor can assist in alleviating crowded aisles and attempts to rush onto the stage.

Performers' Cooperation. In researching the history of prior concerts by the same performer and group, determine if they are cooperative or tend to incite the audience. Do the performers start on time, cooperate in informing the audience that the show will not go on unless aisles are kept clear, and so on? Do the performers demand certain security (for example, that a certain number of officers be deployed in front of the stage, backstage, and while the performers are entering and leaving the hall)?

Other Factors. Numerous other factors should be considered in planning for any rock concert or similar event. One factor would be the type of advance publicity. At times, campus newspapers may focus on some issue or otherwise indicate a situation that could cause trouble.

Another factor would be the type of ushers, ticket takers, and other personnel who will be working the affair. If they are regularly assigned and experienced in handling this type of audience, problems will be minimized.

Other matters such as lighting and the effectiveness of sound equipment should be considered. Some performers demand total darkness. This darkness, coupled with psychedelic lighting, hard-rock music, and the use of marijuana and other drugs, may contribute to stirring up the audience. The failure of the sound system or a poor sound system may also lead to disruptive audience reaction.

CONTROVERSIAL SPEAKERS

In conclusion, campuses also attract many controversial speakers who require security similar in many respects to that for rock artists. Many of the same principles and suggestions mentioned in this chapter can also be applied to such appearances.

Chapter 18

PROTECTION OF CASH
AND VALUABLE OBJECTS

CASH HANDLING

Large amounts of cash are generated and handled on every college or university campus. The security department does not become involved in the collection or management of this money. However, it should become involved in formulating security procedures and overseeing these money-handling operations to protect not only the cash but also the safety and well-being of the people responsible for it.

In conducting a security survey on a campus, considerable time should be devoted to tracing cash flow and auditing security measures utilized to insure the safekeeping of cash. Security procedures pertaining to the handling of cash are usually very weak and at some institutions hardly exist at all.

Common Security Weaknesses

Some security departments do not know where cash is generated on the campus, the amount taken in, security procedures and policies followed by employees handling cash, or the accounting procedures to protect against internal theft. The security department many times does not even become involved in guarding the cash when it is transported from one location to another on campus or to a bank.

In many cases the security department cannot be blamed entirely for this lack of involvement, because those handling the cash have never asked for assistance. However, campus security directors should perform a detailed study of all cash-handling procedures at their institutions and go on record in making recommendations to safeguard cash and protect the personal safety of employees handling money. If this is not done, and a robbery, embezzlement or other loss occurs, there will be no answer to the question that is sure to be asked: "What steps had security taken to prevent this from happening?"

At many institutions, the attitude of persons handling money is that "it can't happen here." Over and over, persons charged with the handling of cash state, "We've been doing it this way for years and never had any trouble. Why should we change now?"

Another common attitude is, "So what? We are insured." However, many of those supervising the handling of cash do not know the degree of insurance coverage or what this insurance is costing the college or university. In recent years two trends regarding insurance for theft or loss of property and cash have emerged. One trend involves increasing the amount of deductible for which the institution is responsible. The other trend involves drastically increasing insurance rates because of accelerating losses. The best way to reverse these trends is to decrease losses through an effective, preventive-oriented security approach.

Many examples of cash-handling procedures at various colleges and universities exist that practically invite robberies and burglaries. Only a few of the more common examples are mentioned here.

On one campus the completely unprotected bursar's office was located on the first floor near the entrance in a building only about two blocks from a main highway. Business was transacted over a low, open counter by two elderly female clerks who kept at least $2,000 in cash in an unlocked drawer at each of their posts. In addition, up to $30,000 was stored in a safe located in a walk-in vault easily observed by anyone at the counter. The vault and safe doors were unlocked in the morning and left open throughout the business day. At lunch time the two elderly ladies relieved each other, so that for approximately two hours the entire operation was staffed by one woman who had no way of summoning assistance except by telephone.

On another campus a sixty-four-year-old maintenance man at the student union brought all receipts to the bank each morning. These receipts often exceeded $15,000. They were merely placed in a canvas money bag and driven to the bank in his personal car. Discreet observations of this procedure revealed that prior to visiting the bank each morning, the maintenance man stopped for coffee at a local diner, where he stayed for at least fifteen minutes talking to friends and diner employees. His unlocked car was left parked outside with the money bag left on the seat. When confronted with this situation, his reply was, "I have been stopping for coffee for years and never lost a cent yet."

Most colleges and universities follow a system in which all cash receipts from dining halls, bookstores, and other sources of revenue are channeled to the business office to be processed. Many times the methods used to transport receipts to the business office are extremely weak from a security standpoint. For example, on some campuses an unescorted young female employee simply puts the money in an envelope and walks it to the business office. Some people try to disguise the operation by putting the money in a brown paper bag, a brief case, or similar container that ordinarily would not be used to carry cash. However, in many instances the money is transported by the same employee in the same manner each day at approximately the same time, making it easy for a robber to case the transaction and snatch the container. Again, the attitude often prevails that the person carrying the money has to walk only a short distance to the business office and is safer on campus than in the outside community.

Finally, at several institutions large sums of money were kept in desk drawers and filing cabinets, and business was transacted in open office space. At one of these institutions, an employee left her unlocked desk for a few minutes and, upon returning, found over $1,000 missing from the drawer in which she kept her cash. Inasmuch as this was a large, public office with many other employees and where considerable business was transacted, the case was never solved.

An even more common loss involves prying open desks or filing cabinets during nonworking hours, particularly over weekend or vacation periods, and taking the cash contained in them. Often many filing cabinets are keyed exactly the same, making illegal entry even more difficult to trace. These cabinets should be keyed individually.

Desks and filing cabinets should be left unlocked unless they contain something of real value. Frequently, desks and cabinets containing nothing of any significant value require expensive repairs as a result of their being pried open even though their contents were of no interest to the thief.

Check Cashing—Pros and Cons

Many colleges and universities provide a check-cashing service for students and employees. Because they must maintain a constant supply of cash on hand, this practice increases their security vulnerability. Check cashing also means almost daily delivery of cash from the bank to the campus and the storage of large amounts of money. Security procedures and equipment must be utilized to protect these assets.

I question whether a college or university should be in the check-cashing business. In recent years, many of the larger universities have provided or rented space to local banks for campus branches. This arrangement usually proves to be ideal for the bank and the university. It certainly reduces the university's responsibility for the security of cash.

Check cashing is a hazardous business these days. Bad checks account for more losses to banks than do bank robberies. Colleges and universities that cash checks are almost as vulnerable. They can also be the target of robbers, burglars, and embezzlers.

Nevertheless, some colleges and universities, because of their location and other reasons, find it necessary to maintain a check-cashing service for the convenience of students, faculty, and staff. In this case, limits should be set on the amount of checks to be cashed so that the amount of cash on hand will be reduced and uncollectible check losses will be minimal. In other words, the check-cashing service would be used for emergency situations in which small amounts of cash are needed in a hurry. Checks would be cashed only for persons displaying a campus identification card. However, remember that even these cards can be stolen or sometimes forged.

Securing the Cashier's Operation

Most colleges and universities have what amounts to a cashier's operation for bill paying, check cashing, and general accounting of all cash generated on campus. These operations should be afforded the same type of security as exists in most banks.

A campus cashier's office should be situated in a secure, conveniently located area isolated from other activities and business. Ideally, it should contain only a small public lobby area and a counter over which the cashiers transact business. This counter should be enclosed above by transparent Plexiglas acrylic plastic to protect the cashiers. This bullet-resisting glazing should extend from the top of the counter to the ceiling. It should be louvered to allow normal voice contact and should contain a small pass-through space. These protective cashier's shields prevent robbers from vaulting over the counter during a holdup, act as a deterrent to would-be robbers, and make the cashiers feel safer.

Cashiers should work out of their own secure metal cash drawer or box that should contain the lowest amount of money possible. These cash boxes should be kept out of sight under the counter and a minimum of cash should be exposed during transactions. Each cashier's station should be equipped with a silent holdup alarm connected to the security department console. This alarm can be a wireless money clip or pressure plate in the cashier's drawer or a double-squeeze or recessed finger-type hard-wired alarm under the counter.

If the cashier's operation is extensive and involves a number of cashiers and high amounts of money, one or more cameras might also be considered. These cameras should be mounted behind the cashiers so as to view the people standing in front of the counter. A calendar and clock should be in camera range to record the date and time of any incident. A sequence-type camera that takes a picture about every thirty seconds is recommended because on many occasions these photos can be used to identify bad check passers. When a holdup alarm is triggered, the camera will automatically change to a rapid picture-taking sequence.

Cashiers should be trained in what to do during and immediately after a robbery. This training would involve such matters as obtaining a good description of the subject, protecting the note passed or other evidence, and how and when to activate the alarm.

Cash should be stored in a secure safe that cannot be easily carried off. Preferably, this safe should be in a secure walk-in vault and out of public view. The safe should be protected by a capacitance alarm monitored at the security console. In large operations in which high sums of money are involved, a time-lock feature should be utilized and the safe clearly marked that it is under such a time lock.

Cash should not be counted in view of the public. A secure, private room should be provided for this purpose and a panic-type alarm considered. This room would be used for counting and auditing cash generated from other campus operations and received from the bank. The room should be contiguous to the cashier's operation and storage safe or vault.

Money Escorts

Most colleges and universities hire professional, qualified money transportation companies to pick up cash and deliver it to the bank. This is undoubtedly the safest and most convenient procedure. However, some institutions still have their own employees make these trips to the bank, often placing the employee and the cash in jeopardy. All too frequently, employees make trips to the bank with no protection even though they are carrying thousands of dollars.

If a money escort is to be truly effective, two trained, armed officers should be assigned. Anything less is extremely risky. If you think otherwise, consider just one example.

A few years ago Duke Vincent, director of safety and security at Southwestern University, Memphis, Tennessee, drove to the bank in a university-owned, unmarked station wagon at 9:30 A.M. to pick up approximately $3,000 in cash for the check-cashing service. Vincent was well known at the bank because he made the same trip twice each day. He usually obtained at least $3,000 that he carried out of the bank in a paper bag.

Immediately after he left, everyone in the bank heard what they believed to be a car backfiring. However, seconds later a customer rushed in saying a man's body was in the parking lot. Vincent was found lying beside the open driver's-side door of the wagon. He had been shot twice in the chest and his gun was still in his holster. The paper bag and some of the cash were strewn about. He had been accosted by three subjects and almost immediately shot down and killed. Although he was a former inspector and veteran officer of the Memphis Police Department, Duke Vincent just didn't have a chance.

VALUABLE COLLECTIONS

Many educational institutions have valuable collections of art objects and memorabilia that require security protection. At Yale University, for example, security must be provided for the following priceless collections:

- Yale Center for British Art (Mellon Collection);
- Yale Art Gallery (valuable paintings, sculptures, and so on);
- Garvan Collection of Early American Art and Furniture (antique furniture, Paul Revere silver, paintings, and so on);
- Peabody Museum of Natural History;
- Beinecke Rare Book and Manuscript Library;
- Numismatic Collection;
- Musical Instruments Collection.

In addition, numerous other smaller collections of valuable art objects, manuscripts, and antiques are at Yale. These collections are sometimes more difficult to protect than the large exhibits because of their insecure locations.

Accountability for Valuable Objects

One of the problems at some colleges and universities is that the security department may not even know that certain valuable objects or collections exist. At times, an alumnus gives or wills some valuable collection or art object to the institution or to a particular department or its chairman. The institution accepts the gift but then does not have any place to display it safely. Therefore, the collection of valuable antiques or art objects is stored, often in insecure closets or similar locations, and sometimes the objects are not properly inventoried or accounted for. The valuables may be stolen, vandalized, or damaged. Many times the security department is never apprised of the receipt of such items and is only notified when they are missing.

At a large eastern university, for example, the security director received a frantic call from a department head regarding a rare Chinese vase worth over $40,000. It was missing from its storage space in a basement closet used to store less valuable china and glass. The security director thus found out for the first time that the vase had been given to the department about a year earlier by an alumnus. No one knew when it had been seen last.

A clear-cut policy and accountability procedures must be established for the protection of valuable objects. This policy should make mandatory a uniform inventory system so that each object or collection is listed and fully described. Photos of valuable pieces should be taken and kept with the inventory list. Such photos are invaluable in the event these pieces are stolen or lost. The security department should be furnished with a copy of this inventory, which should also indicate the location of the property.

The advisability of having a centralized inventory system administered by a full-time property custodian has already been mentioned in Chapter 15. This system would also insure that periodic inventories were made of distinctive and costly property.

The security department should be informed immediately of the receipt of any valuable property and should assist in formulating procedures and determining its location so that it will be secure. Special attention should be given to these areas by patrolling officers, and preventive-oriented inspections should be scheduled by the security department to insure that the property is being afforded proper protection.

Responsibility for the Security of Special Collections

The question often arises as to who should be responsible for security in a campus art gallery, museum, library, or similar collection. All security planning, personnel, and electronic intrusion devices should be the responsibility of the director of security.

Directors of campus art galleries, museums, and libraries will sometimes argue this point, and on many campuses they still hire and administer guards, watchmen, and other personnel whose functions are predominantly security-oriented. They also set up security procedures and sometimes purchase elaborate alarms and other electronic protective systems with no input or direction from the head of security.

The director of security should be responsible for the hiring, training, supervision, and administration of all security personnel such as art gallery or museum guards. He should also be responsible for and have the final say in the purchase of any electronic intrusion system, which should be monitored at the central console in the security office. However, all security planning should be discussed fully with the director of the gallery, museum, library, or other facility, and close cooperation and communication should be maintained. For example, no guard should be hired for a facility unless interviewed and approved by the director of that operation.

Directors of large university galleries usually welcome assistance and direction from the head of security and are willing to have guards and other security personnel administered by him. The only time this assistance would not be welcomed is when the security department is a low-level operation that does not have the confidence and respect of the campus community and when the head of the department is not a professional.

In the recruitment of art gallery guards, some excellent talent is available among retired business executives and other intelligent, well-motivated individuals who are interested in art and want something to keep them busy. Although an art gallery guard's work would be boring to many people, these individuals enjoy their association with the people and cultural and art objects that are part of their working environment. They make conscientious and excellent employees who need only a minimum of supervision. These guards may wear a neat, attractive blazer uniform that clearly identifies them as art gallery guards. They do not have police power. Their main duties are usually to deter visitors from smoking, touching the paintings, allowing children to go unchecked, and similar functions. They also project a good public relations image for the gallery by answering questions and assisting visitors.

Chapter 19

PROTECTION OF SPECIAL CAMPUS FACILITIES

Colleges and universities are in many respects carbon copies of each other in regard to certain facilities and operations. The only difference involves the size of these facilities and the extent of the services they provide.

Each of these facilities requires some special security planning that must be tailored to meet the security needs of that particular operation or service. Some of these services set up their own security programs many years ago before campus security reached the level of performance existing at most institutions today. Some administrators of these specialized operations continue to run their own security programs and only call on the security department for responses to problems they are unable to handle. Providing that the security department is professional and effective, I believe that all security planning for every facility and activity on campus should be the primary responsibility of the head of the security operation.

Specialized facilities and operations that are found on every campus, and that are discussed in this chapter, are the library, bookstore, food service, computer center, and the health center.

LIBRARY

Premise Protection

Campus libraries at most institutions are housed in separate buildings that can be best protected by a proprietary alarm system when the library is closed. Protection involves alarming each perimeter door and making sure that all windows providing access are locked, or better still, that they are of the solid, unbreakable type that cannot be opened.

In order to meet insurance requirements, a watchman will probably have to tour the library when it is closed. Electronic watch tour stations that record at the central console are most desirable and should be planned for in constructing new library facilities.

Premise protection during hours when the library is open involves the alarming of all fire doors, which should have no outside hardware, and controlling access and egress.

One of the vulnerable areas in large libraries are the stacks in which female students often study alone and are often isolated. These students can be the targets of exhibitionists, and there have been cases of their being molested, attacked, and robbed. Emergency telephones or alarm buttons should be strategically placed in these isolated areas that would provide a signal at the security console and the main desk of the library. In large libraries there should be some security presence who would respond immediately to this type of problem, check on alarm violations, patrol, and provide other flexible security coverage.

If a rare book room or section is in the library, this area should be protected by an alarm system (probably ultrasonic), and access should be strictly controlled at all times.

In the event of thefts of rare books or manuscripts, these losses should be registered with the Security Program of the Society of American Archivists (SAA), Box 8198, University of Illinois at Chicago Circle, Chicago, Illinois 60680. Only rare books that can be positively identified may be registered. A brochure regarding this registering program and other material regarding archival security may be obtained from SAA.

The main desk should have an emergency alarm so that those working there could press a strategically located button that would transmit a silent alarm to the security console and insure immediate response. If a security guard or officer is assigned to the library, he should either be equipped to receive this signal or carry a two-way radio and be dispatched by the central console operator/dispatcher.

In large libraries with numerous sexual perversion or similar problems, a hidden portable CCTV camera, monitor, and video recorder might be considered for trouble-spot protection and to record legal evidence. Signs should clearly indicate that the premises may be under electronic surveillance and troublemakers may be prosecuted.

Access Control

After-hours access to the library should be confined to as few people as possible—usually, the director and one or two other administrators. Access can be controlled at one entrance by a card-key reader that prints out the entry at the central console or by an electric strike controlled at the console. If neither of these systems is used, the main entrance locking hardware should be keyed with a system that cannot be easily duplicated, and tight key control should exist.

Access control during library hours is extremely important because without a good access-control system the use of book detection systems (to be discussed later) are ineffective and a waste of money. All persons entering a campus library should be channeled through as few entrances as possible, preferably a single main entrance. They should be directed through a turnstile where a library guard or attendant visually checks their ID before allowing entry. At some libraries this same individual can provide backup for a book detection system.

The reason why a check of ID cards is a good security precaution is because it helps keep unauthorized individuals off the premises and alleviates some of the main problems common to all libraries. These problems involve book thefts or mutilations, exhibitionists and other sex offenders, thefts, and vandalism.

The campus library, unlike the municipal public library, can restrict access to members of the campus community and, in my opinion, at least ID screening should be performed. If necessary, special provisions can be made for members of the outside community to gain access and use the facilities. An established fact is that libraries are often havens for sexual deviants, arsonists, transients and "winos" who are escaping the cold, and other undesirables. Libraries also provide fertile locations for sneak thieves who steal handbags, clothing, and other property while their owners are studying, searching for a book, or otherwise occupied.

All fire and other perimeter doors not being used for authorized and supervised access and egress should be alarmed and clearly marked to prevent egress. These alarms would be registered at the central console but also would be monitored when the library is open at an additional monitor at the main desk so that a library guard or attendant could be immediately dispatched.

Book Detection Systems

The gravity of book thefts from academic libraries is ever increasing and estimates show that libraries at educational institutions lose from 2 to 15 percent of their total collections in a single year. In my experience as a campus security consultant, I have also found that many campus libraries really do not know what their losses are or when they occurred. This problem is caused by the lack of effective inventory controls that, in turn, can sometimes be attributed to low budgets that preclude personnel to administer an inventory system. Some libraries also seem to consider books to be expendable and simply buy others to replace the stolen books.

The first step that should be taken prior to purchasing an electronic book detection system should be to determine the extent of the loss problem and whether it is caused by failure to return charged-out books or failure to charge them out at all. Book detection systems are expensive and can only be justified when the extent of the theft problem reaches proportions that indicate the system will pay for itself in a few years by reducing losses.

In considering the expense of a book detection system, the costs of any current programs to prevent book thefts must be analyzed. The most common book theft deterrent in the past was to station a guard or attendant at the main entrance or entrances who would screen brief cases and other containers and check books being carried out to make sure they had been properly charged out. This type of screening usually proved inconvenient and, at times, annoying to the honest library user, and it also really did not prevent the library book thief from taking out what he or she wanted to. Thieves could hide books under their coats, exit from an unguarded exit, or drop books out windows, for example.

Several book detection systems employ approximately the same scientific principals. All systems utilize sensitive markers attached to books (metal strips, transceiver wafers, metal sheets covered by paper) in such a way so they will not be recognized. When a book is properly charged out the detection marker is desensitized, and when the book is returned it is resensitized. Patrons are channeled through an exitway with a locking exit gate that permits egress when books are properly charged out. A signal is given and the gate locks when a book is carried out that has not been processed.

The use of these book detection systems have dramatically reduced book losses at some college and universities libraries, while at others they have proved ineffective. The reasons why in some cases they are ineffective are:

- No security backup or action taken when detection system identifies a book thief;
- Lax access control that permits the use of other exits including fire doors;
- Multiple open windows that permit books dropped outside to be retrieved later;
- Careless processing of books and administration of the system itself;
- Poor design of the existing and book-screening process that permits books to be sneaked out without going through the channeled exit and detection process.

The American Library Association has considerable material regarding the cost of purchasing or leasing various book detection systems and their effectiveness.

BOOKSTORE

Shoplifting and the internal theft of cash and merchandise are the major security problems faced by campus bookstores. The use of the word campus *bookstore* is also a misnomer because most of these stores sell not only books but also everything from toothpaste to souvenirs.

Shoplifting is one of the major concerns of campus-owned bookstores and, in some cases, accounts for the difference between operating at a profit or loss. Some university-owned and operated bookstores have become so unprofitable due to shoplifting and internal theft that they have been turned over to outside companies on a concession basis.

Consumers pay an estimated five to ten cents more for every dollars' worth of merchandise purchased in retail stores to make up for losses suffered from shoplifting and internal employee theft.

After-Hours Premise Protection

Premise protection after the store is closed can best be accomplished by the use of electronics monitored and recorded on a printout at the security console. This system would include perimeter intrusion-alarm devices as well as internal alarm traps utilizing infrared beams, capacitance alarms on money safes, and space alarms in stock storage rooms.

Internal Theft

Effective supervision and fixing security responsibility are necessary to reduce the opportunity for internal theft and the embezzlement of cash. A good inventory control system of merchandise should be established extending from the time goods are received until they are sold.

Store cashiers should work under procedures similar to those governing bank tellers, which entails working out of an individual cash drawer with each cashier having to balance his or her account against the cash register tape or a computerized record of sales and receipts. No cash should ever be left in cash registers during periods when the store is closed, and register drawers should be left open at these times to reveal that they are empty.

Screening of employees prior to employment should be done (as much as possible) to determine their honesty and prior record.

Spot checks of salespeople should be made if they utilize individual cash registers rather than have customers pay at a checkout cashier. These audits would be made by professional shoppers to insure that salespersons are ringing up sales properly and that they are not pocketing cash, particularly when exact-change payments are made for merchandise. Cashiers should also be checked occasionally by professional shoppers.

After-hours custodial services should always be performed under supervision of the store manager or other supervisor. Occasionally, security officers can be utilized for these assignments that would usually entail payment for these off-duty services by the bookstore.

Management should reserve the right to check any property or containers taken off the premises by employees.

Cash Handling

Most university bookstores use cashier checkouts and few salespersons. Customers obtain the book or merchandise they want and are channeled as in a supermarket by a cashier for payment.

Cashiers should be accountable for their own individual cash drawers and balancing their receipts against the cash register tape. A minimum amount of start-up small bills and change (about $100 to $200) should be given to each cashier at the start of his or her work day. A trusted head cashier would be responsible for giving out, maintaining, and accounting for all cash as well as auditing cashiers' balancing records.

During rush periods cash registers should be emptied frequently and proceeds counted out of sight in a secure counting room. Access to this room should be limited to as few employees as possible, preferably just the head cashier and manager. When cash is being counted the room should be locked from the inside by the person counting the cash, and access should be controlled by that person. This control can involve the use of an electric strike controlled from within the counting room and some means (intercom and viewing peephole or CCTV) of identifying the individual requesting entry. A panic button should also exist in the room that would signal the security department's central console of trouble.

It is preferable form a security standpoint to have an armored car service pick up all currency and checks daily for delivery to a bank. During rush periods this exchange might have to be done twice a day at larger stores.

If cash is to be transported to the bank or business office by other than armored car service, it should be placed in a secure container, and armed security officers (preferably two) should perform this function or accompany the bookstore employee.

In larger stores with a number of cashiers, a roller-type, secure cash drawer cart may be used by the head cashier, supervisor, or a security officer to transport cash drawers to the counting room.

Cash should be stored overnight and at all times when not being counted or balanced in a secure vault or safe that should be locked and alarmed when not being used. One of the major weaknesses noted in campus bookstores is locating this safe or vault in full view of people in the store and failing to secure it during the working day. Often the doors to safes and vaults are closed, but the combination dial is not spun so that the door can be opened. This "fake" locking of safes and vaults is done for the convenience of employees, but professional thieves are also aware of this tactic and most try the doors to see if they are open. Ideally, safes and vaults should be located within the secure counting room that should also be alarmed for additional security.

During rush book-selling periods at the start of each semester it is usually advisable to have a security officer (preferably armed) on the premises. This officer would primarily be there to protect the cashiers' operation but would also be used to detect shoplifting and act as a visible deterrent to the would-be shoplifter.

In larger stores the manager might also use a CCTV camera trained on the cashiers' operation and monitored at his or her desk. This camera would be used as a supervisory tool and to provide better security for the cashiers' operation. A panic button might also be installed at each cash register to be used in the event of a robbery attempt or other problem. These panic buttons should be of the finger-insert or double-squeeze type to prevent accidental triggering.

Shoplifting

Shoplifting is a major problem with many campus bookstores. Textbooks and small items appear to be the main targets of shoplifters. Some campus bookstores no longer expose textbooks to customers but transact business through a window or windows.

One of the main reasons why shoplifting is so prevalent in campus bookstores is because of the lack of any penalties imposed on shoplifters. Many institutions follow a double standard in regard to shoplifting, with outsiders being arrested and students being referred to the disciplinary process, which often means that very little penalty, if any, is imposed. A number of bookstore managers have confided in me that because the university will not permit arrests of student shoplifters and the disciplinary process is so weak, they take no action against student and other campus-related shoplifters but merely absorb their losses.

The only effective way to reduce shoplifting is to emphasize to shoppers that shoplifting is a crime and they may be subject to arrest and prosecution. This policy should be clearly displayed on signs in the store, publicized through the campus media, and made part of the student handbook.

Other measures that can be taken to reduce shoplifting are as follows:

- Channel entering customers through turnstiles and require free locker checking for brief cases, books, and so on.
- Channel customers so that they will have to go by a cashier when they leave.
- Avoid crowding of merchandise displays that provide opportunities for shoplifters to hide merchandise on their person.
- Use of CCTV cameras, the main value of which is as a deterrent. These cameras will only be really effective if they are constantly monitored and immediate action is taken when acts of shoplifting are observed. Excellent CCTV coverage may be provided by a Photo Scan camera system (which can be leased), in which scanning cameras are enclosed in a dome that does not enable the customer to observe if he or she is on camera.

- Larger stores can use elevated, enclosed viewing points or walkways where customers' actions may be observed through two-way mirrors.
- Pricing labels should be of the type that cannot be altered or switched to other merchandise.
- All merchandise should be bagged after payment and the bag stapled closed with the sales receipt. This is especially important if purchases can be made individually in the store and a cashier check system is not utilized.
- Merchandise that is particularly vulnerable, such as stereo tapes, small radios, calculators, and jewelry should be displayed in locked cases that can only be opened by a clerk.
- Professional shoppers should be used occasionally to spot shoplifters.
- Employees should be trained to be alert to shoplifters and report any customers that appear suspicious.
- Larger stores should consider a full-time, trained security officer with arrest power.

FOOD SERVICES

Many colleges and universities now contract with food service companies to provide all food services. These companies are experienced, professionally operated organizations that have established their own security programs. In my opinion, the campus security department should not be involved or responsible for most security functions other than to provide normal patrol and respond to problems. However, I see no objection to bringing in alarms from these operations (e.g., panic alarm in cash counting rooms) into the security central console and having officers respond.

The two vulnerable areas in any food service operation are cash and food storage. Cafeteria cashiers should follow the same security procedures as mentioned in the prior section on bookstore operations. Money handling, counting, and storage would also follow all the same recommendations.

Food products, particularly meat, coffee, and other high-priced foods, are very vulnerable to theft. Most of these thefts are perpetrated by dishonest employees who sometimes even carry out canned hams and similar products in the trash or garbage and retrieve them later (or work with a trash or garbage collector). Spot checks should occasionally be made of trash and garbage containers.

The stock room, freezers, and refrigerators should be securely locked and access to them limited to as few people as possible. In most cases the locks on refrigerators and freezers are not very secure and additional hardened-steel, heavy-duty padlocks or chaining may be needed to prevent after-hours burglary.

Stockrooms should be located in secure, unwindowed areas and be alarmed when not in use. Access should be strictly limited to stockroom employees only. Food products should be immediately inventoried upon being received and not allowed to remain on the loading dock. If the size of the operation justifies it, a CCTV camera might be used on the loading dock monitored by a supervisor in the food service office. Truck drivers should be confined to the loading dock and, if possible, toilet facilities and a telephone should be located on the dock so drivers will not have to enter the premises.

A running inventory of food products should be maintained by the stockroom clerk who would be solely responsible for dispensing supplies. A requisition signed by a supervisor should provide authorization for the release of these supplies.

Keys to food storage rooms, freezers, or refrigerators should not be indiscreetly given to maintenance, security, or food service employees. These keys should be kept under tight control in the security office for after-hours use in emergency situations. Contracted food services should maintain their own keys to these areas, and they should be off the master system.

The right to spot check food service employees when leaving should be made part of the employment process or union contract. These spot checks should probably be the responsibility of security officers, and any employee caught stealing food should be subject to dismissal.

COMPUTER CENTERS

Campus computer centers do not usually approach the size and degree of vulnerability of those in large financial institutions and corporations.

The main problem at campus computer facilities is the unauthorized use of equipment for personal purposes and financial gain. Therefore, security efforts have to be directed at premise security, access control, and supervision of the use of equipment.

The average campus security department should not be expected to have a wide knowledge of computer technology and, therefore, persons in charge of the computer operation should be mainly responsible for monitoring the use of computers and programs to insure they are not compromised. The security department should be involved in the access-control and premise-protection process.

It is usually preferable from a security standpoint to keep programmers out of the machine room and have strict access procedures to that room. A card-key system that records entry and egress on a printout, and in which ID cards can be quickly voided or programmed, is one means of controlling entry. An additional level of access control would be provided by adding a cipher lock requiring that those entering also punch a certain code sequence. In small computer rooms possibly only a mechanical or electronically operated, coded entry system may be sufficient.

The problem of one employee's opening the door and several other individuals' piggybacking is a common weakness. This is primarily a supervision rather than a security department problem. Close supervision and a firm administrative stance regarding violations is the answer.

In larger computer facilities it is usually better to provide a toilet and, possibly, some refreshments (vending machines) in the secure area, to cut down on traffic in and out.

Valuable tapes and disks should be stored in storage vaults under the supervision of the tape librarian. Access should be strictly limited and controlled. If information is extremely critical, back-up tapes should be stored in a secure location elsewhere, possibly off campus.

IBM's publication entitled "42 Suggestions for Improving Security in Data Processing Operations"* produced an excellent list of suggestions as follows:

- Control access to the system area.
- Define responsibilities for the security of data, systems, and programs.
- Involve a number of people in sensitive functions.
- Maintain a data inventory or other measure of the value of your data holdings.
- Take prompt, decisive, corrective action when security is jeopardized or lost.
- Protect yourself against the destructive activities of disgruntled data processing personnel.
- Assess threats to your data holdings.
- Carefully select and implement fire detection and quenching systems and their interconnections, if any, with electrical power.
- Be realistic; don't operate in reaction mode only.
- Establish procedures and instructions for system operators. Use audit trails or transaction logs as security measures.
- Set up emergency security procedures.
- Check the vulnerability of your air-conditioning installations.
- Protect your system against smoke damage.
- Don't put exterior glass walls and windows in vulnerable locations.
- Have instructions and procedures on what to do in the event of fire or fire alarms.
- Maintain good working relations with the local fire department.
- Maintain a good working relationships with local police departments.
- Don't rely too much on guards or a small guard force for protection against civil disturbances.
- Don't identify your data processing centers.
- Indoctrinate data processing personnel with the importance of security and their individual responsibilities in achieving it.
- Take into account any specialized requirements of your data processing center when you establish procedures and instructions for responding to bomb threats.

---

*Courtesy of IBM Corporation.

- Limit access to terminals.
- Assess the need for protection against power failures or voltage reductions.
- Have a realistic understanding of how magnets can damage storage media.
- Set up procedures to control portable transceivers.
- Change keys, combinations, and passwords frequently.
- Limit access to your working tape and disk libraries.
- Maintain adequate backup files.
- Identify or prioritize critical operations in planning for backup facilities and other recovery activities.
- Protect your system against water damage.
- Set up procedures for delivering records to archival storage and recovering them.
- Control the use of information on scratch packs or tapes and other residual data.
- Plan for and test backup data processing facilities.
- Set up security-minded procedures for receiving and storing paper supplies.
- Keep your operating areas clean and neat.
- Set up thorough procedures to protect programs, run instructions, object decks, etc.
- Keep sensitive data out of the outgoing paper trash.
- Test your backup files.
- Tighten up procedures for controlling your application programs.
- Set up procedures to control the use of paper output.
- Test physical security measures and operating procedures to see if they are effective.

HEALTH SERVICES

Campus health services for the most part maintain only limited supplies of narcotics and drugs. These drugs should be dispensed under strict controls and a close inventory record maintained as required by state and federal laws. These substances should be kept in a secure, locked metal container or other secure space to which access would be strictly controlled. If these areas are not staffed at all times, alarm coverage should be considered.

Some campus infirmaries have only a single nurse on duty at night and, therefore, he or she should be afforded protection. Tight after-hours access-control procedures should exist so that this nurse would be able to screen those desiring to enter prior to allowing them to enter. Strategically placed panic buttons should also be located in the premises so that the nurse can summon assistance.

Chapter 20

CONTINGENCY PLANNING AND EMERGENCIES

The importance of effective advance planning to cope with natural disasters, fire, arson, bomb threats, various types of demonstrations, acts of terrorism, potentially volatile events such as rock concerts and similar occurrences cannot be stressed too strongly. The lack of such contingency planning is one of the greatest weaknesses I have found in surveying educational institutions.

Any campus contingency plan must be carefully designed and involve practically every segment of campus life. A central safety committee should be considered that would be responsible for setting up emergency plans to meet any situation. Included on this committee should be representation from the security department, building and grounds, housing, health services, various student life functions, the faculty, employees, and other people who would be involved and/or affected if an emergency occurred. Including a representative from the outside community who would be designated by the mayor or administrative head would also be a good idea. The president of the college or university (or a designate) should chair this committee because his or her input will be vital in decision making.

One of the most important functions of the committee will be to formulate a general plan to meet most emergencies. However, remember that no plan can specifically cope successfully with every incident and situation. Any plan should define the areas of responsibility to be covered by security, buildings and grounds, health, student life, and other groups to insure a team response rather than a fragmentized approach.

This central safety committee would also be charged with the responsibility of producing a manual of emergency plans that would outline the response to emergencies and policies to be followed. However, I would caution here that the existence of a thick and impressive manual does not always indicate an effective response and plan. Many times as a consultant, in reply to my question as to the existence of a contingency plan, such manuals have been displayed. However, upon further research I usually discovered that the plan had never been tested and, in some cases, was outdated and reflected the names of individuals who were no longer employed or involved. It is of vital importance to keep emergency plans current, and dry runs should be made to test planning and make sure the persons involved know their assignments. A complete and current emergency plan manual is necessary but is only one component of being prepared to cope with emergencies and disasters. The main and most important component is still to properly train and prepare the people involved in the plan and educate those who may be affected in the event of an emergency.

The campus security department should serve as the focal point for any emergency planning, because it is probably the only department on campus staffed and functioning twenty-four hours each day of the year. The department also serves as the communication link between the campus community and the emergency plan operation. Electronics form an integral part of this communication network with the security department's monitoring all fire and other alarms at a central console. All emergency phone calls should flow into this central point, and an emergency extension number should be publicized and utilized. Two-way FM radios would be used to communicate with all members of the emergency team from this central console. Specified telephone numbers with full instructions regarding when to contact what members of the team would also exist.

An emergency control headquarters for members of the central safety committee and others administering the emergency plan should be included in advance planning. This central control headquarters should preferably be located in or contingent to the security department space and should be secure and private. It should be equipped with campus and other pertinent maps, floor plans of buildings, blackboards, working documents, and other material that might be needed in event of an emergency. The headquarters should also have constant communication to the central console and outside via radio and telephone.

The importance of backup electrical power cannot be overemphasized. Emergency generators should immediately take over in the event of the loss of power to service the central console, radio transmitter, and various alarms and other equipment. Without this source of backup power, communications will be inoperative and emergency procedures will be difficult, if not impossible, to carry out.

Colleges and universities can be regarded as self-contained communities that face approximately the same types of disasters and hazards as the outside community in which they are located. These disasters can be broken down into the following categories:

- *Natural*—No human involvement as in hurricanes, flooding, earthquakes;
- *Social*—Result from human involvement as in demonstrations, riots, vandalism, arson, bombs, bomb threats, terrorist acts, potentially explosive gatherings (e.g., rock concerts), occupation of buildings or offices, strikes;
- *Technological*—Result from human error or involvement as in explosions, airplane crashes, power failure, fires.

Any disaster plan will have to be designed to cope with these types of emergencies, but the degree of advance planning will depend on many factors such as the location of the campus, the type of buildings, the availability and extent of outside assistance, and similar considerations. For example, the threat of an earthquake would be a prime consideration at a university located in Los Angeles, California, but it would merit little attention at a college in Hanover, New Hampshire.

Any emergency plan has to be tailored to the institution it will serve. No universal emergency plan can be devised that can be applied to every institution. Therefore, this book does not attempt to set out such a plan. However, the following outline shows the general areas and the approach to composing such a plan:

- *Table of Contents;*
- *Distribution List*—Should be on a "need to know" basis;
- *Introduction*—Relates purpose of the plan;
- *Chapter 1, General Comments*—Describes the role of the central safety committee and others participating; provides pertinent data regarding personnel involved, the communications system and how notification of emergencies are handled, an organizational chart, policy and coordination with outside agencies, list of phone numbers of personnel, departments, and outside sources who may be involved, and so on;
- *Chapters 2 to end*—Discuss one service or area of responsibility and the duties and role persons involved will play; organizational-type diagrams are included with lists of personnel; provide lists of resources and equipment.

The remainder of this chapter deals with emergencies and disasters that could be encountered on a campus and some of the preventive measures and effective responses.

NATURAL DISASTER

Any natural disaster will invariably not only effect the college or university campus but also the outside community. Therefore, the college emergency plan will function as part of a larger disaster plan formulated and administered by civil defense, local law enforcement and fire agencies, the Red Cross and medical facilities, and many other segments of the outside community. Therefore, it is most important in pre-planning to set up good liaison with agencies and personnel that are administering these local or state disaster-preparedness procedures. One of the most important factors in effecting a united and coordinated response is to make sure that good emergency communications exist. Immediate and open communication must exist between the campus control headquarters and the outside emergency control center. A direct-line phone may be used with a backup radio system. Monitoring local law enforcement and fire department transmissions and vice versa should be allowed.

Hurricanes (Tornadoes)

Certain areas of the country are more susceptible to hurricanes and tornadoes than other areas. College campuses in these areas are usually more sensitive to this danger, particularly during certain seasons of the year.

Early warning is one of the most important factors in any preparedness program. Early warning can be accomplished by alert monitoring of radio weather reports or by more sophisticated equipment that immediately alerts the central console operator to a warning or actual hurricane. Hurricane warnings are then communicated to members of the emergency team as well as the community. At that time certain procedures to insure the safety of persons on campus may be put in operation such as evacuating buildings and directing people to previously designated safe areas.

Preventive-oriented physical-protection measures are also important factors that should be considered in the design of new facilities. For example, institutions in hurricane-prone sections of the country should avoid large expanses of plate glass and employ reinforced concrete or similar types of sturdy construction. Roof tiles should be avoided, and strong, anchored, wind-resistant roofs should be specified.

The University of Miami, Coral Gables, Florida is an excellent example of a campus that has prepared for the rather frequent hurricanes that plague that section of the country. The U.S. Hurricane Center is also located in one of the campus buildings that provides an immediate early-warning and hurricane-tracking service. The university has installed aluminum hurricane shutters, which can be immediately rolled down in case of a hurricane warning, on the extensive glass walls of the large Richter Library. These shutters could also be used to advantage in case of a riot or demonstration during which vandalism might occur.

Emergency hurricane procedures are also in effect at the University of Miami and are integrated with the preparedness program existing in the outside community.

Earthquakes

Past history would indicate that earthquakes present very little threat to most campuses. Educational institutions in southern California along the San Andreas Fault are most susceptible and should prepare as much as possible for earthquake disaster.

Construction of buildings in earthquake-prone locations should be planned to permit sway and movement without causing the entire structure to crumble.

Emergency planning must include provisions for transportation to medical facilities, emergency first aid procedures, equipment to clear debris, emergency supplies of food and water, firefighting equipment, provisions for temporary housing, and other materials and procedures needed to cope with a major disaster. This type of planning would also be necessary in preparing to handle practically any natural disaster.

Floods

The threat of a flood is also restricted to certain campuses whose location near rivers, the seacoast, reservoirs, dams, or other bodies of water makes them particularly vulnerable.

The same precautionary measures and emergency planning utilized for earthquakes and hurricanes can also be applied here. Again, an early warning of an impending flooding condition is of paramount importance and calls for established lines of communication to outside sources.

Approximately the same equipment to cope with other disasters is necessary but additional equipment such as pumps, small maneuverable boats, sandbags, and similar equipment should also be considered.

SOCIAL

Disasters caused by people are usually not of the magnitude of serious natural disasters. They are diversified in nature and although some of the same emergency planning and procedures can be applied, they also require more specialized planning. They differ from natural disasters in regard to preventive security planning. A hurricane or other natural disaster cannot be stopped by humans but some social disasters such as riots, potentially unruly demonstrations, and gatherings can be prevented by effective preplanning.

People cause these types of problems, and therefore, handling such problems must also involve people. Security officers and others involved in coping with these types of disasters must be well trained and briefed, exercise good judgment and, in certain instances, patience and restraint.

Preparing an emergency plan to meet each of these disaster situations is very difficult. A disaster plan must first be established, and then individual sections of the plan must be tailored to meet the particular danger.

Bombs and Bomb Threats

Bombings have been on the increase and casualties and injuries resulting from such incidents have risen. However, most of these bombings have been politically motivated and perpetrated by terrorist organizations seeking to focus attention on their cause. Most of these acts have been directed at the so-called capitalist establishment. Another type of bombing has involved criminal bombings against people that are usually directed at cars or residences.

Educational institutions have not been the targets of as many bombings during the past few years as they were in the student dissent era. However, colleges and universities could be selected for bombings, particularly if they represent targets in which political causes can be espoused (e.g., a government-financed weapons-research project).

Colleges and universities continue to be plagued by bomb threats, although not to the extent that existed in the early 1970s. One of the reasons for this decline is the fact that institutions have formulated better policies and procedures regarding responses to these bomb threat calls. Evacuation of the building named in the bomb threat or, in some cases, several buildings was formerly a policy followed at some colleges without any evaluation of the call or search of the premises. Proper emergency planning has resulted in selective evacuation policies based on numerous factors that are discussed later.

Two reasons exist for bomb threat calls. The first reason is that the caller has planted a bomb and wants to prevent casualties. The second reason is to disrupt the normal routine of the institution. This latter reason is the one that in most cases can be applied to colleges and universities. Some of the motives for disrupting normal procedures are students who are not ready to take an exam in that building that day or disgruntled employees. On one small college campus I visited some years ago, bomb threat calls were received about noon each Friday so that buildings would be evacuated, classes would be called off, and students would be able to leave campus early for the weekend. At a large university in which evacuation was carried out after every call, so many calls and disruption of classes occurred that a group of students petitioned the university for return of their tuition.

The decision to evacuate should be made by a small, accessible, representative group of the central safety committee based on many factors that the security department would be responsible for quickly acquiring. On most campuses the individuals responsible for making the decision to evacuate would be the head of the institution, the director of security, the fire marshal (if one exists), and the department chairman or administrator of the area involved.

Evacuation Considerations. The most important factor in making a decision to evacuate or not is an evaluation of the call itself. Therefore, it is very important to properly train employees who might be the logical individuals to receive such calls such as the switchboard operator, president's secretary, or security department dispatcher or operator.

An interview form to be used as a guide and that should be filled out immediately by the person receiving the call should be available at logical places and employees taught how to use it.

Figure 20-1 depicts a sample bomb threat call form that contains practically all the information the receiver of the call should try to acquire and be alert to listen for. The most important specific information to obtain is the time and place the bomb is to be detonated. Too often bomb threat callers merely state, "A bomb will go off in the _____ building."

Another prime consideration is whether time permits a search of the area. The search should involve a team that has been previously designated in the emergency plan and trained in regard to responsibilities. Responsible employees and resident halls students should conduct this search with security officers, physical plant employees, and other people familiar with the area affected. Local fire and police agencies should also be notified of each bomb threat and policies agreed on regarding their participation in the search. However, the institution itself will undoubtedly have to make the decision to evacuate or not.

In conducting this search a decision must be made (depending on the area, type of call, and so on) as to whether it will be a covert search without informing and alarming building occupants or a search conducted openly after alerting occupants and possibly leaving it entirely up to them as to whether they want to leave the premises. If the latter tactic is adopted, care must be taken to make it a low-key announcement that relates all known information regarding the call so that panic does not ensue and so individuals can make their own decision. Experience has shown that few people leave when this type of announcement is made.

Make it crystal clear to searchers that if they find any suspicious package or other material, THEY SHOULD NOT TOUCH IT. The local police and/or fire department should be called. If local or state law enforcement agencies do not have a trained bomb disposal unit, the assistance of the nearest Explosive Ordinance Disposal group must be requested.

Another consideration regarding whether to evacuate or not involves preventive bomb searches in a building prior to an athletic contest or special event. For example, when I was director of security at Yale University we often had public figures speaking on campus. Normal procedure was to search the involved auditorium and building as thoroughly as possible, seal off access, and guard the area prior to the individual's appearance. On one occasion I recall former California Governor, and now President, Ronald Reagan speaking before a packed auditorium when a bomb threat was received by the Yale University Police dispatcher. The caller, who sounded young, merely stated, "A bomb is set to go. Clear the auditorium." After

BOMB THREAT CALL

1. CALLER'S IDENTITY: Sex: Male _____ Female _____ Age: Adult _____ Child _____

   Organization _____ Telephone No. _____

   Address _____

2. BOMB FACTS:

   a. Time of Detonation (When will it go off?) _____

   b. Location (Where is it planted?): Building _____ Area _____

   c. Method of Detonation (How will it explode?): Remote Control _____ Timer _____

                          Pressure Release _____ Pressure _____

   d. Type: Powder _____ Nitroglycerin _____ Other _____

                 TNT _____ Dynamite _____

   e. Container (What does it look like?): Box _____ Bottle _____ Can _____

              Carton _____ Paper Bag _____ Brief Case _____

              Package _____ Other _____

   f. Method of Delivery: In Person _____ U.S. Mail _____ Messenger _____

              Other _____ Time of Delivery _____

3. CALL: Local _____ Long Distance _____ Unknown _____

4. VOICE CHARACTERISTICS:

TONE		SPEECH		LANGUAGE	
Loud	_____	Fast	_____	Excellent	_____
Soft	_____	Slow	_____	Good	_____
High Pitch	_____	Distinct	_____	Fair	_____
Low Pitch	_____	Distorted	_____	Poor	_____
Raspy	_____	Stutter	_____	Cursing	_____
Pleasant	_____	Nasal	_____		_____

ACCENT		MANNER			
Local	_____	Calm	_____	Emotional	_____
Not Local	_____	Angry	_____	Rational	_____
Foreign	_____	Coherent	_____	Irrational	_____
Caucasian	_____	Incoherent	_____	Deliberate	_____
Negro	_____	Righteous	_____	Laughing	_____

Figure 20-1. Form used to report a bomb threat call.

5. BACKGROUND NOISES:

Office Machines _____	Quiet _____	Voices _____
Factory Machines _____	Street Traffic _____	Music _____
Bedlam _____	Airplanes _____	Mixed _____
Animals _____	Trains _____	

6. POINTS TO REMEMBER: Keep caller talking. Ask to speak louder, slower, etc.
   Do not interrupt! Ask to repeat.

7. Write out the message in its entirety on the reverse side.

8. Your name _____ Location _____

9. Time call received _____ A.M.–P.M. Date _____

10. Reported to _____ Time _____ A.M.–P.M.

Figure 20-1. Continued

consultation with Reagan's security head, we decided to ignore the threat because the usual preventive search and sealing off of the hall had been conducted.

Other considerations regarding whether to evacuate or not are the number of occupants in the building, the ability to evacuate if necessary, and the past history of similar threats. If a series of similar false alarm calls have been received, the risk of a real bomb being planted diminishes.

Evacuation Procedures. The same evacuation plan for use in case of a fire can usually be applied to bomb threat evacuations. In fact, in the past some colleges receiving bomb threats announced, "This is a fire drill," and evacuated students and others.

A written evacuation plan should be designed so that designated group leaders, stair guards, area wardens, and floor captains will know exactly what their duties are in evacuating students, employees, and others. Posted evacuation directions should also assist in directing the orderly flow of those leaving the premises. Persons leaving the building should be escorted a safe distance away from the area and no one should be allowed to enter the building or cleared perimeter area.

Evacuation procedures in the form of fire drills should be tested periodically—especially in regard to resident halls. The plan should be constantly reviewed for updating. Persons involved in the plan should not only be security personnel but physical plant and office employees, administrators, faculty, various staff members, and students.

The following questions should be asked in regard to an evacuation plan:

- *Communications*—How will the occupants be notified? Ideally, notification should be done by a zoned public address system operated at the security central console. Is the public address system tested periodically?

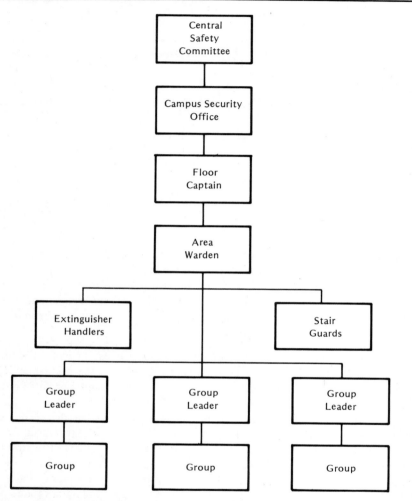

CENTRAL SAFETY COMMITTEE—The Central Safety Committee is charged with the safety of all personnel and shall at all times be available to advise and assist the President. In an emergency, the Committee shall act for the President if that officer is absent or unable to act.

CORPORATE SECURITY—Corporate Security, which is available at any hour, takes charge in an emergency, while the ultimate authority is the Central Safety Committee or the President.

FLOOR CAPTAIN—There is a Floor Captain for each floor in each building. Floor Captains are selected from among the executive personnel on that floor. If the Floor Captain's office

Figure 20-2. Evacuation organizational chart. Courtesy of Corporate Security Office of the Travelers Insurance Companies, Inc., Hartford, Connecticut.

- *Floor Diagrams and Exit Routes*—Are they conspicuously posted with very visible printing? Do they show the location of the reader, and are safe egress routes clearly shown?
- *Emergency Lighting*—Does it exist? Is it sufficient? Has it been tested?
- *Elevators*—Can they be immediately summoned to the first floor and immobilized? Do signs indicate that elevators are not to be used during emergencies and clear routes to emergency fire stairwells displayed?
- *Elderly and Physically Handicapped*—Have provisions been made for their removal and specific individuals trained and designated to handle these individuals?

A sample evacuation organizational chart is depicted in Figure 20-2.

Summary. A great deal more could be written about bombs and bomb threats, but the most important point to be emphasized is that you must have a workable, up-to-date, written plan of action that will involve teamwork and a coordinated approach. Remember that "how to build your own bomb" instructions are very easy to acquire today. The materials to make a bomb (e.g., black powder) are also easy to secure. In fact, many of these materials can be rather easily obtained from campus laboratories and other locations. With acts of terrorism on the increase, colleges and universities might become future targets. Administrators must plan to meet this type of challenge.

Figure 20-2. Continued.

is not centrally located on the floor, another centrally located station, from which he will operate in an emergency, should be selected.

The chart following shows the model of organization for each floor. Variation from the model, in accord with size of the floor and its population, is permissible.

AREA WARDEN—Each of the several defined areas, and its assigned stairway exit is under the control of an Area Warden, selected from among the members of management normally present.

GROUP LEADERS—Within each area there are Group Leaders appointed from among the supervisory personnel. Each Group Leader is responsible for controlling and directing about 15 people, the exact number depending on size and floor layout.

STAIR GUARDS—For each stair opening there are two Stair Guards. They are responsible, in event of emergency, for control of traffic through the exit designated for that area.

EXTINGUISHER HANDLERS—Adjacent to fire extinguishers, an appropriate number of trained Extinguisher Handlers are appointed.

EMPLOYEES—Each employee and particularly each member of the emergency organization must be thoroughly acquainted with the prescribed basic pattern of action and communication. Should any local deviation from standard procedure then become necessary, the alternate action or communication can be carried out so as to serve basic requirements.

Arson and Fire

Arson is caused by human involvement, but fires can sometimes be attributed to other causes (e.g., faulty wiring). However, the emergency response to arson and fire is approximately the same, and therefore, the two hazards are being discussed collectively.

The problem of arson has been growing dramatically during the past several years, particularly in the larger cities. Although school systems have been plagued with acts of arson, our colleges and universities have fortunately not kept pace with the alarming rise in arson statistics. Nevertheless, campus security departments must remain alert to this serious problem and security programs must emphasize prevention in the form of tighter perimeter security and access control, sprinklers, fire sensors, effective early-warning intrusion and fire alarms, alert patrol of facilities, emergency firefighting equipment, and other preventive measures.

We now take a brief look at arson, which is defined as the "willful and malicious burning of property." The following are the usual motives for acts of arson:

- *Concealment of Crime*—Someone wants to destroy evidence of a theft, of communications regarding illegal activities, and so forth.
- *Personal Revenge or Furtherance of a "Cause"*—An employee, former employee, customer, or student has an "ax to grind" and "gets even" by setting a fire. A political or other cause is fostered and spotlighted by committing an act of arson.
- *The Psychologically Imbalanced*—Arson is committed by a firebug or pyromaniac.
- *Financial Gain*—Property is heavily insured and the owner profits. A competitor's establishment is set on fire to put him or her out of business. A professional "torch" is often engaged for these acts.

A college or university could experience any of these motives for an act of arson. However, the motive of financial gain that is most prevalent in urban communities would be highly unlikely on a campus.

The role of the security or public safety department in regard to fire is to (1) reduce the vulnerability by detecting and correcting unsafe hazards and procedures and enforcing fire regulations; (2) utilize preventive procedures and equipment to prevent the arsonist from operating; (3) act as a first line of defense by using fire extinguishers and, if necessary, evacuating dormitories and buildings; (4) investigate to determine cause, origin, and responsibility.

A college or university fire marshal is recommended who is experienced in the fire safety field. He would be responsible for setting up proper fire procedures and regulations and for insuring that fire extinguishers and other equipment is available and operative. This fire marshal would answer to the director of public safety or security. Knowledgeable, retired fire department administrators may be good candidates for these positions.

Evacuation plans and procedures for fires are almost identical to those mentioned previously in the discussion of bombs and bomb threats.

Campus security officers should not be expected to be fire safety experts. However, they should be trained to recognize and report obvious safety hazards such as missing or damaged fire extinguishers, fire doors left open, or chained exit doors and other violations and hazards. This officer would, in effect, back up inspections by the campus fire marshal, safety expert, or other people having primary responsibility.

Demonstrations and Gatherings

If this book were written ten to fifteen years ago I would have included a long chapter on preventing and handling student sit-ins and various other forms of disruptive dissent. However, I do not see a real necessity for a lengthy perusal of the subject at this time.

Campuses for the past few years have been experiencing a period of relative calm as far as unruly demonstrations are concerned. Although students still demonstrate and voice their opinions, they are usually content to work "within the system" to achieve their objectives. I do not see a return to the turmoil and disruption of the late 1960s and early 1970s. However, a local issue on campus could spark a spontaneous demonstration that might be potentially dangerous.

In discussing student demonstrations we must start with the premise that a demonstration in itself is legal and no threat. Usually, these demonstrations are planned ahead, and the security department should be involved in the planning process. Therefore, close liaison and a working relationship should be constantly maintained with student organizatons and their leaders. The image a campus security or public safety department should protect should be one of helping and not one of repression and authority. The department and its officers should not become involved in the issues involved or the causes espoused. Their function is to preserve the peace and protect the demonstrators as well as campus properties and population.

A university or college should incorporate into its student handbook and similar publications clear-cut regulations and policies regarding large gatherings and demonstrations. These regulations should also stress the role of the security officer as one of working to insure that participants will be protected. Such matters as advance notification and location of the demonstration, nature of the demonstration, composition and number of people expected to attend, how long will it last, and identities of leaders are important points to consider in regard to policies and establishing ground rules.

Most universities and colleges prefer to have their own security force and various student life personnel handle demonstrations. Student marshals can also be utilized to advantage. Experience has shown that relying on outside law enforce-ment personnel to oversee campus demonstrations and student gatherings can at times create problems due to a lack of sensitivity and too much dependence on authority. We must also face the fact that at most campuses the local police are not held in very high esteem by students. However, interested local law enforce-ment agencies should know that a demonstration will take place—particularly, if it appears to be a large one that might cause problems. Also, local law enforcement officers should be on standby in the event of a riot or situation that is beyond the capability of the campus security department to control.

Student demonstrations should also be the concern of student affairs personnel, and they should be involved in controlling and, particularly, preventing a demonstration from escalating into a riot. Some deans of students, residence hall staff, and others involved in student life are of the opinion that demonstrations and student gatherings that have any potential for becoming unruly are entirely the responsibility of security to prevent and control. Student affairs people are working with students every day, know student leaders, and do not present as authoritative a presence as a uniformed security officer. They should be present to cool down potentially explosive situations and should be included in the overall plan to handle student demonstrations.

The involvement of student affairs personnel in handling demonstrations should not mean that they would dictate the actions and procedures to be followed by security officers. The director of security or public safety should be solely responsible for the deployment and actions of his staff but also should be receptive to the ideas and suggestions of deans and other student affairs people.

Rock concerts on campus often present a challenge for campus security departments to control. This subject has been discussed in Chapter 17.

Terrorism

Judge William H. Webster, director of the FBI, in an October 1978 speech at the annual conference of the International Chiefs of Police Association stated in regard to terrorism, "It's a different experience than we've had in this country but it's coming closer to our shores." Since then we have seen bombings (usually political in nature) increase, but to date no politically motivated terrorist kidnap-ping has occurred in this country, with the possible exception of the Patricia Hearst kidnapping by the Symbionese Liberation Army. However, American executives have often been the target for kidnappers in Italy, various South American countries, and elsewhere abroad. In fact, the trend has changed from kidnapping government personnel to kidnapping executives and their families. This trend has undoubt-edly been fostered by large corporations having weak security programs, no emer-gency plan, and their willingness to pay millions of dollars in ransom.

Remember also that our intelligence-gathering ability to prevent such terrorist acts has been severely weakened during the past few years because of severe limitations being placed on our intelligence-gathering agencies. These limitations have forced the CIA, FBI, and other intelligence agencies to become largely responders to problems rather than preventers.

Local law enforcement agencies cannot be relied upon because they are usually understaffed and have to direct their efforts to combatting crime. Traditionally, they have always responded to problems rather than preventing them.

This lack of preventive intelligence gathering and the emphasis on response dictates that corporations formulate their own preventive security programs to protect executives and their families. These programs have involved additional, higher quality security personnel, more sophisticated electronic security equipment and communications, tightened security procedures, and educating highly paid executives and their families to preventive security measures. It has also involved formulating an advance plan to respond to the kidnapping of an executive or member of his family, which usually calls for a crisis management team that will decide policy, make decisions, and provide the resource to deal with such an emergency.

Do colleges and universities have to be concerned with these types of executive protection programs to protect their top officials and their families? The answer at this time is no, because college presidents do not command the high salaries of corporate executives, and the ability of an educational institution to pay a ransom on short notice would be difficult, if not impossible. However, I do feel that campus security administrators should afford their presidents, chancellors, and other campus officials, particularly persons who are in the public eye, some security protection to guard principally against an attack or similar act by an emotionally disturbed person.

Campus security directors and administrators should be conversant with what is transpiring throughout the world and especially in the United States as far as terrorism is concerned. They should also be cognizant of preventive security measures and executive protection programs being adapted by large corporations. This knowledge is essential because conceivably some terrorist group could kidnap or attack the president of a prestigious university simply to call public attention to the group's existence and the political cause it espouses. A well-known faculty member (e.g., a renowned nuclear physicist) could also be a target. Even more vulnerable would be students who are the sons or daughters of prominent, wealthy families, well-known politicians or entertainers, or foreign dictators or rulers.

The threat of bombings and disruption has already been discussed in this chapter. The potential for an increase in these acts in the 1980s appears more imminent than kidnapping for ransom, and campus security programs should be designed to prevent and respond to them.

TECHNOLOGICAL

Accidents that may or may not involve human error or involvement can occur on campus, and any security program should be prepared to cope with them. These accidents can involve explosions (e.g., boilers, gas leaks), airplane crashes, power outages, and similar incidents. Fires can also start by accident (e.g., faulty wiring) and can be included in this category.

A campus security department should have a security plan to cope with this type of emergency. Naturally, this plan will have to be somewhat general and will combine many of the procedures, policies, and responses already discussed under natural and social disasters, such as evacuation, availability of medical assistance and transportation to hospital, emergency repairs and equipment, and other matters.

These technological disasters differ somewhat from most other emergencies in that they usually occur suddenly without any advance warning. The security department in most instances can do very little to prevent these accidents but has to be prepared to respond immediately. This is particularly true during the night hours when security provides the only coverage for the entire campus.

Any campus security plan should include the names and phone numbers of persons to be notified in regard to various accidents. Campus emergency planning should be coordinated with the plans of the outside community, particularly in regard to medical assistance, transportation, and hospital availability and preparedness.

Certain emergencies such as power failures should be anticipated beforehand and procedures and equipment utilized to alleviate them. For example, emergency generators should be available to supply electricity to critical campus facilities and operations, and the security department should have sufficient battery-operated portable lights, which can also be used for other nighttime emergencies.

Certain types of catastrophes (e.g., airplane crashes, explosions) call for sealing off the area. Therefore, a sufficient supply of rope, stanchions, warning signs, and similar equipment is necessary.

A battery-operated bullhorn is also most desirable to be used to give warnings and directions to curious sightseers, members of the emergency team, and other involved people. These bullhorns can also be used to control crowds, demonstrators, and to convey orders to campus security officers.

Accidental fires caused by faulty wiring or other problems in which people play no part have to be responded to in the same manner as fires involving human involvement. The main role of a security department is to evacuate the premises quickly, insure that the appropriate fire department is immediately notified, and to assist firefighting personnel by controlling people and traffic. Building plans and full information regarding the contents and activities of each building should also be maintained to be furnished to fire and emergency crews when necessary.

Chapter 21

THE FUTURE OF CAMPUS
AND SCHOOL SECURITY

The initial chapter of this book dealt with the past history of campus security, and subsequent chapters described its progress and present status. Therefore, before closing, it is only proper to project our thinking to the future and what it holds for campus security.

The progress and trend toward professionalism has been most encouraging in the campus field and, in my estimation, has been well ahead of all other fields of private security. One of the brightest aspects has been the trend toward raising educational qualifications so that many campus departments today require a college degree or at least enrollment in a degree program. One of the greatest weaknesses in municipal law enforcement agencies has been lower rather than higher educational qualifications. The future should see even more campus departments demanding college-educated personnel.

Another trend that I see continuing in the future is the hiring of younger, well-motivated, ambitious career officers and the increasing hiring of women and students. More college graduates will become interested in various fields of criminal justice, and campus security will become increasingly attractive—particularly to students who were involved with professional and progressive departments during their undergraduate studies. I see campus departments recruiting more and more of their own students upon graduation.

The younger but proven campus security administrator will largely dominate the campus security scene in the future and replace many of the retiring veteran directors who were the pioneers in the field.

Campus security has been able to adopt its role to meet the challenges of the times and will continue to do so. The present challenge of crime will undoubtedly continue and probably bring new and more serious problems involving extortion, kidnapping, bombings, and other terrorist acts. Therefore, the role will have to continue to embody the best of law enforcement while still remaining sensitive to the academic community. Certainly, this role will mean providing the campus department and its officers with all the needed tools such as effective training, power of arrest, weapons, police vehicles, a good communications system, and an increasing use of proprietary electronic detection, intrusion, and access-control systems. However, all of these tools must be utilized under the strictest of standards and policies by well-trained, intelligent officers.

The future will not only see campus security continuing to improve its position and assume its rightful place in the field of criminal justice but also become a vital and integral part of the campus scene. Graduates will reflect on their college days and include security as one of the more professional and service-oriented departments on campus.

SCHOOL SECURITY

Although this book has not dealt with school security, I feel that in closing I should recognize and mention it because it is closely identified with the campus field. School security is in its infancy but is rapidly growing and will continue to grow and become more professional in the future.

I have often stated that school security presents the greatest challenge and opportunity in a relatively new field of private security, and a young security professional would do well to enter it. Millions of dollars are being spent today because of vandalism, arson, and theft in our school systems. These problems, coupled with personal attacks on teachers and students, drugs, youth gangs, racial conflicts, and many other problems, dictate the urgent need for a professionally directed security program utilizing trained, intelligent, well-supervised personnel, and electronic after-hours protection.

School security is closely following the same path as campus security did during its early days. It has been delegated largely to a maintenance or plant responsibility and in many schools the custodians provide the only security presence. Many school administrators just will not face up to the problem and are unsuccessfully trying to wish it away. Some school principals delay calling for police assistance until situations have gotten completely out of hand and will not admit or report security problems because it might reflect on the principals' ability to administer. They also fail to back up teachers in disciplining unruly students or take any action to prevent troublemaking outsiders from creating problems in the schools.

School security will increasingly need proven security professionals who will answer directly to the superintendent of schools or some other highly placed administrator. Security personnel will have to be hired who will be sensitive to the school and its students, be able to respond to people problems intelligently, prevent incidents from occurring, and formulate access-control procedures to keep trouble-makers from the outside from entering.

Many encouraging trends in the past few years reflect that school security is making progress and is professionalizing. For example, the National Association of School Security Directors (NASSD) and its crusading, energetic founder, Joseph I. Grealy, have done a great deal in a short time to foster professionalism and recognition for school security. *Security World Magazine* is also to be commended for formerly including NASSD's School Security Journal in each issue.

Federal and state governments are also recognizing the costly crime problem in our schools that involves more dollars than are spent on textbooks. Funding to combat and prevent these problems will continue to increase and, hopefully, will be used to create effective programs.

After-hours protection by electronic intrusion systems should be a must in practically every school building, and such systems should be planned for during new construction. The future will see not only these proprietary systems in school facilities but also changes in the design of new schools to lessen the opportunity for vandalism and intrusion.

The future will also see increased community involvement in protecting our schools by parents and others.

The wide gulf that often exists between the local police department and the board of education will narrow as professional school security administrators communicate and coordinate workable and effective security policies with local law enforcement officials.

The crime problems of our times will dictate that boards of education and school administrators recognize the need for a professional security approach. The growth of this new and challenging field of school security will be even more rapid than the campus field. It will have to largely chart its own role but be guided by that of law enforcement, private security and, particularly, the mistakes and successes of campus security.

APPENDIX

Any number of forms can be utilized that can be filled out quickly and easily. These forms are effective because they furnish pertinent information and statistics without unnecessary writing on the part of the officer, dispatcher, or other employee.

Most departments already utilize such forms. Several are reproduced here for the benefit of campus security departments.

ATTENDANCE RECORD

This attendance record is to be accurately filled out and submitted by the supervisor at the end of each shift. Supervisor should also indicate tardiness of any employee.

Use the following symbols after name of absent employee:

O – Regular day off	SO – Sick leave w/o pay	H – Holiday	X – Suspension
S – Sick leave with pay	V – Vacation	D – Death allowance	
CT – Compensatory time	FH – Floating holiday	A – Leave of absence w/o pay	

Shift: _____

Date: _____

OFFICER	GUARD	WATCHMAN	CLERK

SUPERVISOR _____

1. Attendance record. This is a simple form for the shift supervisor to fill out, indicating the absence or tardiness of any employee under his supervision.

CAR TOWING FORM

On _____ , _____ , at _____ (A.M.) (P.M.)
(date)
the following vehicle was towed from the _____

_____

_____

_____

This vehicle had previously been tagged for illegal parking on

_____

_____

_____
(date/s)

The owner of the car (if known) is _____

_____ , _____

(name)   (address)

This car is described as follows:

State	License Plate	Make	Color	Model

Remarks: _____

_____

_____

Officer _____

Date _____

_____
SUPERVISOR

2. Car towing log. The officer ordering the tow usually fills out this form or radios the information to the dispatcher so an immediate record exists for use when the violator calls about the whereabouts of his vehicle.

Injury and Property Damage Report

TIME & PLACE	Date and Time of Accident			A.M. P.M.
	Location			
INJURED PERSON	Name	Class	Age	Phone No.
	Address			
	Occupation			
	Employed by			
	What was injured doing when hurt?			
THE INJURY	Nature and extent of injury			
	Where was injured taken after accident?		By what means?	
	Name of doctor			
	First aid administered by			
PROPERTY DAMAGE	Owner	Address		
	List damage			
WITNESS	Name	Address		Phone No.
	1			
	2			
	3			
PHOTOS	Were photographs taken?		By whom?	
DESCRIPTION OF ACCIDENT AND LOCATION				
INVESTIGATION	By officer		Date	
	Approved by			
	cc:		File No.	

Use reverse side for sketch if necessary

3. Injury and property damage report. This form is particularly beneficial in reporting injuries and property damage in cases in which the university or college may have an interest and which could result in claims or possible civil suits. These reports are of particular value to the institution's insurance carrier.

MEDICAL EMERGENCY

This form is to be filled out by the Clerk-Dispatcher and is to be used only in ROUTINE medical emergencies.

Name of Complainant _____ Time _____ a.m. Telephone _____
p.m. Personal _____

Class or Title _____

Address _____

DETAILS: At _____ a.m.
p.m.' _____ , _____ , _____ , the University patrol car operated by Officer _____ transported

_____ , _____ , _____
(name)   (class)   (address)

_____ from _____ to _____

for treatment of _____

_____

_____

Assignment completed at _____ a.m.
p.m.

REMARKS: _____

_____

_____

_____

_____

Clerk-Dispatcher's Name _____

Date _____

APPROVED _____
SUPERVISOR IN CHARGE

4. Medical emergency report. This form is to be used by the dispatcher in recording routine medical emergency transportation. In serious cases the officer would submit full information in a regular report.

PROPERTY RECEIPT—RECEIVING

This form must be filled out prior to the receipt of any property by the University Police Department to be held for safekeeping. No property will be received unless it is securely sealed.

DATE AND TIME RECEIVED _____ A.M.
_____ P.M.

DESCRIPTION OF PROPERTY _____

_____

_____

OWNER _____

DEPOSITOR _____

DATE AND TIME (APPROXIMATE)
  TO BE CLAIMED _____

CLAIMANT _____

_____

                                     RECEIVING SUPERVISOR

- -

PROPERTY RECEIPT—DELIVERY

Supervisors should make positive identification of claimant prior to delivering property.

DATE AND TIME DELIVERED _____

NAME AND ADDRESS OF CLAIMANT _____

_____

_____

_____

                                             SUPERVISOR

5. Property receipt—receiving. Most campus departments hold valuable property (such as the proceeds of a social affair or athletic event) for short durations. This form records the receipt and delivery of this property.

REMINDER

This is to let you know that the University Police performed the
following special service for you. This service was performed by

Officer _____

on _____ at _____ A.M.
                                                         P.M.

( ) Auto headlights turned off

( ) Auto parking lights turned off

( ) Office door locked

( ) Office lights turned off

( ) Window secured

( ) Other _____

_____

_____

---

6. Reminder. On a distinctively colored, eye-catching card about 4" X 6", this
form is left by the officer after performing a service such as turning off car headlights, securing an office window, and so on.

UNIVERSITY POLICE DEPARTMENT

SPECIAL POLICE SERVICE—TRANSPORTATION—LOCAL ( )
                          TRANSPORTATION—OUT OF TOWN ( )
                          MONEY ESCORT ( )

Date: _____

Time: _____ A.M.
                              P.M.

- -

Person Requesting: _____

Title: _____

Address: _____

- -

Person Transported: _____

Title: _____

Address: _____

From: _____

Time: _____ A.M.
                              P.M.

To: _____

Time: _____ A.M.
                              P.M.

- -

Officer: _____

Clerk: _____

- -

REMARKS: _____

_____

APPROVED _____

SUPERVISOR IN CHARGE

7. Special police service. This form can be filled out by the officer or dispatcher regarding special service involving transportation and money escorts.

VEHICLE ACCIDENT REPORT

			AM	
DATE OF ACCIDENT		TIME	PM DATE OF INVESTIGATION	
	Month Day Year			

LOCATION

UNIVERSITY PROPERTY

OTHER PRIVATE PROPERTY

PUBLIC STREET(S)

MUNICIPALITY _____ STATE

CHECK INJURIES IN RIGHT COLUMN USING CODE BELOW

CODE FOR INJURY
(Use only the most serious one in each space for injury.)
K—Dead before report made.
A—Visible signs of injury, as bleeding wound or distorted member; or had to be carried from scene.
B—Other visible injury, as bruises, abrasions, swelling, limping, etc.
C—No visible injury but complaint of pain or momentary unconsciousness.
O—No indication of injury.

VEHICLE No. 1 (Always List University Vehicle Here)

VEHICLE ___ Year ___ Make ___ Body Style ___ LICENSE PLATE ___ Number ___ State ___ **INJURY CODE**

PARTS OF VEHICLE DAMAGED

VEHICLE REMOVED FROM SCENE BY

INSURED BY _____ ADDRESS

IDENTIFY EACH PERSON LISTED BY SYMBOL AFTER NAME AS FOLLOWS:

STUDENT [Year] FACULTY [Fac] EMPLOYEE [Emp] NON-UNIVERSITY PERSON [NUP]

OWNER _____ ADDRESS

OPERATOR _____ ADDRESS

DRIVER'S LICENSE No. _____ STATE ___ DOB

OCCUPANT _____ ADDRESS

OCCUPANT _____ ADDRESS

OCCUPANT _____ ADDRESS

VEHICLE No. 2 (Also Use For Bicyclist or Pedestrian)

VEHICLE ___ Year ___ Make ___ Body Style ___ LICENSE PLATE ___ Number ___ State ___ **INJURY CODE**

PARTS OF VEHICLE DAMAGED

VEHICLE REMOVED FROM SCENE BY

INSURED BY _____ ADDRESS

IDENTIFY EACH PERSON LISTED BY SYMBOL AFTER NAME AS FOLLOWS:

STUDENT [Year] FACULTY [Fac] EMPLOYEE [Emp] NON-UNIVERSITY PERSON [NUP]

OWNER _____ ADDRESS

OPERATOR _____ ADDRESS

DRIVER'S LICENSE No. _____ STATE ___ DOB

OCCUPANT _____ ADDRESS

OCCUPANT _____ ADDRESS

OCCUPANT _____ ADDRESS

PROPERTY DAMAGE

DESCRIBE DAMAGE TO PROPERTY OTHER THAN VEHICLES

NAME AND ADDRESS OF OWNER OF PROPERTY

WITNESSES

NAME _____ ADDRESS

NAME _____ ADDRESS

NAME _____ ADDRESS

UNIVERSITY OFFICER

APPROVED BY _____ FILE No.

---

8. Vehicle accident report. To be used in reporting motor vehicle accidents occurring on university property.

Appendix 8. Continued

ROAD SURFACE (Check one)	WEATHER (Check one)	WHAT DRIVERS WERE GOING TO DO BEFORE ACCIDENT

ROAD SURFACE (Check one)
☐ Dry
☐ Wet
☐ Snowy or icy
☐ _____ Specify other

LIGHT CONDITIONS (Check one)
☐ Daylight
☐ Dawn or dusk
☐ Darkness

ROAD TYPE (Check one or more)
Driver 1 2
☐ ☐ 1 driving lane
☐ ☐ 2 driving lanes
☐ ☐ 3 driving lanes
☐ ☐ 4 or more lanes
☐ ☐ Divided roadway
☐ ☐ Expressway, parkway, toll road

WEATHER (Check one)
☐ Clear
☐ Raining
☐ Snowing
☐ Fog
☐ _____ Specify other

TRAFFIC CONTROL (Check one or more)
☐ Stop sign
☐ Stop-and-go signal
☐ Officer or watchman
☐ R.R.gates or signals
☐ _____ Specify other
☐ No traffic control

ROAD CHARACTER (Check two)
☐ Straight road
☐ Curve
☐ Level
☐ On grade
☐ Hillcrest

WHAT DRIVERS WERE GOING TO DO BEFORE ACCIDENT

Driver No. 1 was headed ☐ ☐ ☐ ☐ on _____
                        North S E W   (Street or highway)
Driver No. 2 was headed ☐ ☐ ☐ ☐ on _____
                                              (Street or highway)

Driver 1 2 (Check one for each driver)
☐ ☐ Go straight ahead   ☐ ☐ Make left turn   ☐ ☐ Start in traffic lane   ☐ ☐ Remain stopped in traffic lane
☐ ☐ Overtake   ☐ ☐ Make U turn   ☐ ☐ Start from parked position ☐ ☐ Remain parked
☐ ☐ Make right turn   ☐ ☐ Slow or stop   ☐ ☐ Back

WHAT PEDESTRIAN WAS DOING   ☐ Along
Pedestrian was going ☐ ☐ ☐ ☐   ☐ Across or into.................. From.............. To..............
(Check one)   N S E W   Street name, highway No.) (N.E. corner to S.E. corner, or west to east side, etc.)
☐ Crossing or entering at intersection ☐ Walking in roadway—with traffic ☐ Pushing or working on   ☐ Other in roadway
☐ Crossing or entering not at   ☐ Walking in roadway—against   ☐ Other working in roadway ☐ Not in roadway
  intersection   traffic   vehicle
☐ Getting on or off vehicle   ☐ Standing in roadway   ☐ Playing in roadway

CONTRIBUTING CIRCUMSTANCES
Driver 1 2 (Check one or more for each driver)
☐ ☐ Speed too fast   ☐ ☐ Disregarded stop sign   ☐ ☐ Other improper driving
☐ ☐ Failed to yield right of way ☐ ☐ Disregarded traffic signal ☐ ☐ Inadequate brakes
☐ ☐ Drove left of center   ☐ ☐ Followed too closely   ☐ ☐ Improper lights
☐ ☐ Improper overtaking   ☐ ☐ Made improper turn   ☐ ☐ Under infl. of liquor or drugs

WAS ACCIDENT ALSO INVESTIGATED BY LOCAL POLICE? YES ☐ NO ☐

IF "YES," GIVE NAME OF OFFICER AND DEPARTMENT _____

ARRESTS NAME _____ CHARGE _____

         NAME _____ CHARGE _____

OTHER ACTION TAKEN _____

DESCRIBE WHAT HAPPENED (REFER TO VEHICLES BY NUMBER) _____

INDICATE ON THIS DIAGRAM WHAT HAPPPENED

SHOW NORTH BY ARROW

Street or highway

Street or highway

Street or highway

ALARM LOG

This log should be maintained by the Clerk-Dispatcher for twenty-four hours starting with the 8:00 A.M. to 4:00 P.M. shift. It should be sent to the Office of the Security Director every morning by 8:00 A.M.

DATE	TIME	ALARM	ACTION TAKEN

Clerk-Dispatcher (8:00 A.M. to 4:00 P.M.): _____

(4:00 P.M. to 12:00 midnight): _____

(12:00 midnight to 8:00 A.M.): _____

9. Alarm log. This log should be the responsibility of the dispatcher or other employee responsible for monitoring the alarm console. It furnishes the director with a history of all alarms and action taken.

☐ INCIDENT REPORT
☐ ARREST REPORT

HARVARD UNIVERSITY POLICE DEPARTMENT

DATE OF OFFENSE	TIME OF OFFENSE	DATE REPORTED	OBJECT OF ATTACK	
TIME REPORTED	DATE OF ARREST	TIME OF ARREST	POINT OF ENTRY	INCIDENT NO.

OFFENSES	MEANS OF ATTACK (WEAPON, TOOL USED)
	METHOD OF ATTACK
	01 ☐ UNIV. ☐ STOLEN PROPERTY TYPE
	☐ EVIDENCE ☐ RECOV.
	(DESC., SER #, ETC.)
LOCATION OF ARREST (NO. STREET - APT. /BOX)	VALUE
LOCATION OF OFFENSE (NO. STREET - APT. /BOX) RA	02 ☐ UNIV. ☐ STOLEN PROPERTY TYPE
	☐ EVIDENCE ☐ RECOV.
VICTIM NAME (LAST, FIRST, MI) OR (PROPER BUSINESS NAME - INC., CO.) ☐ AFFILIATION	(DESC., SER #, ETC.)
VICTIM ADDRESS (NO. STREET - APT. /BOX)	VALUE
CITY, STATE PHONE	03 ☐ UNIV. ☐ STOLEN PROPERTY TYPE
	☐ EVIDENCE ☐ RECOV.
ARREST/SUSPECT NAME (LAST, FIRST, MI) JUV. ☐ ADULT ☐	(DESC., SER #, ETC.)
A/S ADDRESS (NO. STREET - APT. /BOX)	VALUE
CITY STATE	04 ☐ UNIV. ☐ STOLEN PROPERTY TYPE
	☐ EVIDENCE ☐ RECOV.
DATE OF BIRTH AGE SEX M☐ F☐ RACE	(DESC., SER #, ETC.)
HEIGHT WEIGHT PECULIARITY	VALUE
COLOR HAIR COLOR EYES COMPLEXION ☐ LIGHT ☐ MED. ☐ DARK	☐ UNIV. ☐ STOLEN ☐ VEHICLE
	☐ EVIDENCE ☐ RECOV. ☐ LICENSE PLATE
WITNESS (1) NAME (LAST, FIRST, MI)	LIC. PLATE TYPE STATE LIC. PLATE NO.
ADDRESS (NO. STREET - APT. /BOX)	VIN #
CITY, STATE PHONE	YEAR MAKE MODEL
WITNESS (2) NAME (LAST, FIRST, MI)	STYLE COLOR VALUE
ADDRESS (NO. STREET - APT. /BOX)	TOTAL VALUE OF PROPERTY TAKEN $
CITY, STATE PHONE	PHOTOS BY: PRINTS BY:

NARRATIVE

CLEARED BY ARREST OF:	ARREST NO.	DISPOSITION	SUPPLEMENTS NARRATIVE ☐ OFF/PROP ☐
REPORTING OFFICER	DATE	APPROVED BY:	DATE

SM 017

10. Incident and arrest report and narrative supplement. Courtesy of Harvard University Police Department, Cambridge, Massachusetts.

Appendix 10. Continued

NARRATIVE SUPPLEMENT

HARVARD UNIVERSITY POLICE DEPARTMENT

☐ INCIDENT REPORT   ☐ ARREST REPORT   ☐ INVESTIGATION REPORT   ☐ _____

INCIDENT NO

REPORTING OFFICER	DATE	APPROVED BY	DATE

UNIVERSITY OF MIAMI
DEPARTMENT OF PUBLIC SAFETY
REPORT

OFFICER	POST	SHIFT

SUBJECT'S NAME	Address of subject	Classification of case

COMPLAINANT'S NAME	Complainant's address & telephone number	Complaint received:
		Personal Telephone Other
		_____ _____ _____
		_____ _____ _____
		Date: _____
		Time: _____

FACTS OF COMPLAINT AND ACTION TAKEN:

_____

_____

_____

_____

_____

_____

(Use plain paper for subsequent pages)

(Following spaces for office use)

Copies To:	

File Number _____

C.G.P.D. Case Number _____

11. Incident report and supplemental report. Courtesy of University of Miami Department of Public Safety, Coral Gables, Florida.

Appendix 11. Continued

UNIVERSITY OF MIAMI
DEPARTMENT OF PUBLIC SAFETY

SUPPLEMENTAL REPORT

Reporting Officer: _____ Date: _____

Name of subject: _____

Name of complainant: _____

Classification of case: _____

_____

_____

_____

_____

_____

_____

_____

_____

_____

_____

_____

_____

_____

(Use plain paper for subsequent pages)

(Following spaces for office use)

Copies To:

File Number _____

HARVARD UNIVERSITY POLICE DEPARTMENT

Daily Activity Sheet

Date _____ Officer _____ Shift _____ Start _____

Area_____ Call No. _____ Mileage Start _____ Mileage Finish _____

Supervisor _____ Car # _____ Repairs Needed ☐ Yes ☐ No
             Signature

Rec'd	Arr	Cl	Incd. #	Information

Incidents_____ Reports _____ Security Checks _____

Arrests_____ Warnings_____ On Sites _____

UHS Runs_____ MV Tags_____ MV Towed _____

Accidents_____ Alarms_____ Other _____

Over for Patrol Cars and Car Light and Light Repairs ☐ Yes ——————————
                                                              SIGNATURE

12. Daily activity sheet. Courtesy of Harvard University Police Department, Cambridge, Massachusetts.

VOLUNTARY STATEMENT

Date _____ Time _____ Place _____

I, _____ , Date of Birth _____ ,

am _____ years of age and my address is _____

_____ .

I have been read my rights and have read my rights as herein described by _____

_____ , who has identified himself as _____ .

1. You have the right to remain silent and not incriminate yourself in any manner.
2. Anything you say to us can be used against you in a court of law.
3. You have the right to talk to an attorney before answering any questions and to have an attorney present with you during questioning.
4. You have this same right to the advice and presence of an attorney whether you can afford to hire one or not. We have no way of furnishing you with an attorney, but one will be appointed for you, if you wish, if and when you go to court.
5. If you decide to answer questions now without an attorney present, you will still have the right to stop answering at any time until you talk to an attorney.

Initials _____ Date _____   Page No. _1_

---

13. Voluntary signed statement and waiver of rights form. Courtesy of University of Miami Department of Public Safety, Coral Gables, Florida.

Appendix 13. Continued

WAIVER

I have read the foregoing statement of my rights, and it has been read to me. I understand what my rights are. I do not want an attorney at this time. No force, threats, or promises of any kind or nature have been used by anyone in any way to influence me to waive my rights. I am signing this waiver after having been advised of my rights before any questions have been asked of me by the police.

_____   _____   _____
          Date   Time   Signature

CERTIFICATION

I hereby certify that the foregoing warning and waiver were read by me to the person who has affixed his (her) signature above, and that he (she) also read it and signed it in my presence this _____ day of _____ , 19__ at _____ o'clock __ M. at _____

_____

POLICE OFFICER

_____

WITNESS

Initials _____ Date _____   Page No. _2_

Appendix 13. Continued

STATEMENT

I declare that the following statement is made of my own free will without promise or hope of reward, without fear or threat of physical harm, without coercion, favor or offer of favor, without leniency or offer of leniency, by any person or persons whomsoever.

I have read this statement consisting of ___ page(s), and I affirm to the truth and accuracy of the facts contained therein.

This statement was completed at ____ M, on the _____ day of _____, 19___.

_____

SIGNATURE OF PERSON GIVING
VOLUNTARY STATEMENT

Page _____ of _____ pages

_____

WITNESS

_____

WITNESS

Date _____ Page No. 3

DEPARTMENT OF SECURITY

VEHICLE INSPECTION REPORT

VEHICLE NUMBER _____

DATE _____

TIME _____

MILEAGE_____

The above vehicle has been personally inspected by me. There is no new damage to the vehicle. Required equipment (spare tire, jack, CO_2 and water-type fire extinguishers, first aid kit, blanket) is present and in proper condition. Interiors of the vehicle and trunk are in keeping with regulations.

REMARKS: _____

_____

_____

_____

_____

_____

_____

_____

_____

_____

_____   _____
OFFICER TURNING VEHICLE IN   OFFICER ABOUT TO USE VEHICLE

14. Vehicle inspection report to be filled out by patrol vehicle operators. Courtesy of University of Miami Department of Public Safety, Coral Gables, Florida.

DAILY PATROL SHEET

Officer _____ Post Number _____

On duty at—Date _____ Time _____

Off duty at—Date _____ Time _____

Vehicle No. _____ Mileage out _____ in _____ Time serviced _____

Call Code	Time Rec'd.	Time Arrived Scene	Time Ret'd. Patrol	ACTIVITY

Turned following equipment: Over to:

15. Daily patrol sheet for patrol vehicles.

PERSONNEL EVALUATION REPORT

LAST NAME	FIRST	M.I.	BADGE #

	RATING PERIOD		
RANK		FROM	TO

PERFORMANCE OF DUTY 1. (A) When reporting on this officer, consider him/her with all other officers of the same grade whose professional ability is known to you personally and indicate your estimate of this officer by marking "A" in the appropriate spaces below. (B) Any element rated outstanding, needs improvement, or unsatisfactory must be commented on in the narrative.	OUTSTANDING	EXCELLENT	SATISFACTORY	NEEDS IMPROVEMENT	UNSATISFACTORY	UNABLE TO RATE
1. Patrol duties—prevention and apprehension						
2. Operation and maintenance of cruisers						
3. Care and upkeep of equipment						
4. Safety duties						
5. Property security duties						
6. Contact with public						
7. Contact with suspects						
8. Investigative ability						
9. Knowledge and application of law						
10. Case preparation						
11. Ability on the witness stand						
12. Traffic duties						

16. Personnel evaluation report.

Appendix 16. Continued

	OUTSTANDING	EXCELLENT	SATISFACTORY	NEEDS IMPROVEMENT	UNSATISFACTORY	UNABLE TO RATE
13. Service duties						
14. Special details						
15. Performance under hazardous conditions						
16. Compliance with department rules						
17. Attendance and promptness						
2. To what degree has he/she exhibited the following:						
1. Personal Appearance (Habitually appearing neat, smart, and well groomed in uniform and civilian attire)						
2. Endurance (Physical and mental ability for carrying on under fatiguing conditions)						
3. Attention to Duty (Industry — the trait of working thoroughly and conscientiously)						
4. Cooperation (The faculty of working in harmony with others, police and civilians)						
5. Initiative (The trait of taking necessary or appropriate action on own responsibility)						
6. Judgement (The ability to think clearly and arrive at logical conclusions)						
7. Leadership (The capacity to direct, control, influence others and maintain high morale)						
8. Loyalty (The quality of rendering faithful and willing services)						

Appendix 16. Continued

3. Were deficiencies indicated by you brought to the attention of this officer?
   Explain. _____

   _____

   _____

   _____

   _____

   _____

4. Can you report improvements? _____

   _____

   _____

   _____

   _____

   _____

5. Give a short appraisal (in not less than fifty words) of the professional character of this
   officer.

   _____

   _____

   _____

   _____

   _____

   _____

   _____

   _____

   _____

   _____

   _____

Appendix 16. Continued

SIGNATURE OF RATING OFFICER

SIGNATURE OF REVIEWING OFFICER

RANK   DATE

OFFICER'S COMMENTS: _____

I have been given an opportunity to
examine the contents of this report:

SIGNATURE OF OFFICER RATED   DATE

APPENDIX - RELATED READINGS

This list of related readings was compiled mainly from computer printouts prepared for the International Association of Campus Law Enforcement Administrators and reprinted here with permission from Jerry Hudson, Director of Security, University of North Carolina at Charlotte, N.C.

ADMINISTRATION

A Housing President's Observations
 Quick, Jerry
 Campus Law Enforcement Journal
 Mar–Apr 1980, Vol. 10, No. 2, P 36
A Small Police Facility on a Shoestring Budget
 Nielsen, Robert C.
 Campus Law Enforcement Journal
 May–June 1978, Vol. 8, No. 3, P 26–27
A Usable College Security Shift Tour Schedule
 Johnson, Herman B. & Felicetta, Michael J.
 Campus Law Enforcement Journal
 Nov–Dec 1977, Vol. 7, No. 6, P 21
Academic Internship: An Operating Lab Approach
 McEntee, A.P.
 Campus Law Enforcement Journal
 March–April 1979, Vol. 9, No. 2, P 21

Administrator's View of the Public Safety Division
 Armstrong, Richard C.
 Campus Law Enforcement Journal
 Nov–Dec, 1979, Vol. 9, No. 6, P 46
Alternative to Chaos: The Need for Professional . . .
 Kassinger, Edward T.
 New Directions in Campus Law Enforcement. . .
 1971
Awards: Not Just for Heroes
 Nielsen, Robert C.
 Campus Law Enforcement Journal
 Jan–Feb 1980, Vol. X, No. I, P 8
Blazers: A National Survey of Police Attitudes
 Wiley, Ronald E. & Cochran, C.D.
 Police Chief
 Jul 1972, Vol. 2, No. 7, P 68

Bringing University Police into the Academic Community
  The Journal of the College & University Personnel
  April–May, 1976
Campus Autonomy
  Cox, David C.
  Campus Law Enforcement Journal
  Apr–May–June 1974, Vol. 4, No. 2
Campus Law Enforcement and Student Affairs: A Definition
  Sims, O. Suthern
  New Directions in Campus Law Enforcement: A Handbook
  1971
Campus Security
  Yale Alumni Magazine
  Dec 1961, P 15
Campus and School Security
  Powell, John W.
  School Security
  April 1974
Campus Security – A Perspective
  Powell, John W.
  American School & University
  July 1971
Campus Security . . . Take More Than Locks and Cops
  Post, Richard S.
  College and University Business
  Aug 1971, Vol. 51, No. 2, P 33
Campus Security—Responsibilities of Students, Faculty
  Wilson, Etsel A.
  Campus Law Enforcement Journal
  May–June 1976
Campus Security Today: Progressive But Sensitive
  Powell, John W.
  American School and University
  Oct 1972, P 17
Concentrate Your Security . . . Aid in Allocating . . .
  Miller, Floyd G., Ph.D
  Security World
  May 1973, Vol, 10, No. 5, P 30
Contract Security
  Yon, Stephen E.
  Campus Law Enforcement Journal
  May–June 1977, Vol. 7, No. 3, P 17

Cops on Campus: A Handbook
  College and University Personnel Assn Journal
  April–May 1976, Vol. 27, No. 2
Cops or Guards
  Gorda, Bernard L.
  Security Management
  Nov 1975
Day-To-Day Dealing with the Union
  Leggat, Al and McNamara, Joseph P.
  Campus Law Enforcement Journal
  Sept–Oct 1976, Vol. 6, No. 5, P 28
Death & Disability Benefits for Public Safety Employees
  Heath, Edwin D.
  The Police Chief
  May 1978, Vol. XLV, No. 5, P 33
Department Growth and Development
  Johnson, Herman B.
  Campus Law Enforcement Journal
  Sept–Oct 1976
Designing the Job to Motivate
  Baker, Thomas J.
  Campus Law Enforcement Journal
  Jan–Feb 1977, Vol. 7, No. 1
Education or Preservation? The Educator's View
  Kmet, Mary A.
  Security Management
  Feb 1979, Vol. 22, No. 2, P 36
Effectiveness of Campus Security . . . An Analysis
  Willard, Nesley
  Campus Law Enforcement Journal
  Sept–Oct 1979, Vol. 9, No. 5, P 18
Employee Discipline—Punishment or Education?
  Thomas, Gerald S.
  Campus Law Enforcement Journal
  May–June 1980, Vol. 10, No. 3, P 31
Factors Affecting the Relationship Between Public
  Neilson, Francis B.
  Security Management
  Jan 1977, P 22
Friends or Foes? The Changing Relationship . . . .
  Nielsen, Robert C.
  Campus Law Enforcement Journal
  Nov–Dec 1974, Vol. 4, No. 4, P 30

General Organizational and Administrative Concepts
Nielsen, Swen
1971
Georgia's Security Staff Stresses Services
American School & University
Jan 1973, Vol. 42, No. 11, P 28
Guard Forces (Direct Hire or Contract)
Shurr, Robert
Security Management
Jan 1976, Vol. 19, No. 6, P 42
Handbook of College and University Administration
Knowles, Asa S.
McGraw-Hill Book Co.
1970
Helping Police with Emotional Problems
Arkin, Joseph
Campus Law Enforcement Journal
Apr-May-June 1974, Vol. 4, No. 2, P 6
In-service Training & the Four Day Week
Strunk, Daniel M.
The Police Chief
July 1978, Vol. XLV, No. 7
International Encyclopedia of Higher Education
Knowles, Asa S.
1977, Jossey-Bass Publishers
LEEP Funding Threatened
Guinn, Robert E.
Campus Law Enforcement Journal
Oct 1976, Vol. XIII, No. 5
Lost, Stolen, Missing or Counterfeit Securities
Kassinger, Edward T.
Campus Law Enforcement Journal
May-June 1978, Vol. 8, No. 3, P 32
Make Everyone a Manager
Nielsen, Robert C.
Campus Law Enforcement Journal
Jan-Feb 1977, Vol. 7, No. 1
Manpower: Make the Most of What You've Got
Nielsen, Robert C.
Police Chief
Jan 1970, Vol. XLV, No. 1 P 23
Management-by-Objectives in Law Enforcement Agencies . . .
Skinner, Gilbert and Sullivan, John
Campus Law Enforcement Journal
Sept-Oct 1976, Vol. 6, No. 5, P 20

New Test for Successful Security
Otis, Robert W.
June 1973
Organization of a Campus Security and Safety Unit
Posey, Robert W.
School of Law Enforcement Eastern Kentucky University
1968
Police Sue State Union
Shelton, Pat
Campus Law Enforcement Journal
Nov-Dec 1977, Vol. 7, No. 6, P 20
Policing a University Campus —Approach
Brug, Richard C.
Campus Law Enforcement Journal
May-June 1978, Vol. 8, No. 3, P 19-21
Problems in Police Management Transition
Kimble, Joseph P.
Campus Law Enforcement Journal
Nov-Dec 1976
Professionalizing Campus Security
Powell, John W.
Security World
May 1967, P 23
Protective Services Objectives . . . MSU
Campus Law Enforcement Journal
Sept-Oct 1974, Vol. 4, No. 3
Rise and Fall of Colleges as Insurance Risks
Kloman, H.F.
College and University Business
Jan 1971, Vol. 50, No. 1, P 42
Security
College and University Business Administration
July 1974, Third Ed., P 125.
Security Director Examines Police Budget Concept
McCue, Edward C.
Campus Law Enforcement Journal
Jan-Feb 1975
Setting Up a Strong University Security Department
Kennedy, Verne C.
American School & University
Feb 1972, Vol. 44, No. 6, P 30
Special Orders for Special Events
Owens, James
Campus Law Enforcement Journal
Jan-Feb 1976, Vol. 6, No. 1, P 37

Suggestion for Gaining Objectives ...
  Security
    Andraf, Reed
    College and University Business
      Administration Office
    Nov 1974, Vol. 4, No. 3
Surveying School Security and Costs
    Carlton, Stephen A.
    Security World
    Jan 1974, Vol. 11, No. 2, P 26
Tackling Scheduling & Deployment
  Problems
    Security Management
    May 1978, Vol. 22, No. 5, P 24
The Campus Police
    Iannarelli, Alfred V.
    1968 Precision Photo Form
The Chief's Challenge: Providing a Full
  Range ...
    Van Eepoel, Vicki V.
    Campus Law Enforcement Journal
    Sept–Oct 1975
The Future of Campus Security
    Powell, John W.
    Security World
    Feb 1966, P 30
The Law and Private Police
    Kakalik, James S. and Wildhorn, Sorrel
    Nat'l Institute of Law Enforcement and
      Criminal Justice
The Necessity for Developing a Statement
  of Policy
    Engel, Robert E.
    Campus Law Enforcement Journal
    Nov–Dec 1976, P 17
The Need to Be Recognized
    Gonson, Harvey D.
    Campus Law Enforcement Journal
    Sept–Oct 1974, Vol. 4, No. 3
The New Breed: College and University
  Police
    Hollomon, Frank C.
    Police Chief
    Feb 1972, P 41
The Part-time Student Employee ...
    Walker, Wynn C.
    Campus Law Enforcement Journal
    May–June 1976
The Role of Campus Security in the College
  Setting
    Gelber, Seymour
    U.S. Government Printing Office
    1972

Trying to Be Objective About Our
  Objectives
    Kimble, Joseph P.
    Campus Law Enforcement Journal
    May–June 1977, Vol. 7, No. 3, P 36
Trying to Be Objective About Our Objective
    Kimble, Joseph P.
    Campus Law Enforcement Journal
    Sept–Oct 1978, Vol. 8, No. 5, P 28
University Police, Are They Necessary?
    Cox, Berry D.
    Campus Law Enforcement Journal
    May–June 1977, Vol. 7, No. 3, P 4
Western Illinois Occupies New Facility
    Campus Law Enforcement Journal
    Sept–Oct 1974, Vol. 4, No. 3, P 13
What a Corporate Security ... Know About
  Insurance
    Beck, Sanford E.
    Security Management
    May 1974, Vol. 18, No. 2, P 25
What Does Management Expect of Its
  Security Operation
    Jaffe, James A.
    Security Product News
    Nov, Dec 1974, P 16

APPLICANT SELECTION

... Criteria for Selecting Police Chiefs
    Fenlon, Tim D.
    Campus Law Enforcement Journal
    Jan–Feb 1977, Vol. 7, No. 1
... Guidelines ... Training ... Qualifica-
  tions ... Clep
    Boynton, Asa T.
    Campus Law Enforcement Journal
    Mar–Apr 1980, Vol. 10, No. 2, P 30
A Model for Recruiting and Training
  Campus Security
    Richer, T.
    The Police Chief
    July 1974, P 76
Attracting College Grads to Police
  Department
    Hamilton, Lander C. and Bimstein,
      Donald
    Police Chief
    Aug 1972, Vol. XXXIX, No. 8, P 40

Campus Security Needs Professionals With
  Emphasis on People Problems
  Powell, John W.
  College and University Business
  April 1970, P 94
Careers in Campus Policing
  Kimble, Joseph P.
  Campus Law Enforcement Journal
  Jan-Feb 1975
Going Beyond Handcuffs 101
  McGrath, Noreen
  The Chronicle of Higher Education
  Nov 27, 1978, P 3
Prediction Personnel Behavior — It's in the
  Stars
  Nielsen, Robert C.
  Campus Law Enforcement Journal
  Nov-Dec 1979, Vol. 9, No. 6, P 26
Screening Police Applicants with Group
  Interview
  Kaplan, Gene
  The Police Chief
  Jan 1978, Vol. XLV, No. 1, P 27
Selecting Police Recruits
  McCue, Ed
  Campus Law Enforcement Journal
  Jan-Feb 1979, Vol. 9, No. 1, P 24
University Police Selection Procedures
  Sewell, James D. and Bromley, Max L.
  Campus Law Enforcement Journal
  Mar-Apr 1980, Vol. 10, No. 2, P 18
What Makes a Good Police Executive
  Gugas, Chris, Sr.
  Security World
  Jun 1977, Vol. 14, No. 6, P 24
With Whom Would You Share the Risk?
  Hudson, Jerry E.
  Campus Law Enforcement Journal
  Mar-Apr 1978, Vol. 8, No. 2, P 12

ARRESTS, LAWS OF: PROCEDURE

Campus Apprehensions of College Students
  Milander, H.M.
  Police Chief
  Nov 1971, Vol. XXXIX, No. 11, P 70
Case Law for College Security Officers
  Gehring, Donald D.
  Campus Law Enforcement Journal
  Sept-Oct 1975

Citizen's Arrest: The Law of Arrest, Search,
  and
  Bassiount, M.C.
  Charles C. Thomas, Publisher
  1977, P 144
College Student and the Courts
  Young, D., Parker
  Published by College Admin . . . Publica-
  tions, Inc. 1973, with quarterly
  supplements
Legal Aspects of Student Dissent and
  Discipline
  Young, D., Parker
  Institute of Higher Education, University
  of Georgia
  1971
Probable Cause
  Stevens, E.H.
  Campus Law Enforcement Journal
  March-April 1976, Vol. 6, No. 2, P 6
The Law and Private Police
  Kakalik, James S. and Wildhorn, Sorrel
  Nat'l Institute of Law Enforcement and
  Criminal Justice
The Law of Arrest and Search and Seizure:
  A State's . . .
  Markle, Arnold
  Charles C. Thomas, Publisher
  1974, 320 pages

ATHLETICS/ATHLETIC EVENTS

Campus Concerts . . . Some Guidelines and
  Precautions
  Nielsen, Robert C.
  Campus Law Enforcement Journal
  Jan-Feb 1976
Controlling Visitor and Special Event
  Parking
  Beebe, Richard S.
  25th Annual IMPC Workshop
  Proceedings
  Apr 8-11 1979, P 139
Drugs and Athletic Performance
  Williams, Melvin H.
  Charles C. Thomas, Publisher
  1974, 212 pages
Football: Oklahoma Style
  Eaton, Everett
  Campus Law Enforcement Journal
  Sept-Oct 1979, Vol. 9, No. 5, P 6

Managing Vandalism . . . Parks and Recreation Facilities
Center for Urban Affairs
1978, P 59

Planning for Large-Scale Special Events
Jands, Jack M.
The Police Chief
Jan 1980, Vol. XLVII, No. 1, P 59

Pre-game Planning
Kmet, Mary A.
Security Management
Oct 1979, P 17

Rock Festival or Fiasco?
Tuler, Roy A.
Police Chief
Mar 1973, Vol. XL, No. 3, P 34

Security Tightened for the U. MD Inter . . . Olympics
Dickey, Sandra L.
Campus Law Enforcement Journal
Sept-Oct 1975

Stadium Parking in Gator Bowl — Problems & Solutions
23rd IMPC Workshop Proceedings
June 5-8 1977, 109 pages

Stadium Rock Concerts
McEntee, Andrew P.
Campus Law Enforcement Journal
May-June 1977, Vol. 7, No. 3, P 46

Protection Against Bombs and Incendiaries: For . . .
Pike, Earl A.
Charles C. Thomas, Publisher
1973, 92 pages

Short-notice Bomb-scare Warning System
Gupta, Om T.
Security World
Apr 1972, Vol. 9, No. 4

Stadium Security Doesn't Clown Around
Howard, Gordon C.
Security Mangement
Oct 1979, P 6

The Fifth Quarter: Law Enforcement and . . . Sports
Deaver, Mick
The Police Chief
Sept 1978, Vol. 1, XLV, No. 9

The Saturday Afternoon Invasion
Blacklock, Thomas G.
Campus Law Enforcement Journal
Sept-Oct 1974, Vol. 4, No. 3, P 4

BOMB THREATS

A Campus Plan for Bombs and Bomb Threats
Owens, James
Campus Law Enforcement Journal
May-June 1976

Beware: New Terrorist Weapons
Voue, H.T.
Security World
Feb 1972, Vol. 9, No. 2

Bomb Threat Response
Cox, David L. and DeMarco, John M.
Security Management
Jan 1977, P 8

Bombings, Vandalism & Arson
Powell, John W.
Burns Security Institute

BUDGETING

A Small Police Facility on a Shoestring Budget
Nielsen, Robert C.
Campus Law Enforcement Journal
May-June 1978, Vol. 8, No. 8 P 26-27

Management-by-Objectives in Law Enforcement Agencies . . .
Skinner, Gilbert and Sullivan, John
Campus Law Enforcement Journal
Sept-Oct 1976, Vol. 6, No. 5, P 20

Security Director Examines Police Budget Concept
McCue, Edward C.
Campus Law Enforcement Journal
Jan-Feb 1975

Surveying School Security and Costs
Carlton, Stephen A.
Security World
Jan 1974, Vol. 11, No. 2, P 26

CIVIL DISORDERS

. . . Terrorists Getting Ready
Campus Law Enforcement Journal
Sept-Oct 1975, Vol. 5, P 10

Beware: The New Terrorist Weapons
Voue, H.T.
Security World
Feb 1972, Vol. 9, No. 2

State Legislation and Campus Disorders
   Rouland,
   1, *Journal of Law and Education,* 231
State Legislative Response to Campus
   Disorder . . .
   10, *Houston Law Review,* 930
Strike Procedures for the Campus Security
   Dept.
   Stump, William
   Campus Law Enforcement Journal
   Mar–Apr 1978, Vol. 8, No. 2, P 32
Student Conduct and Campus Law
   Enforcement
   Sims, O., Suthern
   New Directions in Campus Law
      Enforcement: . . .
   1971
Students Are Invited to Riot at City Hall
   Hansen, David A.
   Police Chief
   May 1974, Vol. XLI, No. 5, P 54
Terrorist Attacks Present Another
   Dimension for EM
   D'Addario, Francis M.
   Security Management
   May 1978, Vol. 22, No. 5, P 31
The American Student Left
   Rosenthal, Carl F.
   National Criminal Justice Reference
   Service
The Law of Dissent and Riots
   Bassiount, M.C.
   Charles C. Thomas, Publisher
   1971, 510 pages
The President's Commission on Campus
   Unrest
   U.S. Government Printing Office
   1970

COMPUTERS

Assets Protection
   International Journal of Security &
      Investigation
   P.O. Box 5327, Madison Wi, 53705
Breach of Campus Computer Results in
   Convictions
   Perry, Gordon
   Campus Law Enforcement Journal
   March–April 1979, Vol. 9, No. 2, P 16

Commuter Crime Prevention
   Bromley, Max L.
   Campus Law Enforcement Journal
   March–April 1976, Vol. 6, No. 2, P 33
Computer Safety Goes Down to Final Wire
   Zaiden, Dennis J.
   College and University Business
   Aug 1971
Computers and Campus Law at Conn State
   Conners, Kevin
   Campus Law Enforcement Journal
   Nov–Dec 1975, Vol. 5, No. 6, P 33
Foozles & Frauds
   Russell, Harold F.
   Institute of Internal Auditors, Inc.
   1972
Impact & Use of Computer Technology by
   the Police
   Colton, Kent W.
   Communications of the A.C.M.
   Jan 1979, Vol. 22, No. 1, P 10

COMMUNICATIONS

An Old Familiar Story . . . . with a Happy
   Ending
   Hudson, Jerry E.
   Campus Law Enforcement Journal
   Jan–Feb 1978, Vol. 8, No. 1, P 38
Automated Dispatch System for Small
   Department
   Klein, William G.
   The Police Chief
   Feb 1978, Vol. XLV, No. 2, P 22
Best's Safety Directory (Updated Annually)
   A.M. Best Co.
   1976, 16th Ed.
Campus Communication Network Shrinks
   Crime Network
   Security Industry and Product News
   Aug 1976
Dictionary of Security Terms
   Fuss, Eugene
   Campus Law Enforcement Journal
   May–June 1973, Vol. 3, No. 3, P 41
Freshman Orientation Program Revisited
   McAuliffe, John D.
   Campus Law Enforcement Journal
   Jan–Feb 1979, Vol. 9, No. 1, P 26

CRIME ON CAMPUS

Controlling Crime in the School—Handbook
  for Admin
    Vestermark, S.D, and Blauvelt, P.D.
    Parker Publishing Co. Inc., West Nyack,
    NY 10994
    1978, 354 pages
Crime Goes to College
    Meyer, Pamela
    Campus Law Enforcement Journal
    Nov–Dec 1977, Vol. 7, No. 6, P 12
Crime on Campus
    Strunk, Daniel
    The Police Chief
    May 1980, P 39
Crime on the Campus
    Campus Law Enforcement Journal
    March–April 1976, Vol. 6, No. 2, P 9
Crime on the Campus
    Fox, James W.
    Journal of College Student Personnel
    Sept 1977, P 345–351
Crime on the Campus (U.C.R.S.)
    Campus Law Enforcement Journal
    Nov–Dec 1976, Vol. 6, No. 6,
Crime on the Campus 1977
    McGovern, James L.
    Campus Law Enforcement Journal
    Jan–Feb 1979, Vol. 9, No. 1, P 30
Crime on the Campus, 1978
    McGovern, James L.
    Campus Law Enforcement Journal
    Jan–Feb 1980, Vol. X, No. I, P 34
Crime Rate on the Decline at Tufts
    Stuart, Gould, and Stuart, Cynthia
    Campus Law Enforcement Journal
    May–June 1973, Vol. 3, No. 3, P 44
Foozles & Frauds
    Russell, Harold F.
    Institute of Internal Auditors, Inc.
    1972
Numbers Can Be Misleading
    Rideout, John
    Campus Law Enforcement Journal
    Mar–Apr 1980, Vol. 10, No. 2, P 34
Rutgers Intensifies Its Fight on Crime
    Campus Law Enforcement Journal
    May–June 1973, Vol. 3, No. 3, P 21
School Security Survey
    Morton, Roger
    School Product News
    Jun 1977

Student's Faculty Want Protection
  Against . . .
    Burner, A.W.
    Campus Law Enforcement Journal
    May–June 1973, Vol. 3, No. 3, P 68
The Changing Campus Crime Scene
    Powell, John W.
    Burns Security Institute
Univ. of Texas Police Reverse Crime Trend
    Campus Law Enforcement Journal
    May–June 1973, Vol. 3, No. 3, P 18
Wayne State Univ. Police Report
  Substantial . . .
    Foss, Vern
    Campus Law Enforcement Journal
    May–June 1973, Vol. 3, No. 3, P 25

CRIME PREVENTION

. . . Letters Judge Dept. Performance
    McAuliffe, John C.
    Campus Law Enforcement Journal
    Nov–Dec 1974, Vol. 4, No. 4,
. . . Terrorists Getting Ready
    Campus Law Enforcement Journal
    Sept–Oct 1975, Vol. 5, P 10
A Long Hard Look at Bicycle Safety
    Cleckner, Robert M.
    Police Chief
    Jun 1976, Vol. XCII, No. 6, P 58
A Money Mover
    Chafin, Saul
    Campus Law Enforcement Journal
    Mar–Apr 1978, Vol. 8, No. 2, P 36
A New Service Concept – and It's Free
    Burke, Mary E.
    Campus Law Enforcement Journal
    Mar–Apr 1980, Vol. 10, No. 2, P 38
A Note on Campus Security Transporting
  Money
    Chafin, Saul
    Police Chief
    Dec 1978, Vol. XLV, No. 12, P 91
A University Computer-controlled Security
  System
    The Chronicle of Higher Education
    Oct 1976, Vol. XIII, No. 5
A University to the Challenge of Crime
  Prevention
    Nix, Ernest M. and Stansel, Paul L.
    Campus Law Enforcement Journal
    Nov–Dec 1978, Vol. 8, No. 6, P 19

Alarms Deter Crime
  Distelhors, Garis F.
  The Police Chief
  June 1978, Vol. XLV, No. 6, P 43
Art Theft and the Need for Central Archive
  Mason, Donald L.
  The Police Chief
  June 1977, Vol. XLIV, No. 6
Auditor Security Officer Relationships
  Marsh, Quinton N.
  Security Management
  Nov 1975, Vol. 19, No. 5, P 22
Better Lighting with Less Energy
  Meyers, Alan R.
  American School and University
  Sept 1979, P 30
Better Security Through LPS Lighting
  Lewis, Robert A.
  Security Management
  April 1978, Vol. 22, No. 4
Big Results with Little Motorcycles
  Nielsen, Robert C.
  Police Chief
  Sept 1978
*Bike Theft: One of America's Fastest
  Growing Crime*
  Seaken, Raymond N.
  Campus Law Enforcement Journal
  1975
*Campus Communication Network Shrinks
  Crime Network*
  Security Industry and Product News
  Aug 1976
Campus Police in Disguise
  Dumas, Paul J.
  Campus Law Enforcement Journal
  Jan–Feb 1977, Vol. 7, No. 1,
*Campus Shoplifters—Some Approaches to
  the Problem*
  Nielsen, Robert C.
  College Store Executives
  October 1976
Camp Vandalism—Who Pays?
  Gardner, John
  American School & University
  Jul 1973, Vol. 42, No. 11, P 14
Campus White Collar Crime
  Kleberg, John
  Campus Law Enforcement Journal
  Nov–Dec 1977, Vol. 7, No. 6, P 15

CCTV System Design for School Security
  Kravontka, Stanley J.
  Security World
  Jan 1974, Vol. 11, No. 2, P 22
CMU Uses Bookmark to Curb Larcenies
  McAuliffe, John C.
  Campus Law Enforcement Journal
  Sept–Oct 1976, Vol. 6, No. 5, P 23
*Colleges to Give Crime Some Competition
  on Campus*
  LEAA Newsletter
  April 1978, Vol. 7, No. 3, P 10
*Colorado Security Department Combats
  Crime*
  Lindbloom, Kenneth D.
  American School & University
  Mar 1978, Vol. 50, No. 6
*Community Awareness—the Key to Campus
  Safety*
  Gross, Phillip
  Campus Law Enforcement Journal
  May–June 1973, Vol. 3, No. 3, P 45
Commuter Crime Prevention
  Bromley, Max L.
  Campus Law Enforcement Journal
  March–April 1976, Vol. 6, No. 2, P 33
Computer Safety Goes Down to Final Wire
  Zaiden, Dennis J.
  College and University Business
  Aug 1971
*County Defeats Campus but Cindy Is Real
  Winner*
  Campus Law Enforcement Journal
  Jan–Feb 1975
Crime Goes to College
  Meyer, Pamela
  Campus Law Enforcement Journal
  Nov–Dec 1977, Vol. 7, No. 6, P 12
Crime Is Minimal on New Member's Campus
  Roberts, D.F.
  Campus Law Enforcement Journal
  July–Aug 1977, Vol. 7, No. 4
Crime Prevention and the Architects
  Fennelly, Lawrence J.
  Assets Protection
  May–June 1979, Vol. 4, No. 2, P 30
Crime Prevention at UCLA
  Security Industry and Product News
  Oct 1979, Vol. 8, No. 10, P 35
Crime Prevention Headquarters in Texas
  Horwitz, David
  Campus Law Enforcement Journal
  Nov–Dec 1978, Vol. 8, No. 6, P 14

*Crime Prevention in University Residence
Halls*
    Handley, Jackson R.
    Campus Law Enforcement Journal
    May–June 1980, Vol. 10, No. 3, P 24
Crime Prevention 1977/1978
    Wehner, Joseph
    Campus Law Enforcement Journal
    Nov–Dec 1978, Vol. 8, No. 6, P 24
*Crime Reduction at Eastern Washington
University*
    Campus Law Enforcement Journal
    Nov–Dec 1978, Vol. 8, No. 6, P 29
*Crime Unreported on Campus . . .
    Victimization . . .*
    Wagner, Michael C.
    Campus Law Enforcement Journal
    Sept–Oct 1975
*Crises Avoidance and Prevention: Com-
munity Approach*
    Hudson, Jerry E.
    Campus Law Enforcement Journal
    May–June 1980, Vol. 10, No. 3, P 40
Design to Reduce School Property Loss
    Strobel, Walter M.
    School Product News
    June 1977
Designing a Slide-tape Presentation
    Low, William C.
    Campus Law Enforcement Journal
    May–June 1977, Vol. 7, No. 3, P 49
Designing Security In
    Post, Richard S.
    American School & University
    July 1971
Do You Have a Drug Problem?
    Freund, Richard G.
    Campus Law Enforcement Journal
    Oct–Nov–Dec 1973, Vol. 3, No. 3
*Electronic Watchdogs Guard Minnesota
Campus*
    Security Management
    Jan 1974, Vol. 17, No. 6, P 45
Entire District Wired for Security
    American School & University
    June 1978, Vol. 50, No. 10
Foozles & Frauds
    Russell, Harold F.
    Institute of Internal Auditors, Inc.
    1972

*Freshmen . . . Crime Prevention Slide
Program*
    McAuliffe, John C.
    Campus Law Enforcement Journal
    May–June 1977, Vol. 7, No. 3, P 52
*Greek System: Internal Theft . . . How to
Approach It*
    Roling, Ann
    Campus Law Enforcement Journal
    Sept–Oct 1979, Vol. 9, No. 5, P 3
*Handbook of Building Security – Planning
and Design*
    Powell, John W. and Burton, Lucius W.
    McGraw-Hill Book Co.
    1979, Educational Facilities Chapter
How Explorers Can Help Your Department
    Stearns, Arthur L. and Archimbaud,
    Brian D.
    Campus Law Enforcement Journal
    Sept–Oct 1979, Vol. 9, No. 5, P 22
Improved Pedestrian Lighting on Campus
    Molte, John
    Security Management
    May 1977, Vol. 2, No. 2, P 30
Innovative Crime Prevention at M.I.T.
    Downes, Terrence B.
    Campus Law Enforcement Journal
    Mar–Apr 1977, Vol. 2, No. 2, P 1
*Interception of the Alcohol Influenced
Driver*
    Stormer, David E.
    Campus Law Enforcement Journal
    Jan–Feb 1977, P 34
K-9 Corps and Student Marshalls Syracuse
    Bernstein, Marilyn
    Campus Law Enforcement Journal
    Mar–Apr 1977, Vol. 7, No. 2
*Larcenies Reduced by New Project at
South Florida*
    Mueller, Scott
    Campus Law Enforcement Journal
    Jan–Feb 1975
Lighting for Safety and Security
    McGowan, T.K.
    *Reviews in College and University
    Business*
    Aug 1971, Vol. 51, No. 2, P 42
*Michigan Snow: 'Sno Worry to CMO Public
Safety Dept*
    Bruce, Bob
    Campus Law Enforcement Journal
    May–June 1973, Vol. 3, No. 3, P 24

Microwaves Stop School Vandals
  Kolstad, Ken C.
  Security World
  Jan 1974, Vol. 11, No. 2, P 20
Mobile Crime Unit: Model for Community Involvement
  Lambert, Donald F.
  Campus Law Enforcement Journal
  Sept–Oct 1979, Vol. 9, No. 5, P 25
Model School Security System Cuts Crime
  Burton, Lucius W.
  Security World
  June 1975
Moon Over the United States
  Christian, Charles V.
  Campus Law Enforcement Journal
  Jan–Feb 1977, Vol. 7, No. 1
New Approach to Building Security at Georgetown U
  Lamb, Charles E.
  Campus Law Enforcement Journal
  May–June 1976
New Test for Successful Security
  Otis, Robert W.
  June 1973
North Carolina Continues Campus Awareness Program
  Campus Law Enforcement Journal
  Mar–Apr 1978, Vol. 8, No. 2, P 8
NRTA/AARP Crime Prevention Cartoons
  Campus Law Enforcement Journal
  Sept–Oct 1979, Vol. 9, No. 5, P 29
Numbers Can Be Misleading
  Rideout, John
  Campus Law Enforcement Journal
  Mar–Apr 1980, Vol. 10, No. 2, P 34
Operation Identification Prevents . . .
  Campus Law Enforcement Journal
  Nov–Dec 1974,
Photo Identification Inevitable for Schools
  Kuhns, Roger
  Security Management
  March 1977, P 10
Positive Results in Crime Prevention
  Howard, William B., and Creekmore, Edward
  Campus Law Enforcement Journal
  Sept, Oct 1975
Pound of Prevention . . . Is Pushed for ECU Students
  Bunch, Margaret
  Campus Law Enforcement Journal
  Jul–Aug 1979, Vol. 9, No. 4, P 30

PR Department Assists in Crime Prevention
  Campus Law Enforcement Journal
  Sept–Oct 1975
Protecting Against Fire and Vandalism
  Reeves, David
  American School & University
  May 1972, Vol. 44, No. 9, P 62
Quick Quiz on the Subject of Campus Life
  Haight, William H.
  National Campus Report
  621 Sherman Ave., Madison, WI
Rape Crisis Counseling at . . . Minn.
  Kirby, Arthur G.
  Campus Law Enforcement Journal
  Sept–Oct 1974, Vol. 4, No. 3
Reducing School Violence . . . Drug Abuse
  Harris, Karl B.
  Security World
  Jan 1974, Vol. 11, No. 2, P 18
Rise and Fall of Colleges as Insurance Risks
  Kloman, H.F.
  College and University Business
  Jan 1971, Vol. 50, No. 1, P 42
Risk Management . . . Guidelines for Higher Education
  Adams, John F.
  Nacubo Publication
  1972
Round-up Shows Colleges Secure with Technology
  College and University Business
  Aug 1971, Vol. 51, No. 2, P 40
Rutgers Intensifies Its Fight on Crime
  Campus Law Enforcement Journal
  May–June 1973, Vol. 3, No. 3, P 21
Santarelli Says Rise in Crime is Due to Society
  Byrd, J.M.
  Campus Law Enforcement Journal
  Jan–Feb 1975
School Security Survey
  Morton, Roger
  School Product News
  Jun 1977
School System Cuts Its Losses–Drastically
  Siden, David M.
  Security Management
  Nov 1978, Vol. 22, No. 11, P 52
School Vandalism Can Be Stopped
  Young, George P. and Soldatis, Steven
  American School & University
  Jan 1973, Vol. 42, No. 11, P 22

Security Minded Faculty & Students Support SEMO.
  Campus Law Enforcement Journal
  Mar–Apr 1978, Vol. 8, No. 2, P 30
Security Planning for New Library Facilities
  Powell, John W.
  Library Security
  Sept–Oct 1975, Vol. 1, No. 5, P 1
Security Surveys
  Fennelly, Lawrence J.
  Assets Protection
  July–Aug 1979, Vol. 4, No. 3, P 19
Security: And the Small Business Retailers
  Ewing, Blair G. and Dogin, Henry S.
  Nat. Inst of Law Enforcement and Criminal Justice
  1978
Selecting Intrusion Detectors for Your School
  Reiss, Martin H.
  Security World
  Jan 1974, Vol. 11, No. 2, P 24
State Universities Cooperate to Prevent Crime
  Gilmore, Daniel
  Campus Law Enforcement Journal
  May–June 1978, Vol. 8, No. 3, P 28–29
Stopping School Property Damage
  Zeisel, John
  AASA . . EFL
  1976
Students' Faculty Want Protection Against . . .
  Burner, A.W.
  Campus Law Enforcement Journal
  May–June 1973, Vol. 3, No. 3, P 68
Surveying School Security and Costs
  Carlton, Stephen A.
  Security World
  Jan 1974, Vol. 11, No. 2, P 26
The Crime of Arson
  Flanders, David A.
  Campus Law Enforcement Journal
  Mar–Apr 1977, Vol. 7, No. 2,
The Museum Security Officer
  Ward, Roland L.
  Security Management
  Mar 1976, Vol. 20, No. 1, P 30
The Property Office: More Than Inventory Control
  Edwards, Ralph and Silver, David B.
  American School & University
  Mar 1978, Vol. 50, No. 6

Univ. of Texas Police Reverse Crime Trend
  Campus Law Enforcement Journal
  May–June 1973, Vol. 3, No. 3, P 18
University of Texas Acts to Curb Rape
  Campus Law Enforcement Journal
  Jan–Feb 1975
Vandalism: Recovery and Prevention
  Furno, O.F. and Wallace L.B.
  American School & University
  July 1972, Vol. 44, No. 11, P 19
Verne's Views
  McClurg, Verne H.
  Campus Law Enforcement Journal
  May–June 1978, Vol. 8, No. 3, P 42
Violence & Vandalism in Public Education . . .
  Ban, J.R. and Climinillo, L.M.
  Interstate Printers & Publishers, Inc.
  1977 172 pages
What A Corporate Security . . . Know About Insurance
  Beck, Sanford E.
  Security Management
  May 1974, Vol. 18, No. 2, P 25
What Are College Students Into These Days?
  Haight, William H.
  National On Campus Report
  March 1978
What Can a Security Check Do for You?
  Powell, John W.
  College Management
  Oct 1969, Vol. 4, No. 10, P 40
Who Is Afraid of the Dark? Vandals That's Who!
  American School & University
  May 1978, P 38
Workshop on Student Housing Security
  Foulre, David M.
  Campus Law Enforcement Journal
  Nov–Dec 1975, Vol. 5, No. 6
Yale Univer Crime Prevent Program: An Overview
  Campus Law Enforcement Journal
  Nov–Dec 1978, Vol. 8, No. 6, P 12

DORMITORIES

Dormitory Searches: A Legal Viewpoint
  Williams, Kristi
  Campus Law Enforcement Journal
  Jan–Feb 1976, Vol. 6, No. 1, P 39

A Long Hard Look at Bicycle Safety
  Cleckner, Robert M.
  Police Chief
  Jun 1976, Vol. XCII, No. 6, P 58
Bicycle Parking
  Campus Law Enforcement Journal
  Apr–May, June 1974, Vol. 4, No. 2, P 1
Bike Theft: One of America's Fastest Growing Crimes
  Seaken, Raymond N.
  Campus Law Enforcement Journal
  1975
Campus Apprehensions of College Students
  Milander, H.M.
  Police Chief
  Nov 1972, Vol. XXXIX, No. 11, P 70
Campus Interviews of College Students
  Milander, H.M.
  Campus Law Enforcement Journal
  May–June 1973, Vol. 3, No. 3, P 9
Courage, Skill Meet Crisis
  Johnson, Alex K.
  Campus Law Enforcement Journal
  Jul–Aug 1979, Vol. 9, No. 4, P 29
Crime Prevention in University Residence Halls
  Handley, Jackson R.
  Campus Law Enforcement Journal
  May–June 1980, Vol. 10, No. 3, P 24
Design to Reduce School Property Loss
  Strobel, Walter M.
  School Product News
  Jun 1977
Designing Security in
  Post, Richard S.
  American School & University
  July 1971
Handbook of Building Security Planning and Design
  Powell, John W. and Burton, Lucius W.
  McGraw-Hill Book Co.
  1979, Educational Facilities Chapter
Indecent Exposure
  MacDonald, John M.
  Charles C. Thomas, Publisher
  1973
Searches and Seizures
  Hollister, C.A.
  College Management
  Dec 1972

Trespassing Laws: Can They Be Enforced
  Auman, F.C.
  Campus Law Enforcement Journal
  March–April 1970, Vol., No. 2, P 30
Workshop on Student Housing Security
  Foulre, David M.
  Campus Law Enforcement Journal
  Nov–Dec 1975, Vol. 5, No. 6

DRUGS/CONTROL'D SUBSTANCES

Cocaine Monograph of a User
  Downing, Stephen M.
  The Police Chief
  June 1977, Vol. XLIV, No. 6
Do You Have a Drug Problem?
  Freund, Richard G.
  Campus Law Enforcement Journal
  Oct–Nov–Dec 1973, Vol. 3, No. 3
Drugs and Athletic Performance
  Williams, Melvin H.
  Charles C. Thomas, Publisher
  1974, 212 pages
Licit and Illicit Drugs
  Brecher, Edward M.
  Consumers Union Report
  1972
Phencyclidine–Angel of Death
  Gordon, Roger K.
  Campus Law Enforcement Journal
  Sept–Oct 1978, Vol. 8, No. 5, P 18
Reducing School Violence . . . Drug Abuse
  Harris, Karl B.
  Security World
  Jan 1974, Vol. 11, No. 2, P 18
Street Drugs New Hazards from an Old Problem
  Woodhouse, Edward J.
  Security World
  July–Aug 1972, Vol. 9, No. 7

ELECTRONIC MONITORING

A New Approach to Problems of Technical Security
  Brunskill, Charles
  Campus Law Enforcement Journal
  Jan–Feb 1976, Vol. 6, No. 1, P 43
A University Computer-Controlled Security System
  The Chronicle of Higher Education
  Oct 1976, Vol. XIII, No. 5

Alarms Deter Crime
    Distelhors, Garis F.
    The Police Chief
    June 1978, Vol. XLV, No. 6, P 43
Best's Safety Directory (Updated Annually)
    A.M. Best Co.
    1976, 16th Edition
Design to Reduce School Property Loss
    Strobel, Walter M.
    School Product News
    Jun 1977
Designing Security In
    Post, Richard S.
    American School & University
    July 1971
*Electronic Watchdogs Guard Minnesota
Campus*
    Security Management
    Jan 1974, Vol. 17, No. 6, P 45
Entire District Wired for Security
    American School & University
    June 1978, Vol. 50, No. 10
*Handbook of Building Security Planning
and Design*
    Powell, John W. and Burton, Lucius W.
    McGraw–Hill Book Co.
    1979 Educational Facilities Chapter
Model School Security System Cuts Crime
    Burton, Lucius W.
    Security World
    June 1975
*New Approach to Building Security at
Georgetown U*
    Lamb, Charles E.
    Campus Law Enforcement Journal
    May–June 1976
*Round-up Shows Colleges Secure with
Technology*
    College and University Business
    Aug 1971, Vol. 51, No. 2, P 40
Security Problem? Listen In
    Marshall, Stanley
    American School and University
    Oct 1979, P 92

EMERGENCY PLANNING

. . . Terrorists Getting Ready
    Campus Law Enforcement Journal
    Sept–Oct 1975, Vol. 5, P 10

. . . Utilization of State Police . . . Campus
    Campus Law Enforcement Journal
    Apr–May–June 1974, Vol. 4, No. 2, P 1
*A Campus Plan for Bombs and Bomb
Threats*
    Owens, James
    Campus Law Enforcement Journal
    May–June 1976
*Basic Goal of Emergency Planning
Avoidance*
    Daughters, David L.
    Security Management
    May 1978, Vol. 22, No. 5, P 14
Bomb Threat Response
    Cox, David L. and Demarco, John M.
    Security Management
    Jan 1977, P 8
Bombings, Vandalism and Arson
    Powell, John W.
    Burns Security Institute
*Campus Communication Network Shrinks
Crime Network*
    Security Industry and Product News
    Aug 1976
*Campus Concerts . . . Some Guidelines and
Precautions*
    Nielsen, Robert C.
    Campus Law Enforcement Journal
    Jan–Feb 1976
*Campus Emergency Planning: Some
Suggestions*
    Bernitt, Richard O, and Sims, O.Suthern
    *New Directions in Campus Law
    Enforcement . . .*
    1971
*Civil Defense Director Outlines Contingency
Method*
    Boucher, Roger
    Campus Law Enforcement Journal
    July–Aug 1978, Vol. 8, No. 4, P 15
Countering Terrorism
    Security Suggestions for U.S. Business
    Rep. Abroad
    Jan 1977
*Design for Emergency Response: Facility
Self-Prote*
    Cox, David L.
    Security Management
    May 1978, Vol. 22, No. 5, P 44

First Aid for Emergency Crews: A Manual on Emer . . .
  Young, Carl B., Jr.
  Charles C. Thomas, Publisher
  1970, 192 pages
Industrial Security for Strikes, Riots and Disasters
  Momboisse, Raymond M.
  Charles C. Thomas, Publisher
  1977, 516 pages
Our River Went Wild
  Lenahan, Francis E.
  Campus Law Enforcement Journal
May–Jun 1973, Vol. 3, No. 3
Planning for Large-scale Special Events
  Jands, Jack M.
  The Police Chief
  Jan 1980, Vol. XLVII, No. 1, P 59
Preparing for Disaster with Contingency Planning
  Young, James H. and Smith, Sigmund A.
  College and University Business
  Aug 1971, Vol. 51, No. 2, P 35
Project M.E.D.I.C. Underway at Oklahoma
  Holladay, Tish
  Campus Law Enforcement Journal
  May, Jun 1975
Protecting Against Fire and Vandalism
  Reeves, David
  American School & University
  May 1972, Vol. 44, No. 9, P 62
Protection Against Bombs and Incendiaries: For . . .
  Pike, Earl A.
  Charles C. Thomas, Publisher
  1973, 92 pages
Special Orders for Special Events
  Owens, James
  Campus Law Enforcement Journal
  Jan–Feb 1976, Vol. 6, No. 1, P 37
Strike Procedures for the Campus Security Dept.
  Stump, William
  Campus Law Enforcement Journal
  Mar–Apr 1978, Vol. 8, No. 2, P 32
Terrorist Attacks Present Another Dimension for Em
  D'Addario, Francis M.
  Security Management
  May 1978, Vol. 22, No. 4, P 31

INVESTIGATIONS

. . . Fatal Vehicle Accidents . . . Okla
  Campus Law Enforcement Journal
  Sept, Oct 1974, Vol. 4, No. 3,
A Case for/of Cooperation: It Won't Happen . . .
  Hudson, Jerry E.
  Campus Law Enforcement Journal
  Jan–Feb 1980, Vol. X, No. I, P 30
Arson—A National Crisis
  Gately, Glenn S.
  Security Management
  Aug 1979, P 53
Campus Homicide One Universitys Admin Response
  Tanner, William A. and Sewell, James D.
  Campus Law Enforcement Journal
  Nov–Dec 1978, Vol. 8, No. 6, P 25
Campus Police in Disguise
  Dumas, Paul J.
  Campus Law Enforcement Journal
  Jan–Feb 1977, Vol. 7, No. 1,
Cocaine Monograph of a User
  Downing, Stephen M.
  The Police Chief
  June 1977, Vol. XLIV, No. 6
Colorado State Establishes Human Identification
  Campus Law Enforcement Journal
  May–June 1979, Vol. 9, No. 3, P 20
Hypnosis: An Investigative Tool
  Robinson, Lawrence W.
  Campus Law Enforcement Journal
  Jul–Aug 1979, Vol. 9, No. 4, P 15
Indecent Exposure
  MacDonald, John M.
  Charles C. Thomas, Publisher
  1973
Is FBI Able to Cope with Organized Terror Now?
  Schipp, Bill
  Campus Law Enforcement Journal
  May–June 1978, Vol. 8, No. 3, P 36
Juvenile Delinquency—A Campus Problem
  Bottomly, Edward J.
  Campus Law Enforcement Journal
  Sept–Oct 1978, Vol. 8, No. 5, P 16
Licit and Illicit Drugs
  Brecher, Edward M.
  Consumers Union Report
  1972

Misconceptions Deter Reporting of Sexual
Assaults
   Campus Law Enforcement Journal
   May–June 1978, Vol. 8, No. 3, P 39
Rape Crisis Training
   Nielsen, Robert C.
   Campus Law Enforcement Journal
   Nov, Dec 1976, Vol. 6, No. 6
Street Drugs New Hazards from an Old
Problem
   Woodhouse, Edward J.
   Security World
   July–Aug 1972, Vol. 9, No. 7
The Crime of Arson
   Flanders, David A.
   Campus Law Enforcement Journal
   Mar–Apr 1977, Vol. 7, No. 2
The University Response Team: An
Assessment
   Tanner, William A. and Sewell, James D.
   Campus Law Enforcement Journal
   Nov–Dec 1979, Vol. 9, No. 6, P 28

LAW/LEGAL MATTERS

Dormitory Searches: A Legal Viewpoint
   Williams, Kristi
   Campus Law Enforcement Journal
   Jan–Feb 1976, Vol. 6, No. 1, P 39
. . . State Legislation Affecting Private
Security
   Security Management
   April 1980, Vol. 24, No. 4, P 54
A Legal Overview of the New Student: As
Educational
   Laudicina, Robert A. and Tramutola,
   Joseph L., Jr.
   Charles C. Thomas, Publisher
   1976, P 316
Campus Interviews of College Students
   Milander, H.
   Campus Law Enforcement Journal
   May–June 1973, Vol. 3, No. 3, P 9
Campus Police Liability
   Schmidt, Wayne W.
   Campus Law Enforcement Journal
   May–June 1978, Vol. 8, No. 3, P 33
Canadian News–Dateline Ontario
   McCormick, R.
   Campus Law Enforcement Journal
   May–June 1980, Vol. 10, No. 3, P 35

Case Law for College Security Officers
   Gehring, Donald D.
   Campus Law Enforcement Journal
   Sept, Oct 1975
Citizen's Arrest: The Law of Arrest, Search
and . . .
   Bassiouni, M.C.
   Charles C. Thomas, Publisher
   1977, P 144
College Student and the Courts
   Young, D. Parker
   Published by College Admin . . . Publica-
   tions, Inc.
   1973, With Quarterly Supplements
Confessions and Interrogations After
Miranda
   National District Attorneys Association
   Jan 1972, Revised Dec 1972
Constitutional Parameters of Student
Protest
   Smith
   1, *Journal of Law and Education*, 39
Illinois Supreme Court Upholds U. Ill.
Action . . .
   Campus Law Enforcement Journal
   May–June 1973, Vol. 3, No. 3, P 16
Judicial Remedies for Student Protest
Problems: . . . .
   Hill, Harold N.
   New Directions in Campus Law
   Enforcement: . . .
   1971
Juvenile Delinquency–A Campus Problem
   Bottomly, Edward
   Campus Law Enforcement Journal
   Sept–Oct 1978, Vol. 8, No. 5, P 16
Law and Order on the Campus: Problems
of . . . Police
   Berman
   49, *J. Urban L.*, 513
Legal Aspects of Hospital Security
   Olmstead, John A.
   Security Management
   Sept 1974, Vol. 18, No. 4, P 25
Legal Aspects of Student Dissent and
Discipline
   Young, D. Parker
   Institute of Higher Education Univ of
   Georgia
   1971

Legal Considerations Relative to the
   Authority . . .
      Clancy, Daniel T.
      The Police Chief
      June 1978, Vol. XLV, No. 6, P 26
National Organization in Legal Position of
   Educato
      5401 Southwest Seventh Ave, Topeka,
      Kansas 66606
Police Sue State Union
      Shelton, Pat
      Campus Law Enforcement Journal
      Nov–Dec 1977, Vol. 7, No. 6, P 20
Possible Challenge to Freedom of
   Expression
      Campus Law Enforcement Journal
      July–Aug 1978, Vol. 8, No. 4, P 14
Private Security and Your Local Prosecutor
      Salit, Robert-Ian
      Security Management
      Feb 1978, Vol. 22, No. 2, P 39
Probable Cause
      Stevens, E.H.
      Campus Law Enforcement Journal
      March–April 1976, Vol. 6, No. 2, P 6
Proposed Unified Appeal Procedures
      Nichols, H.E.
      Campus Law Enforcement Journal
      May–June 1980, Vol. 10, No. 3, P 20
Search & Seizure Law Report
      Clark Boardman Co Ltd
      435 Hudson St, NY, NY 10014
Searches and Seizures
      Hollister, C.A.
      College Management
      Dec 1972
State Legislation and Campus Disorders
      Rouland
      1, *Journal of Law and Education,* 231
State Legislative Response to Campus
   Disorder . . .
      10, *Houston Law Review,* 930
The Education Court Digest
      Bund, Emanuel
      Juridical Digests Instit, 1860 Broadway,
      NY, NY, 10023
      Nov 1978, Vol. 22, No. 11
The Law and Private Police
      Kakalik, James S. and Wildhorn, Sorrel
      Nat'l Institute of Law Enforcement and
      Criminal Justice

The Law of Arrest and Search and Seizure:
   A State
      Markle, Arnold
      Charles C. Thomas, Publisher
      1974, 320 pages
The Law of Dissent and Riots
      Bassiouni, M.C.
      Charles C. Thomas, Publisher
      1971, 510 pages
The President's Commission on Campus
   Unrest
      U.S. Government Printing Office
      1970
The Yearbook of Higher Education Law–
   1978
      Young, Parker D.
      National Organization on Legal Problems
      of Educat.
      1978, 209 pages
Trespassing Laws: Can They Be Enforced
      Auman, F.C.
      Campus Law Enforcement Journal
      March–April 1976, Vol. No. 2, P 30

MANUALS/HANDBOOKS

A Basic Manual for Physical Plant
   Administration
      Weber, George O. and Fincham,
      Michael W.
      1974
A Legal Overview of the New Student: As
   Educationa
      Laudicina, Robert A. and Tramutola,
      Joseph L., Jr.
      Charles C. Thomas, Publisher
      1976, P 316
Alternative to Chaos: The Need for
   Professional . . .
      Kassinger, Edward T.
      New Directions in Campus Law
         Enforcement . . .
      1971
Campus Disorders A Symposium of Rel-
   evant Papers
      Assn. of Physical Plant
         Administrators . . . Journal
      1969

*Campus Emergency Planning: Some
Suggestions*
  Bernitt, Richard O. and Sims, O.Suthern
  *New Directions in Campus Law
  Enforcement . . .*
  1971
Campus Fire Safety
  Juillerat, Ernest
  National Fire Prevention Association
  1977, 86 P
*Campus Law Enforcement and Student
Affairs: A Defi*
  Sims, O.Suthern
  *New Directions in Campus Law
  Enforcement: A Handb*
  1971
*Campus Law Enforcement: Town-Gown
Relations*
  Bernitt, Richard O.
  *New Directions in Campus Law
  Enforcement . . .*
  1971
College and University Police Agencies
  Scott, Eric
  Police Services Study Technical Report,
  Ind. Univ.
  Aug 1976
College Student and the Courts
  Young, D. Parker
  Published by College Admin . . .
  Publications, Inc.
  1973, With Quarterly Supplements
*Confessions and Interrogations After
Miranda*
  National District Attorneys
  Association
  Jan 1972, Revised Dec 1972
*Controlling Crime in the School—Handbook
for Admin*
  Vestermark, S.D. and Blauvelt, P.D.
  Parker Publishing Co. Inc., West Nyack,
  NY 10994
  1978, 354 P
Cops on Campus: A Handbook
  College and University Personnel
  Assn. Journal
  April, May 1976, Vol. 27, No. 2
*Educational Aids for Police & Fire Science
Instruc*
  Lansford Publishing Co. PO Box 8711
  San Jose, CA
  March 1978

*Fundamentals of Training for Security
Officers*
  Peel, John D.
  Charles C. Thomas, Publisher
  1975, 340 pages
Guidelines for Security Education
  Kingsbury, Arthur J.
  American Society for Industrial Security
*Handbook of Building Security Planning
and Design*
  Powell, John W. and Burton, Lucius W.
  McGraw-Hill Book Co.
  1979 Educational Facilities Chapter
*Handbook of College and University
Administration*
  Knowles, Asa S.
  McGraw-Hill Book Co.
  1970
Indecent Exposure
  MacDonald, John M.
  Charles C. Thomas, Publisher
*International Encyclopedia of Higher
Education*
  Knowles, Asa S.
  1977, Jossey-Bass Publishers
  1973
Policing Metropolitan America
  Ostrom, Elinor
  Dept. of Political Science, Indiana Univ.
  1977
*Privacy & Security of Criminal History
Information*
  Trubow, G.B.
  National Criminal Justice Information
  & Statistics
  1978, 112 pages
*Risk Management . . . Guidelines for Higher
Education*
  Adams, John F.
  Nacubo Publication
  1972
Search & Seizure Law Report
  Clark Boardman Co., Ltd,
  435 Hudson St. NY, NY 10014
Special Purpose Public Police
  National Institute of Law Enforcement
  and Criminal
  Vol. V; R-873/DOJ

Student Conduct and Campus Law
    Enforcement
    Sims, O.Suthern
    New Directions in Campus Law
        Enforcement: . . .
    1971
The Law and Private Police
    Kakalik, James S. and Wildhorn, Sorrel
    Nat'l Institute of Law Enforcement and
        Criminal Justice
The Law of Arrest and Search and Seizure:
    A State
    Markle, Arnold
    Charles C. Thomas, Publisher
    1974, 320 pages
The Law of Dissent and Riots
    Bassiouni, M.C.
    Charles C. Thomas, Publisher
    1971, 510 pages
The President's Commission on Campus
    Unrest
    U.S. Government Printing Office
    1970
The Role of Campus Security in the College
    Setting
    Gelber, Seymour
    U.S. Government Printing Office
    1972
The Yearbook of Higher Education Law—
    1978
    Young, Parker D.
    National Organization on Legal Problems
        of Educat.
    1978, 209 pages
What Are College Students into These Days?
    Haight, William H.
    National On Campus Report
    March 1978

MEDIA RELATIONS

Campus Homicide One Universitys Admin
    Response
    Tanner, William A. and Sewell, James D.
    Campus Law Enforcement Journal
    Nov–Dec 1978, Vol. 8, No. 6, P 25
Campus Officers Need Recognition
    Sherman, Robert E.
    Campus Law Enforcement Journal
    May–June 1977, Vol. 7, No. 3, P 18

County Defeats Campus But Cindy Is Real
    Winner
    Campus Law Enforcement Journal
    Jan–Feb 1975
Crises Avoidance and Prevention: Com-
    munity Approach
    Hudson, Jerry E.
    Campus Law Enforcement Journal
    May–June 1980, Vol. 10, No. 3, P 40
Excellence A Search . . .
    Shanahan, Michael G.
    Campus Law Enforcement Journal
    May–June 1977, Vol. 7, No. 3, P 22
Local Scouts Explore Police Work
    Fell, Sharon
    Campus Law Enforcement Journal
    Jan–Feb 1976, Vol. 6, No. 1, P 46
PR Department Assists in Crime Prevention
    Campus Law Enforcement Journal
    Sept–Oct 1975
Students Are Invited to Riot at City Hall
    Hansen, David A.
    Police Chief
    May 1974, Vol. XLI, No. 5, P 54
The Necessity for Developing a Statement
    of Policy
    Engel, Robert E.
    Campus Law Enforcement Journal
    Nov–Dec 1976, P 17
The Need to be Recognized
    Gonson, Harvey D.
    Campus Law Enforcement Journal
    Sept, Oct 1974, Vol. 4, No. 3,
The University Response Team: An
    Assessment
    Tanner, William A. Sewell, James D.
    Campus Law Enforcement Journal
    Nov–Dec 1979, Vol. 9, No. 6, P 28
Verne's Views
    McClurg, Verne H.
    Campus Law Enforcement Journal
    May–June 1978, Vol. 8, No. 3, P 42

MEDICAL SCHOOL SECURITY

A Security Dilemma—Medical Institutions
    on Campus
    Cox, Berry, and Sutherland, Donald
    Campus Law Enforcement Journal
    Sept–Oct 1979, Vol. 9, No. 5, P 16

Contemporary Changes in Hospital Security
Glassman, S.A. and Fitzgerald, W.J.
Security Management
Sept 1974, Vol. 18, No. 4, P 18
Hospital Security Guard Training Manual
Wanat, John A. and Brown, John F.
Charles C. Thomas, Publisher
1977, 168 pages
Legal Aspects of Hospital Security
Olmstead, John A.
Security Management
Sept 1974, Vol. 18, No. 4, P 25
Med College of GA Gets Top Safety Award
Campus Law Enforcement Journal
Sept-Oct 74, Vol. 4, No. 3, P 7
Security on a New Medical Campus
McCue, Edward C.
Campus Law Enforcement Journal
Aug-Sept 1975, Vol. 5

MUNICIPAL POLICE RELATIONS

. . . *Utilization of State Police . . . Campus*
Campus Law Enforcement Journal
Apr-May-June 1974, Vol. 4, No. 2, P 1
A Campus Plan for Bombs and Bomb
  Threats
Owens, James
Campus Law Enforcement Journal
May-June 1976
A Message From the Chief: The Commu-
nity's Responsi
Sides, Eugene
Campus Law Enforcement Journal
Nov-Dec 77, Vol. 7, No. 6, P 28
Campus Apprehensions of College Students
Milander, H.M.
Police Chief
Nov 1972, Vol. XXXIX, No. 11, P 70
Factors Affecting the Relationship Between
Public
Neilson, Francis B.
Security Management
Jan 1977, P 22
Juvenile Delinquency—A Campus Problem
Bottomly, Edward J.
Campus Law Enforcement Journal
Sept-Oct 1978, Vol. 8, No. 5, P 16
Kent State Story
Malone, Robert and Eastman, George D.
Police Chief
Nov and Dec Editions

Mass. State Police Academy Supports
  Campus Police
Peckham, Allen
Campus Law Enforcement Journal
Jan-Feb 1976
Police Training Cooperation
Peterson, John A.
Campus Law Enforcement Journal
May-June 1977, Vol. 7, No. 3, P 30
Policing a College Town
Epstein, David G.
Police Chief
Sept 1974, P 20
Preparing for Disaster with Contingency
  Planning
Young, James H. and Smith, Sigmund A.
College and University Business
Aug 1971, Vol. 51, No. 2, P 35
Stadium Rock Concerts
McEntee, Andrew P.
Campus Law Enforcement Journal
May-June 1977, Vol. 7, No. 3, P 46
Students Are Invited to Riot at City Hall
Hansen, David A.
Police Chief
May 1974, Vol. XLI, No. 5, P 54
The Value of Mutual Assistance
Wilson, Etsel A.
Campus Law Enforcement Journal
Jan-Feb 1976, Vol. 6, No. 1, P 47

ORGANIZATION/MANAGEMENT

. . . *Houston Police Standards and Goals*
Kimble, Joseph P.
Campus Law Enforcement Journal
Nov-Dec 1975, Vol. 5, No. 6,
. . . *Methods of Establishing an*
  Intelligence . . .
Weyant, James M.
Campus Law Enforcement Journal
Aug-Sept 1975, Vol. 5, No. 4
. . . *Questions Colleges Are Asking About*
  Security . . .
Powell, John W.
College Management
Oct 1960, Vol. 4, No. 10, P 35
. . . *Threat to Vital Intelligence Opns . . .*
Rampton, Ralph J.
Campus Law Enforcement Journal
Aug-Sept 1975, Vol. 5, No. 4,

A Basic Manual for Physical Plant Administration
   Weber, George O. and Fincham, Michael W.
   1974
A Usable College Security Shift Tour Schedule
   Johnson, Herman B. and Felicetta, Michael J.
   Campus Law Enforcement Journal
   Nov–Dec 1977, Vol. 7, No. 6, P 21
Advantages of State of Florida's Organization Conc
   Fenlon, Timothy P.
   Campus Law Enforcement Journal
   Mar–Apr 1978, Vol. 8, No. 2, P 16
Assessing Your Executive Style
   Nielsen, Robert C. and Shea, Gordon
   Campus Law Enforcement Journal
   Nov–Dec 1979, Vol. 9, No. 6, P 24
Automated Dispatch System for Small Department
   Klein, William G.
   The Police Chief
   Feb 1978, Vol. XLV, No. 2, P 22
Blazers: A National Survey of Police Attitudes
   Wiley, Ronald E. and Cochran, C.D.
   Police Chief
   Jul 1972, Vol. 2, No. 7, P 68
Change in Approach for the Calif. State Univ. & . . .
   Campus Law Enforcement Journal
   May–June 1973, Vol. 3, No. 3, P 70
College and University Police Agencies
   Scott, Eric
   Police Services Study Technical Report, Ind. Univ.
   Aug 1976
Colorado Security Department Combats Crime
   Lindbloom, Kenneth D.
   American School & University
   Mar 1978, Vol. 50, No. 6
Concentrate Your Security . . . Aid in Allocating . . .
   Miller, Floyd G., Ph.D.
   Security World
   May 1973, Vol. 10, No. 5, P 30
Contract Security
   Yon, Stephen E.
   Campus Law Enforcement Journal
   May–June 1977, Vol. 7, No. 3, P 17

Controlling Crime in the School—Handbook for Admin
   Vestermark, S.D. and Blauvelt, P.D.
   Parker Publishing Co. Inc., West Nyack, NY 10994
   1978, 354 P
Democracy in Action for Student Security
   Grossman, Robert J. and MacGregor, Archie
   Campus Law Enforcement Journal
   Aug 1977, Vol. 14, No. 8, P 16
Department Growth and Development
   Johnson, Herman B.
   Campus Law Enforcement Journal
   Sept–Oct 1976
Designing the Job to Motivate
   Baker, Thomas J.
   Campus Law Enforcement Journal
   Jan–Feb 1977, Vol. 7, No. 1
Drastic Change Made at University of Nebraska
   Keith, Tom
   Campus Law Enforcement Journal
   Sept–Oct 1975
Field Placement—Its Use at Niagara College
   Milligan, Bruce C.
   Police Chief
   Nov 1972, Vol. XXXIX, No. 11, P 32
General Organizational And Administrative Concepts
   Nielsen, Swen
   1971
In-service Training & the Four Day Week
   Strunk, Daniel M.
   The Police Chief
   July 1978, Vol. XLV, No. 7
Innovation in Education at New England College
   Powell, Jack and Stuart, Cynthia
   Campus Law Enforcement Journal
   May–June 1973, Vol. 3, No. 3, P 24
Integrated Function—The Role of the Campus Police
   Gunson, Harvey P.
   Campus Law Enforcement Journal
   Nov–Dec 1979, Vol. 9, No. 6, P 40
Keystone Cops—They're Not
   Wykes, Leslie J.
   Campus Law Enforcement Journal
   March–April 1976, Vol. 6, No. 2, P 46

Make Everyone a Manager
  Nielsen, Robert C.
  Campus Law Enforcement Journal
  Jan-Feb 1977, Vol. 7, No. 1,
Management Development: Filling a Need
  Nielsen, Robert C.
  Campus Law Enforcement Journal
  March-April 1979, Vol. 9, No. 2, P 10
Manpower: Make the Most of What You've Got
  Nielsen, Robert C.
  Police Chief
  Jan. 1970, Vol. XLV, No. 1, P 23
Moorhead State University Student Security Program
  Pehler, Michael J.
  Campus Law Enforcement Journal
  Nov-Dec 1977, Vol. 7, No. 6, P 24
Motorcycle Patrol on Campus
  Gunson, Harvey P.
  Campus Law Enforcement Journal
  Mar-Apr 1978, Vol. 8, No. 2, P 10
New Concept Spurs Staffing Survey
  Lloyd, Norman
  Campus Law Enforcement Journal
  March-April 1976, Vol. 6, No. 2, P 46
New Directions in Campus Law Enforcement . . .
  Kassinger, Edward T.
  Law Enforcement Journal
  May-June 1973, Vol. 3, No. 3, P 5
New Security Plan for Univ. of Maryland
  Campus Law Enforcement Journal
  May-June 1973, Vol. 3, No. 3, P 29
Open & Shut Case for Sound Security
  Schnabolk, Charles
  Campus Law Enforcement Journal
  May-June 1973, Vol. 3, No. 3, P 35
Organization of a Campus Security and Safety Unit
  Posey, Robert W.
  School of Law Enforcement Eastern
    Kentucky Univ
  1968
Organization of the Patrol Car
  Kelshaw, Robert W.
  Campus Law Enforcement Journal
  Mar-Apr 1978, Vol. 8, No. 2, P 38
Policing a University Campus—One Approach
  Brug, Richard C.
  Campus Law Enforcement Journal
  May-June 1978, Vol. 8, No. 3, P 19-21

Policing and Securing the Campus . . .
  Calder, James D.
  Police Chief
  Nov 1976, Vol. XLI, No. 11, P 60
Policing Metropolitan America
  Ostrom, Elinor
  Dept. of Political Science, Indiana
    Univ.
  1977
Prediction Personnel Behavior—It's in the Stars
  Nielsen, Robert C.
  Campus Law Enforcement Journal
  Nov-Dec 1979, Vol. 9, No. 6, P 26
Protective Services Objectives . . . MSU
  Campus Law Enforcement Journal
  Sept, Oct 1974, Vol. 4, No. 3,
Public Safety and Security: Combining Concepts at
  Campus Law Enforcement Journal
  Sept-Oct 1975
Public Safety Concern in Higher Education
  Kassinger, Edward T.
  Campus Law Enforcement Journal
  Jan-Feb 1979, Vol. 9, No. 1, P 6
Risk Management for Public Schools
  Betterley, Delbert A.
  American School and University
  Oct 1978, Vol. 51, No. 2, P 60
Safety and Security in a School Environment
  Grealy, Joseph
  Security World
  Jan 1974, Vol. 11, No. 2, P 16
Safety and Security Must Go Hand in Hand
  Loyd, E.R.
  Security Management
  Nov 1978, Vol. 22, No. 11, P 21
Seattle's Satellite Campus
  Moloney, Niel W.
  Police Chief
  Sept 1973, Vol. XL, No. 9, P 34
Security
  College and University Business
    Administration
  July 1974
Security on a New Medical Campus
  McCue, Edward C.
  Campus Law Enforcement Journal
  Aug-Sept 1975, Vol. 5

Security or Police Services or Public Safety . . .
Kassinger, Edward T.
Campus Law Enforcement Journal
March–April 1976, Vol. 6, No. 2, P 16

Setting Up a Strong Univ Security Department
Kennedy, Verne C.
American School & University
Feb 1972, Vol. 44, No. 6, P 30

Student Auxiliary . . . *Penn State*
Seip, David P.
Campus Law Enforcement Journal
Nov–Dec 1975, Vol. 5, No. 6,

Student Employees Ease Manpower Problem at U. Conn.
Nielsen, Robert C.
Campus Law Enforcement Journal
May–June 1973, Vol., 3, No. 3, P 30

Students Provide Their Own Security
Hickey, John M.
Campus Law Enforcement Journal
Nov–Dec 1976, Vol. 6, No. 6

Tackling Scheduling & Deployment Problems
Security Management
May 1978, Vol. 22, No. 4, P 24

The Future of Campus Security
Powell, John W.
Security World
Feb 1966, Vol. 3, No. 2, P 30

The Part-Time Student Employee . . .
Walker, Wynn C.
Campus Law Enforcement Journal
May–June 1976

The Private Security and Public Police Interface
Deck, Carol
Security World
Aug 1977, Vol. 14, No. 8, P 16

The Training, Licensing and Guidance of Private . .
Peel, John D.
Charles C. Thomas, Publisher
1973, P 288

The Use of Student Patrols in 1975
Drapeau, Robert F.
Campus Law Enforcement Journal
Jan–Feb 1977, Vol. 7, No. 1,

The UWPD/NFL Draft (Re: Shift Assignments – Editor)
Shanahan, Michael G.
Police Chief
Aug 1979, Vol. XLVI, No. 8, P 59

There's a New Look in L . . . *E* . . . *at Pima College*
Guynn, Arnold and Leon, Moses A.
Police Chief
Nov 1973, Vol. XL, No. 11, P 61

Trying to be Objective About Our Objectives
Kimble, Joseph P.
Campus Law Enforcement Journal
May–June 1977, Vol. 7, No. 3, P 36

Trying to be Objective About Our Objective
Kimble, Joseph P.
Campus Law Enforcement Journal
Sept–Oct 1978, Vol. 8, No. 5, P 28

PERIODICALS/PUBLICATIONS

American School and University
North American Publishing Company
401 N. Broad St., Phil., Pa 19018

Assets Protection
International Journal of Security & Investigation
P.O. Box 5327 Madison, WI 53705

College & University Business
McGraw-Hill Publications
230 W. Monroe, Chicago IL 60606

I.A.C.P. Law Enforcement Review
I.A.C.P., 11 Firstfield Rd, Gaithersburg, MD
Monthly

LEAA Newsletter, Published Monthly by
U.S. Dept of Justice, LEAA Division
Washington, D.C. 20531

National Organization in Legal Position of Educato
5401 Southwest Seunth Ave, Topeka, KS 66606

Police Chief
Official Publication of the I.A.C.P.
I.A.C.P., Gaithersburg, MD 20760

Police on Campus, Parts 1 and 2
Smith, Eugene N.
Motorola Teleprograms, Inc.
Film, 18 minutes each, 1976

School Product News
  P.O. Box 91368, Cleveland, Ohio, 44101
  Monthly
Security Industry and Product News
  PTN Publishing Corp, 250 Fulton Ave,
  Hampstead, NY
Security Industry and Product News
  PO Box 13240, Philadelphia, PA 19101
  Monthly (free)
Security Management
  American Society of Industrial Security
  2000 K St. N.W., Wash., D.C. 20006
Security World
  The Magazine of Professional Security
  Administrato
  PO. Box 272, Culver City, CA 90230
The Education Court Digest
  Bund, Emanuel
  Juridical Digests Institute, 1860 Broad-
  way, NY, NY 10023
  Nov 1978, Vol. 22, No. 11

PHYSICAL PLANT

Better Lighting With Less Energy
  Meyers, Alan R.
  American School and University
  Sept 1979, P 30
Crime Prevention and the Architects
  Fennelly, Lawrence J.
  Assets Protection
  May–June 1979, Vol. 4, No. 2, P 30
Design to Reduce School Property Loss
  Strobel, Walter M.
  School Product News
  Jun 1977
Designing Security in
  Post, Richard S.
  American School and University
  July 1971
Improved Pedestrian Lighting on Campus
  Molte, John
  Security Management
  May 1977, Vol. 2, No. 2, P 30
Lighting for Safety and Security
  McGowan, T.K.
  *Reviews in College and University
  Business*
  Aug 1971, Vol. 51, No. 2, P 42

*Security for Colleges, Universities and
  Schools*
  Powell, John W.
  *Designer's Handbook of Building
  Security*
  McGraw–Hill, 1979, Chapter 24
Workshop on Student Housing Security
  Foulre, David M.
  Campus Law Enforcement Journal
  Nov–Dec 1975, Vol. 5, No. 6

POLICE AS EDUCATORS

*Academic Internship: An Operating Lab
  Approach*
  McEntee, A.P.
  Campus Law Enforcement Journal
  March–April, 1979, Vol. 9, No. 2, P 21
*Bringing University Police into the
  Academic Comm*
  Evangelide, Alice S. and Browner,
  Kathleen S.
  Campus Law Enforcement Journal
  July–Aug 1976, Vol. 4
*Bringing University Police into the
  Academic Commu*
  The Journal of the College & University
  Personnel
  April–May 1976
Designing a Slide-Tape Presentation
  Low, William C.
  Campus Law Enforcement Journal
  May–June 1977, Vol. 7, No. 3, P 49
*Freshmen . . . Crime Prevention Slide
  Program*
  McAuliffe, John C.
  Campus Law Enforcement Journal
  May–June 1977, Vol. 7, No. 3, P 52
*Integrated Function–The Role of the
  Campus Police*
  Gunson, Harvey P.
  Campus Law Enforcement Journal
  Nov–Dec 1979, Vol. 9, No. 6, P 40
Law Enforcement: The Officer as Educator
  McDaniel, William E.
  *New Directions in Campus Law
  Enforcement: . . .*
  1971
Student and Teacher The Dual Role
  Nielsen, Robert C.
  Campus Law Enforcement Journal
  Oct–Nov–Dec 1973, Vol. 3, No.4, P 5

*Student Conduct and Campus Law
  Enforcement*
  Sims, O. Suthern
  *New Directions in Campus Law
    Enforcement:* . . .
  1971

POLICE VS. GUARDS

*. . . State Legislation Affecting Private
  Security*
  Security Management
  April 1980, Vol. 24, No. 4, P 54
A Short History of Private Security
  Chamberlin, Charles S.
  Assets Protection
  July-Aug 1979. Vol. 4, No. 3, P 35
*Advantages of State of Florida's Organiza-
  tion Conc*
  Fenlon, Timothy P.
  Campus Law Enforcement Journal
  Mar-Apr 1978, Vol. 8, No. 2, P 16
Are We Private Police or Security Guard
  Kirkley, James A.
  The Police Chief
  June 1978, Vol. XLV, No. 6, P 36
*Building a Professional Complement to
  Law* . . .
  Criscuoli, E.J.
  The Police Chief
  June 1978, Vol. XLV, No. 6, P 28
*Change in Approach for the Calif. State
  Univ. &* . . .
  Campus Law Enforcement Journal
  May-June 1973, Vol. 3, No. 3, P 70
Choosing Contract or Proprietary Security
  Cohen, Joseph
  Security Management
  Oct 1979, P 26
*Code of Ethics for Private Security
  Management* . . .
  The Police Chief
  June 1978, Vol. XLV, No. 6, P 49
Contract Security
  Yon, Stephen E.
  Campus Law Enforcement Journal
  May-June 1977, Vol. 7, No. 3, P 17
Cops or Guards
  Gorda, Bernard L.
  Security Management
  Nov 1975

*Don't Call Him a Guard . . . Unless That's
  All He Does*
  Lang, James C.
  Security Industry and Product News
  June 1979, Vol. 8, No. 6, P 24
*Getting Off on the Right Foot With
  Contract* . . .
  Cumbow, Thomas L.
  Security Management
  Nov 78, Vol. 22, No. 11, P 14
Guard Forces (Direct Hire or Contract)
  Shurr, Robert
  Security Management
  Jan 1976, Vol. 19, No. 6, P 42
In-House Guards or Contract Service
  Security Industry and Product News
  Dec 1979, Vol. 8, No. 12, P 24
In-House Guards or Contract Service
  Essey, Richard P.
  Security Industry and Product News
  Sept 1979, Vol. 8, No. 9, P 26
Keystone Cops—They're Not
  Wykes, Leslie J.
  Campus Law Enforcement Journal
  March-April 1976, Vol. 6, No. 2, P 46
*Legal Considerations Relative to the
  Authority* . . .
  Clancy, Daniel T.
  The Police Chief
  June 1978, Vol. XLV, No. 6, P 26
*New Directions in Campus Law
  Enforcement* . . .
  Kassinger, Edward T.
  Law Enforcement Journal
  May-June 1973, Vol. 3, No. 3, P 5
*Personal Privacy in an Information
  Society*
  Privacy Protection Study Commission
  1977 (Available Govt. Prnt. Off.)
Police & Private Security
  Shook, Howard C.
  The Police Chief
  June 1978, Vol. XLV, No. 6, P 8
Private and Public Security: Three Views
  Spain, Norman M. and Elkin, Gary L.
  Security World
  Aug 1979, Vol. 16, No. 8, P 32-42
Private Guards: A Viewpoint
  Rockwell, Robert R.
  Security Management
  Sept 1975, Vol. 19, No. 4, P 2

Private Security
  LEAA
  Report of the Task Force on Private
    Security
  Dec 1976
Private Security and Your Local Prosecutor
  Salit, Robert-Ian
  Security Management
  Feb 1978, Vol. 22, No. 2, P 39
Private Security—Some Comments
  Gray, Harold W.
  The Police Chief
  June 1978, Vol. XLV, No. 6, P 34
*Security or Police Services or Public
  Safety . . .*
  Kassinger, Edward T.
  Campus Law Enforcement Journal
  March–April 1976, Vol. 6, No. 2, P 16
Special Purpose Public Police
  National Institute of Law Enforcement
    and Crimnal
  Vol. V; R-873/DOJ
  The Law and Private Police
  Kakalik, James S. and Wildhorn, Sorrel
  Nat'l Institute of Law Enforcement and
    Criminal Justice
*The Private Security and Public Police
  Interface*
  Deck, Carol
  Security World
  Aug 1977, Vol. 14, No. 8, P 16
*The Training, Licensing and Guidance of
  Private . .*
  Peel, John D.
  Charles C. Thomas, Publisher
  1973, P 288
Two Armies: One Flag
  Kobetz, Richard W. and Cooper, H.H.
  The Police Chief
  June 1978, P 31
*Which Guard Service to Use? Its Simple
  Arithmetic*
  Doughty, Norman E.
  Security Management
  Nov 1978, Vol. 22, No. 11, P 18
Why You Should Not Rent a Cop
  Powell, John W.
  College Management
  Nov–Dec 1974, P 33

PRIVACY OF INFORMATION

Case Law for College Security Officers
  Gehring, Donald D.
  Campus Law Enforcement Journal
  Sept, Oct 1975
College Student and the Courts
  Young D. Parker
  Published by College Admin . . .
    Publications, Inc.
  1973, With Quarterly Supplements
Federal Register Report . . . Privacy
  Campus Law Enforcement Journal
  May, Jun 1975
*Feds Publish Final Regulations . . .
  Privacy Rights*
  Campus Law Enforcement Journal
  July–Aug 1976, Vol. 4
*No More "Brats" or "Bastards" for the
  Record*
  Campus Law Enforcement Journal
  Jan–Feb 1975
*Norwood Gets Clarification on Buckley
  Amendment*
  McFee, Thomas S.
  Campus Law Enforcement Journal
  Nov, Dec, 1976, Vol. 6, No. 6
*Privacy & Security of Criminal History
  Information*
  Trubow, G.B.
  National Criminal Justice Information
    & Statistics
  1978, 112 pages
Privacy Buckley Amendment
  Campus Law Enforcement Journal
  July–Aug 1976, Vol. 4,
*Public Welfare, "Federal Register Explains
  . . . Privacy*
  Campus Law Enforcement Journal
  May–June 1976
*Recent Developments & Trends in the
  Field of . . .*
  Eavenson, Chandler
  Campus Law Enforcement Journal
  Jan–Feb 1976, Vol. 6, No. 1, P 33

PROFESSIONALISM/CAREERS

A Giant Step Toward Professionalism
  Hudson, Jerry E.
  Campus Law Enforcement Journal
  Sept–Oct 1976, P 25

A Short History of Private Security
  Chamberlin, Charles S.
  Assets Protection
  July–Aug 1979, Vol. 4, No. 3, P 35
Aims and Achievement Committee Report
  Stormer, David E. and Brook, John E.
  Campus Law Enforcement Journal
  Aug–Sept 1975, Vol. 5
*Alternative to Chaos: The Need for
  Professional . . .*
  Kassinger, Edward T.
  *New Directions in Campus Law
  Enforcement . . .*
  1971
Assessing Your Executive Style
  Nielsen, Robert C. and Shea, Gordon
  Campus Law Enforcement Journal
  Nov–Dec 1979, Vol. 9, No. 6, P 24
*Attracting College Grads to Police
  Department*
  Hamilton, Lander C. and Bimstein,
  Donald
  Police Chief
  Aug 1972, Vol XXXIX, No. 8, P 40
*Be Practical Imaginative, and Resourceful
  (Keynote)*
  McAuliffe, John C.
  Campus Law Enforcement Journal
  Jul–Aug 1979, Vol. 9, No. 4, P 6
*Bringing University Police into the Aca-
  demic Comm*
  Evangelide, Alice S. and Browner,
  Kathleen S.
  Campus Law Enforcement Journal
  July–Aug 1976, Vol. 4
*Bringing University Police into the Academic
  Commu*
  *The Journal of the College & University
  Personnel*
  April–May 1976
Campus Officers Need Recognition
  Sherman, Robert E.
  Campus Law Enforcement Journal
  May–June 1977, Vol. 7, No. 3, P 18
Campus Police: The New Professionals
  Nichols, David
  American School and University
  Oct 1979, P 70
Campus Security–A Perspective
  Powell, John W.
  American School and University
  July 1971

*Campus Security Needs . . . Emphasis on
  People Probs.*
  Powell, John W.
  College and University Business
  April 1970, Vol. 48, No. 4, P 94
*Campus Security Today: Progressive But
  Sensitive*
  Powell, John W.
  American School and University
  Oct 1972, Vol. 44, No. 14, P 17
*Campus Security . . . Take More Than
  Locks and Cops*
  Post, Richard S.
  College and University Business
  Aug 1971, Vol. 51, No. 2, P 33
Campus Security: Professionalism Counts
  American School and University
  Dec 1977, Vol. 50, No. 4, P 40
Careers in Campus Policing
  Kimble, Joseph P.
  Campus Law Enforcement Journal
  Jan–Feb 1975
*Change in Approach for the Calif. State
  Univ. & . . .*
  Campus Law Enforcement Journal
  May–June 1973, Vol. 3, No. 3, P 70
*Changing the Program . . "Changing
  Responsibility. ."*
  Norwood, Billy T.
  Campus Law Enforcement Journal
  July–Aug 1978, Vol. 8, No. 4, P 11
*Code of Ethics for Private Security
  Management . . .*
  The Police Chief
  June 1978, Vol. XLV, No. 6, P 49
*Death & Disability Benefits for Public
  Safety Empl*
  Heath, Edwin D.
  The Police Chief
  May 1978, Vol. XLV, No. 5, P 33
Department Growth and Development
  Johnson, Herman B.
  Campus Law Enforcement Journal
  Sept–Oct 1976
Designing the Job to Motivate
  Baker, Thomas J.
  Campus Law Enforcement Journal
  Jan–Feb 1977, Vol. 7, No. 1
*Effectiveness of Campus Security . . .:
  An Analysis*
  Willard, Nesley
  Campus Law Enforcement Journal
  Sept–Oct 1979, Vol. 9, No. 5, P 18

Emerging Challenges . . . In a Changing
World
Nielsen, Robert C. and Shea, Gordon F.
The Police Chief
Nov 1979, P 28
Excellence A Search . . .
Shanahan, Michael G.
Campus Law Enforcement Journal
May–June 1977, Vol. 7, No. 3, P 22
Feedback–Perspectives
Vanderklis, C.A.
Campus Law Enforcement Journal
Mar–Apr 1980, Vol. 10, No. 2, P 28
General Organizational and Administrative
Concepts
Nielsen, Swen
1971
Georgia's Security Staff Stresses Services
American School and University
Jan 1973, Vol. 42, No. 11, P 28
Going Beyond Handcuffs 101
McGrath, Noreen
The Chronicle of Higher Education
Nov 27, 1978, P 3
Helping Police with Emotional Problems
Arkin, Joseph
Campus Law Enforcement Journal
Apr–May–Jun 1974, Vol. 4, No. 2, P 6
Hood Reflects on 40-Year Career
Hood, Burrel S.
Campus Law Enforcement Journal
Jan–Feb 1978, Vol. 8, No. 1, P 42
How Big Cities Train for Security . . .
Creekmore, Edward L.
Security World
Jan 1974, Vol. 11, No. 2, P 28
IACUSD & Other Professional Organization
Kassinger, Edward T.
Campus Law Enforcement Journal
Jan–Feb 1978, Vol. 8, No. 1, P 33
IACUSD: In Our Nations Service
Witsil, Jerry
Campus Law Enforcement Journal
July–Aug 1977, Vol. 7, No. 4
Integrated Function–The Role of the
Campus Police
Gunson, Harvey P.
Campus Law Enforcement Journal
Nov–Dec 1979, Vol. 9, No. 6, P 40

Kent State Response: Professionalism and
Patience
Malone, Robert and Winkler, Robert
Campus Law Enforcement Journal
Jan–Feb 1978, Vol. 8, No. 1, P 6
Professionalizing Campus Security
Powell, John W.
Security World
May 1967, P 23
Professional Standards Committee Report
Campus Law Enforcement Journal
July–Aug 1976, Vol. 4
Protective Services Objectives . . . MSU
Campus Law Enforcement Journal
Sept, Oct 1974, Vol. 4, No. 3,
Puritan Dilemma Is 74 Challenge
Kassinger, Edward T.
Campus Law Enforcement Journal
Jul–Aug 1974, Vol. 4, No. 3,
Rambling on "Professionalism"
Hudson, Jerry E.
Campus Law Enforcement Journal
May–June 1978, Vol. 8, No. 3, P 24–25
Retreads, Movers, and Shakers, Keynote
Address
McDaniel, William E.
Campus Law Enforcement Journal
Aug–Sept 1975, Vol. 5, No. 4, P 22
School Security Association Starts Up
Grealy, Joseph
American School and University
July 1972, Vol. 44, No. 11, P 16
School Security: An Emerging
Professionalism
Powell, John W.
American School and University
July 1972, Vol. 44, No. 11, P 12
Security
College and University Business
Administration
July 1974, Third Edition, P 125
Security for Colleges, Universities and
Schools
Powell, John W.
Designer's Handbook of Building
Security
McGraw–Hill, 1979
Special Purpose Public Police
National Institute of Law Enforcement
and Crimnal
Vol. V: R-873/DOJ

*Student Conduct and Campus Law
Enforcement*
    Sims, O. Suthern
    *New Directions in Campus Law
    Enforcement: . . .*
    1971
*The Chief's Challenge: Providing a Full
Range . . .*
    Ven Eepoel, Vicki V.
    Campus Law Enforcement Journal
    Sept–Oct 1975
The Future of Campus Security
    Powell, John W.
    Security World
    Feb 1966, Vol. 3, No. 2, P 30
*The History and Proper Role of Campus
Secty. , Pt I*
    Powell, John W.
    Security World
    Mar 1971, Vol. 8, No. 4, P 18
*The History and Proper Role of Campus
Secty., Pt II*
    Powell, John W.
    Security World
    Apr 1971, Vol. 8, No. 4, P 19
*The New Breed: College and University
Police*
    Hollomon, Frank C.
    Police Chief
    Feb 1972, P 41
Law Enforcement: The Officer as Educator
    McDaniel, William E.
    *New Directions in Campus Law
    Enforcement: . . .*
    1971
*Liberating Lawyers: Remembering Mr.
Vogel*
    Trachtenbe, Stephen J.
    Campus Law Enforcement Journal
    Nov–Dec 1977, Vol. 7, No. 6, P 17
Make Everyone a Manager
    Nielsen, Robert
    Campus Law Enforcement Journal
    Jan–Feb 1977, Vol. 7, No. 1,
Management Development: Filling a Need
    Nielsen, Robert C.
    Campus Law Enforcement Journal
    Sept–Oct 1979. Vol. 9, No. 5, P 26
Management Development: Filling a Need
    Nielsen, Robert C.
    Campus Law Enforcement Journal
    March–April 1979, Vol. 9, No. 2, P 10

*Mgt-By-Objectives in Law Enforcement
Agencies . . .*
    Skinner, Gilbert and Sullivan, John
    Campus Law Enforcement Journal
    Sept–Oct 76, Vol. 6, No. 5, P 20
*New Directions in Campus Law
Enforcement . . .*
    Kassinger, Edward T.
    Law Enforcement Journal
    May–June 1973, Vol. 3, No. 3 P 5
Of Profiles and Accreditation
    Eastman, George D. and Malone, Robert
    Campus Law Enforcement Journal
    May–June 1980, Vol. 10, No. 3, P 48
*Police Professionalism: A New Look at an
Old Topic*
    Mecum, Richard V.
    Police Chief
    Aug 1979, Vol. XLVI, No. 8, P 46
*Police Training The Quest for
Professionalism*
    Nielsen, Robert C.
    Campus Law Enforcement Journal
    Apr–May–Jun 1974, Vol. 4, No. 2, P 6
Policing a College Town
    Epstein, David G.
    Police Chief
    Sept 1974, P 20
Problems in Police Management Transition
    Kimble, Joseph P.
    Campus Law Enforcement Journal
    Nov–Dec 1976
Professional Campus Law Enforcement . . .
    Kassinger, Edward T.
    *New Directions in Campus Law
    Enforcement . . .*
    1971
Professional Programs . . . Atlanta
    Hopewell, Walter C.
    Campus Law Enforcement Journal
    Mar–Apr 1977, Vol. 7, No. 2,
Professional Standards Committee Report
    Campus Law Enforcement Journal
    Aug–Sept 1975
*Professionalism of Police: Proceed With
Caution*
    Brown, Gary E.
    The Police Chief
    Nov 1979, P 22

The Policeman's Image
Daniels, Charles B.
Campus Law Enforcement Journal
Apr–May–Jun 1974, Vol. 4, No. 2, P 3
The Role of Campus Security in the College Setting
Gelber, Seymour
U.S. Government Printing Office
1972
The Well Trained Professional Police Officer
Campus Law Enforcement Journal
Aug–Sept 1975, Vol. 5
Training for Effective Supervision: A Model Program
Jennings, Stephen G. and Dileo Etal, Jean C.
Campus Law Enforcement Journal
Nov–Dec 1978, Vol. 8, No. 6, P 35
Trying To Be Objective About Our Objectives
Kimble, Joseph P.
Campus Law Enforcement Journal
May–June 1977, Vol. 7, No. 3, P 36
Trying To Be Objective About Our Objective
Kimble, Joseph P.
Campus Law Enforcement Journal
Sept–Oct 1978, Vol. 8, No. 5, P 28
University Police Selection Procedures
Sewell, James D. and Bromley, Max L.
Campus Law Enforcement Journal
Mar–Apr 1980, Vol. 10, No. 2, P 18
Wayne State Dept of Public Safety Highly Prof . . .
Foss, Vern
Campus Law Enforcement Journal
May–June 1973, Vol. 3, No. 3, P 31
What Makes a Good Police Executive
Gugas, Chris, Sr.
Security World
Jun 1977, Vol. 14, No. 6, P 24
What Professor Learned When He Became a Cop
Kirkham, George L.
Campus Law Enforcement Journal
Sept 1974, Vol. 4, No. 3,
With Whom Would You Share the Risk?
Hudson, Jerry E.
Campus Law Enforcement Journal
Mar–Apr 1978, Vol. 8, No. 2, P 12

PUBLIC SAFETY

. . . Guidelines: Police Role in Environmental Safety
Greenberg, Martin A.
The Police Chief
Nov 1979, P 48
Administrator's View of the Public Safety Division
Armstrong, Richard C.
Campus Law Enforcement Journal
Nov–Dec 1979, Vol. 9, No. 6, P 46
Advantages . . . Combining Security and Safety . . .
Okaty, George J.
Campus Law Enforcement Journal
Jan–Feb 1980, Vol. X, No. I, P 27
Med College of Ga Gets Top Safety Award
Campus Law Enforcement Journal
Sept–Oct 1974, Vol. 4, No. 3, P 7
New Directions in Campus Law Enforcement . . .
Kassinger, Edward T.
Law Enforcement Journal
May–June 1973, Vol. 3, No. 3, P 5
Preparing for Disaster with Contingency Planning
Young, James H. and Smith, Sigmund A.
College and University Business
Aug 1971, Vol. 51, No. 2, P 35
Protective Services Objectives . . . MSU
Campus Law Enforcement Journal
Sept, Oct 1974, Vol. 4, No. 3,
Public Safety and Security: Combining Concepts at
Campus Law Enforcement Journal
Sept–Oct 1975
Public Safety Concern in Higher Education
Kassinger, Edward T.
Campus Law Enforcement Journal
Jan–Feb 1979, Vol. 9, No. 1, P 6
Public Safety for the Small College
Schachtsie, David
Campus Law Enforcement Journal
May–June 1980, Vol. 10, No. 3, P 6
Public Safety on the Private Campus
Dumas, Paul J.
Campus Law Enforcement Journal
Jan–Feb 1975

Security or Police Services or Public Safety . . .
  Kassinger, Edward T.
  Campus Law Enforcement Journal
  March–April 1976, Vol. 6, No. 2, P 16

REPORTING/RECORDKEEPING

Crime on the Campus 1977
  McGovern, James L.
  Campus Law Enforcement Journal
  Jan–Feb 1979, Vol. 9, No. 1, P 30
Development of a Model Records System
  Schleich, Howard H.
  Campus Law Enforcement Journal
  Sept–Oct 1976, Vol. 6, No. 5, P 15
Dictionary of Security Terms
  Fuss, Eugene
  Campus Law Enforcement Journal
  May–June 1973, Vol. 3, No. 3, P 41

SAFETY

. . . Guidelines: Police Role in Environmental Safety
  Greenberg, Martin A.
  The Police Chief
  Nov 1979, P 48
A Campus Plan for Bombs and Bomb Threats
  Owens, James
  Campus Law Enforcement Journal
  May–June 1976
Advantages . . . Combining Security and Safety . . .
  Okaty, George J.
  Campus Law Enforcement Journal
  Jan–Feb 1980, Vol. X, No. I, P 27
Best's Safety Directory (Updated Annually)
  A.M. Best Co.
  1976, 16th Edition
Better Security Through LPS Lighting
  Lewis, Robert A.
  Security Management
  April 1978, Vol. 22, No. 4
Bomb Threat Response
  Cox, David L. and DeMarco, John M.
  Security Management
  Jan 1977, P 8

Campus Fire Safety
  Juillerat, Ernest
  National Fire Prevention Association
  1977, 86 pages
Fire Safety Education at University of Conn.
  Kohrs, Kevin
  Campus Law Enforcement Journal
  Jan–Feb 1979, Vol. 9, No. 1, P 14
First Aid for Emergency Crews: A Manual on Emer . . .
  Young, Carl B., Jr.
  Charles C. Thomas: Publisher
  1970, 192 pages
Helping the Handicapped—An Ongoing Program
  Nielsen, Robert C.
  Campus Law Enforcement Journal
  July–Aug 1977, Vol. 7, No. 4
Lighting for Safety and Security
  McGowan, T.K.
  Reviews in College and University Business
  Aug 1971, Vol. 51, No. 2, P 42
Med College of Ga Gets Top Safety Award
  Campus Law Enforcement Journal
  Sept–Oct 1974, Vol. 4, No. 3, P 7
Organization of a Campus Security and Safety Unit
  Posey, Robert W.
  School of Law Enforcement Eastern Kentucky Univ
  1968
Pre-Planning for Fire at the College Community
  Baldanza, Mauro V.
  Campus Law Enforcement Journal
  Nov–Dec 1979, Vol. 9, No. 6, P 14
Protecting Against Fire and Vandalism
  Reeves, David
  American School and University
  May 1972, Vol. 44, No. 9, P 62
Protection of Public Figures: A Challenge for Univ
  Saye, David
  Campus Law Enforcement Journal
  Nov–Dec 1977, Vol. 7, No. 6, P 6
Public Safety and Security: Combining Concepts at
  Campus Law Enforcement Journal
  Sept–Oct 1975

SECURITY HARDWARE

SEX CRIMES

University of Texas Acts to Curb Rape
  Campus Law Enforcement Journal
  Jan–Feb 1975

  ❧

SPECIAL APPLICATIONS

. . . Methods of Establishing an
  Intelligence . . .
  Weyant, James M.
  Campus Law Enforcement Journal
  Aug–Sept 1975, Vol. 5, No. 4,
. . . Threat to Vital Intelligence Opns . . .
  Rampton, Ralph J.
  Campus Law Enforcement Journal
  Aug–Sept 1975, Vol. 5, No. 4,
A Case for/of Cooperation: It Won't
  Happen . . .
  Hudson, Jerry E.
  Campus Law Enforcement Journal
  Jan–Feb 1980, Vol. X, No. 1, P 30
A Long Hard Look at Bicycle Safety
  Cleckner, Robert M.
  Police Chief
  Jun 1976, Vol. XCII, No. 6, P 58
A Money Mover
  Chafin, Saul
  Campus Law Enforcement Journal
  Mar–Apr 1978, Vol. 8, No. 2, P 36
A New Service Concept—And It's Free
  Burke, Mary E.
  Campus Law Enforcement Journal
  Mar–Apr 1980, Vol. 10, No. 2, P 38
Art Theft and the Need for Central Archive
  Mason, Donald L.
  The Police Chief
  June 1977, Vol. XLIV, No. 6
Auditor Security Officer Relationships
  Marsh, Quinton N.
  Security Management
  Nov 1975, Vol. 19, No. 5, P 22
Big Results with Little Motorcycles
  Nielsen, Robert C.
  Police Chief
  Sept 1978
Bike Theft: One of Americas Fastest Grow-
  ing Crime
  Seaken, Raymond N.
  Campus Law Enforcement Journal
  1975

Blazers: A National Survey of Police
  Attitudes
  Wiley, Ronald E. and Cochran, C.D.
  Police Chief
  Jul 1972, Vol. 2, No. 7, P 68
Campus Police in Disguise
  Dumas, Paul J.
  Campus Law Enforcement Journal
  Jan–Feb 1977, Vol. 7, No. 1,
Campus Security Problems and Solutions
  Wilson, Etsel A.
  Campus Law Enforcement Journal
  Jan–Feb 1976
CCTV System Design for School Security
  Kravontka, Stanley J.
  Security World
  Jan 1974, Vol. 11, No. 2, P 22
CMU Uses Bookmark to Curb Larcenies
  McAuliffe, John C.
  Campus Law Enforcement Journal
  Sept–Oct 1976, Vol. 6, No. 5, P 23
Colorado Security Department Combats
  Crime
  Lindbloom, Kenneth D.
  American School and University
  Mar 1978, Vol. 50, No. 6
Colorado State Establishes Human
  Identification
  Campus Law Enforcement Journal
  May–June 1979, Vol. 9, No. 3, P 20
Courage, Skill Meet Crisis
  Johnson, Alex K.
  Campus Law Enforcement Journal
  Jul–Aug 1979, Vol. 9, No. 4, P 29
Decalcomanias on Campus
  Hendricks, Jerry P. and Jackson, S.W.
  Campus Law Enforcement Journal
  Jan–Feb 1979, Vol. 9, No. 1, P 22
Experts Probe Solutions to Art Theft
  Security Management
  Oct 1979, P 25
Forcible Rape: Influence of the Victim
  Sewell, James D.
  Campus Law Enforcement Journal
  Sept–Oct 1975
Freshmen . . . Crime Prevention Slide
  Program
  McAuliffe, John C.
  Campus Law Enforcement Journal
  May–June 1977, Vol. 7, No. 3, P 52

Georgia's Security Staff Stresses Services
    American School and University
    Jan 1973, Vol. 42, No. 11, P 28
Greek System: Internal Theft . . . How to
    Approach it
    Roling, Ann
    Campus Law Enforcement Journal
    Sept–Oct 1979, Vol. 9, No. 5, P 31
Helping the Handicapped–An Ongoing
    Program
    Nielsen, Robert C.
    Campus Law Enforcement Journal
    July–Aug 1977, Vol. 7, No. 4
Hypnosis: An Investigative Tool
    Robinson, Lawrence W.
    Campus Law Enforcement Journal
    Jul–Aug 1979, Vol. 9, No. 4, P 15
Industrial Security for Strikes, Riots and
    Disaste
    Momboisse, Raymond M.
    Charles C. Thomas, Publisher
    1977, 516 pages
Interception of the Alcohol Influenced
    Driver
    Stormer, David E.
    Campus Law Enforcement Journal
    Jan–Feb 1977, P 34
Investigating the Crime Scene at . . .
    Sports Event
    Deaver, Mick
    Campus Law Enforcement Journal
    Nov–Dec 1978, Vol. 8, No. 6, P 6
Juvenile Delinquency–A Campus Problem
    Bottomly, Edward
    Campus Law Enforcement Journal
    Sept–Oct 1978, Vol. 8, No. 5, P 16
K-9 Corps and Student Marshalls Syracuse
    Bernstein, Marilyn
    Campus Law Enforcement Journal
    Mar–Apr 1977, Vol. 7, No. 2
Kent State Response: Professionalism and
    Patience
    Malone, Robert and Winkler, Robert
    Campus Law Enforcement Journal
    Jan–Feb 1978, Vol. 8, No. 1, P 6
Larcenies Reduced by New Project at
    South Florida
    Mueller, Scott
    Campus Law Enforcement Journal
    Jan–Feb 1975

Michigan Snow: 'Sno Worry to CMU Public
    Safety Dept
    Bruce, Bob
    Campus Law Enforcement Journal
    May–June 1973, Vol. 3, No. 3, P 24
Model School Security System Cuts Crime
    Burton, Lucius W.
    Security World
    June 1975
Moon Over the United States
    Christian, Charles V.
    Campus Law Enforcement Journal
    Jan–Feb 1977, Vol. 7, No. 1
Motorcycle Patrol on Campus
    Gunson, Harvey P.
    Campus Law Enforcement Journal
    Mar–Apr 1978, Vol. 8, No. 2, P 10
Mounted Campus Patrol
    Koegel, Patricia
    Campus Law Enforcement Journal
    May–June 1973, Vol. 3, No. 3, P 22
New Concept Spurs Staffing Survey
    Lloyd, Norman
    Campus Law Enforcement Journal
    March–April 1976, Vol. 6, No 2, P 46
New Publication to Relieve Plight of
    Handicapped
    Campus Law Enforcement Journal
    May–June 1979, Vol. 9, No. 3, P 24
North Carolina Continues Campus Aware-
    ness Program
    Campus Law Enforcement Journal
    Mar–Apr 1978, Vol. 8, No. 2, P 8
Operation Identification Prevents . . .
    Campus Law Enforcement Journal
    Nov–Dec 1974, Vol. No. 4, P 3
Organization of the Patrol Car
    Kelshaw, Robert W.
    Campus Law Enforcement Journal
    Mar–Apr 1978, Vol. 8, No. 2, P 38
Photo Identification Inevitable for Schools
    Kuhns, Roger
    Security Management
    March 1977, P 10
Planning for Large-Scale Special Events
    Jands, Jack M.
    The Police Chief
    Jan 1980, Vol. XLVII, No. 1, P 59
Police on Campus, Parts 1 and 2
    Smith, Eugene N.
    Motorola Teleprograms, Inc.
    Film, 18 Minutes Each, 1976

Professors on Strike
    Roush, Ronald E.
    Campus Law Enforcement Journal
    March–April 1979, Vol. 9, No. 2, P 8
Reducing School Violence . . . Drug Abuse
    Harris, Karl B.
    Security World
    Jan 1974, Vol. 11, No. 2, P 18
School System Cuts its Losses Drastically
    Siden, David M.
    Security Management
    Nov 1978, Vol. 22, No. 11, P 52
Security and the Fine Arts
    Security Industry and Product News
    June 1979, Vol. 8, No. 6, P 30
Security at Princeton Is Low-Keyed
    Witsil, Jerrold L.
    Campus Law Enforcement Journal
    March–April 1979, Vol. 9, No. 2
Security Planning for New Library Facilities
    Powell, John W.
    Library Security
    Sept–Oct 1975, Vol. 1, No. 5, P 1
Security Tightened for the U. Md Inter . . .
    Olymphi
    Dickey, Sandra L.
    Campus Law Enforcement Journal
    Sept, Oct 1975
Security and the Small Business Retailers
    Ewing, Blair G. and Dogin, Henry S.
    Nat. Inst. of Law Enforcement and
        Criminal Justice
    1978
Texas High on Electric Vehicles
    Campus Law Enforcement Journal
    Sept–Oct 1975
The Fifth Quarter: Law Enforcement and
    . . . Sports
    Deaver, Mick
    The Police Chief
    Sept. 1978, Vol. 1, XLV, No. 9
The Mounted Patrol: Reviving an Old
    Tradition
    Nielsen, Robert C.
    The Police Chief
    Oct. 1974
The Museum Security Officer
    Ward, Roland L.
    Security Management
    Mar 1976, Vol. 20, No. 1, P 30

The Need To Be Recognized
    Gonson, Harvey D.
    Campus Law Enforcement Journal
    Sept, Oct 1974, Vol. 4, No. 3,
The Property Office: More Than Inventory
    Control
    Edwards, Ralph and Silver, David B.
    American School and University
    Mar 1978, Vol. 50, No. 6
The University Response Team: An
    Assessment
    Tanner, William A. and Sewell, James D.
    Campus Law Enforcement Journal
    Nov–Dec 1979, Vol. 9, No. 6, P 28
The UWPD/NFL Draft (Re: Shift Assign-
    ments – Editor)
    Shanahan, Michael G.
    Police Chief
    Aug 1979, Vol. XLVI, No. 8, P 59
University of Texas Acts to Curb Rape
    Campus Law Enforcement Journal
    Jan–Feb 1975
What Can a Security Check Do for You?
    Powell, John W.
    College Management
    Oct 1969, Vol. 4, No. 10, P 40
What Happened to the Buffalo
    Trachtenbe, Stephen J.
    Campus Law Enforcement Journal
    May–June 1973, Vol. 3, No. 3, P 3

STUDENT PATROLS

Academic Internship: An Operating Lab
    Approach
    McEntee, A.P.
    Campus Law Enforcement Journal
    March–April 1979, Vol. 9, No. 2, P 21
Campus Security Bolstered by Student
    Volunteers
    American School and University
    May 1978, Vol. 50, No. 9, P 27
Democracy in Action for Student Security
    Grossman, Robert J. and MacGregor,
        Archie
    Campus Law Enforcement Journal
    Aug 1977, Vol. 14, No. 8, P 16
K-9 Corps and Student Marshalls Syracuse
    Bernstein, Marilyn
    Campus Law Enforcement Journal
    Mar–Apr 1977, Vol. 7, No. 2

Moorhead State University Student Security Program
  Pehler, Michael J.
  Campus Law Enforcement Journal
  Nov–Dec 1977, Vol. 7, No. 6, P 24
North Carolina Continues Campus Awareness Program
  Campus Law Enforcement Journal
  Mar–Apr 1978, Vol. 8, No. 2, P 8
Project M.E.D.I.C. Underway at Oklahoma
  Holladay, Tish
  Campus Law Enforcement Journal
  May, Jun 1975
Student Auxiliary . . . Penn State
  Seip, David P.
  Campus Law Enforcement Journal
  Nov–Dec 1975, Vol. 5, No. 6,
Student Employees Ease Manpower Problem at U. Conn.
  Nielsen, Robert C.
  Campus Law Enforcement Journal
  May–June 1973, Vol. 3, No. 3, P 30
Students Provide Their Own Security
  Hickey, John M.
  Campus Law Enforcement Journal
  Nov–Dec 1976, Vol. 6, No. 6.
Students Rescue Service Stirs Controversy
  The Atlanta Constitution, Oct 9, 1975
    Quoted in CLEJ
    Jan–Feb 1976
Syracuse Univ. Honors Philip Gross
  Campus Law Enforcement Journal
  May–June 1973, Vol. 3, No. 3, P 48
The Use of Student Patrols in 1975
  Drapeau, Robert F.
  Campus Law Enforcement Journal
  Jan–Feb 1977, Vol. 7, No. 1,

STUDENT/POLICE RELATIONS

A Housing President's Observations
  Quick, Jerry
  Campus Law Enforcement Journal
  Mar–Apr 1980, Vol. 10, No. 2, P 36
A New Service Concept—and It's Free
  Burke, Mary E.
  Campus Law Enforcement Journal
  Mar–Apr 1980, Vol. 10, No. 2, P 38

Bringing University Police into the Academic Commu
  The Journal of the College and University Personnel
  April–May 1976
Campus Law Enforcement and Student Affairs: A Defi
  Sims, O. Suthern
  New Directions in Campus Law Enforcement: A Handb
  1971
Campus Security—Responsibilities of Students, Facul
  Wilson, Etsel A.
  Campus Law Enforcement Journal
  May–June 1976
Coming of Age in the Seventies: Is Anybody Ready . .
  Fernandez, Thomas L.
  College and University Personnel Assn Journal
  July–Aug 1975, Vol. 26
Courage, Skill Meet Crisis
  Johnson, Alex K.
  Campus Law Enforcement Journal
  Jul–Aug 1979, Vol. 9, No. 4, P 29
Democracy in Action for Student Security
  Grossman, Robert J. and MacGregor, Archie
  Campus Law Enforcement Journal
  Aug 1977, Vol. 14, No. 8, P 16
Freshman Orientation Program Revisited
  McAuliffe, John D.
  Campus Law Enforcement Journal
  Jan–Feb 1979, Vol. 9, No. 1, P 26
Friends or Foes? The Changing Relationship . . . .
  Nielsen, Robert C.
  Campus Law Enforcement Journal
  Nov–Dec 1974, Vol. 4, No. 4, P 30
Greek System: Internal Theft . . . How to Approach It
  Roling, Ann
  Campus Law Enforcement Journal
  Sept–Oct 1979, Vol. 9, No. 5, P 31
Innovation in Education at New England College
  Powell, Jack and Stuart Cynthia
  Campus Law Enforcement Journal
  May–June 1973, Vol. 3, No. 3, P 24

*Legal Aspects of Student Dissent and
  Discipline*
    Young D. Parker
    Institute of Higher Education Univ
      of Georgia
    1971
*Pigs Off Campus: Police and Student
  Demonstrators*
    Gaddy, Dale
    *New Directions in Campus Law
      Enforcement . . .*
    1971
*Security Minded Faculty & Students Sup-
  port SEMO.*
    Campus Law Enforcement Journal
    Mar–Apr 1978, Vol. 8, No. 2, P 30
Students Provide Their Own Security
    Hickey, John
    Campus Law Enforcement Journal
    Nov–Dec 1976, Vol. 6, No. 6.
*Students, Faculty Want Protection
  Against . . .*
    Burner, A.W.
    Campus Law Enforcement Journal
    May–June 1973, Vol. 3, No. 3, P 68
*The Necessity for Developing a Statement
  of Policy*
    Engel, Robert E.
    Campus Law Enforcement Journal
    Nov–Dec 1976, P 17
The Part-Time Student Employee . . .
    Walker, Wynn C.
    Campus Law Enforcement Journal
    May–June 1976
The Policeman's Image
    Daniels, Charles B.
    Campus Law Enforcement Journal
    Apr–May, Jun 1974, Vol. 4, No. 2, P 3
*The Student and the University Traffic
  Authority*
    Finch, Daniel P.
    Campus Law Enforcement Journal
    Jan–Feb 1979, Vol. 9, No. 1, P 25
University Police, Are They Necessary?
    Cox, Berry D.
    Campus Law Enforcement Journal
    May–June 1977, Vol. 7, No. 3, P 4
*What Are College Students Into These
  Days?*
    Haight, William H.
    National on Campus Report
    March 1978

Workshop on Student Housing Security
    Foulre, David M.
    Campus Law Enforcement Journal
    Nov–Dec 1975, Vol. 5, No. 6,

TOWN-GOWN

. . . Letters Judge Dept. Performance
    McAuliffe, John C.
    Campus Law Enforcement Journal
    Nov–Dec 1974, Vol. 4, No. 4
*A Message from the Chief: The
  Community's Responsi*
    Sides, Eugene
    Campus Law Enforcement Journal
    Nov–Dec 1977, Vol. 7, No. 6, P 28
*Bringing University Police into the Aca-
  demic Comm*
    Evangelide, Alice S. and Browner,
      Kathleen S.
    Campus Law Enforcement Journal
    July–Aug 1976, Vol. 4
Campus Autonomy
    Cox, David C.
    Campus Law Enforcement Journal
    Apr–May–June 1974, Vol. 4, No. 2
*Campus Law Enforcement: Town-Gown
  Relations*
    Bernitt, Richard O.
    *New Directions in Campus Law
      Enforcement . . .*
    1971
Campus Officers Need Recognition
    Sherman, Robert E.
    Campus Law Enforcement Journal
    May–June 1977, Vol. 7, No. 3, P 18
*Community Awareness–The Key to
  Campus Safety*
    Gross, Phillip
    Campus Law Enforcement Journal
    May–June 1973, Vol. 3, No. 3, P 45
Excellence a Search . . .
    Shanahan, Michael G.
    Campus Law Enforcement Journal
    May–June 1977, Vol. 7, No. 3, P 22
*Factors Affecting the Relationship
  Between Public*
    Neilson, Francis B.
    Security Management
    Jan 1977, P 22

Enforcement and Collection of Fines
Markle, Howard W.
*24th Annual Institutional & Municipal
Parking Cong*
June 11-14, 1978, P 159

EPA's Updated Policy, Its Effect on Parking
Donoghue, J.L.
Campus Law Enforcement Journal
Sept, Oct 1975

*Factors in Planning the Campus Parking
System*
Donoghue, Larry
*25th Annual IMPC Workshop
Proceedings*
April 8-11, 1979, P 167

*How Georgia Tech Solves Enforcement of
Campus Park*
Auman, F.C.
23rd IMPC Workshop Proceedings
June 5-8, 1977, P 109

How Traffic Tickets Can Work
Wearstler, Dale A.
American School and University
Jan 1973, Vol. 42, No. 11, P 27

Improved Pedestrian Lighting on Campus
Molte, John
Security Management
May 1977, Vol. 2, No. 2, P 30

*Interception of the Alcohol Influenced
Driver*
Stormer, David E.
Campus Law Enforcement Journal
Jan-Feb 1977, P 34

*Is a Multi-Leveled Parking Deck . . .
Solution*
Sharitz, Charles J.
Campus Law Enforcement Journal
Nov-Dec 1975, Vol. 5, No. 6,

Lighting for Safety and Security
McGowan, T.K.
*Reviews in College and University
Business*
Aug 1971, Vol. 51, No. 2, P 42

*Master Planning for Campus Traffic &
Parking*
Donoghue, J.L.
23rd IMPC Workshop Proceedings
June 5-8, 1977, P 96

Parking Control: Gates or Meters
Martin, James F.
*25th Annual IMPC Workshop
Proceedings*
Apr 8-11, 1979, P 10

Parking Control: Gates or Meters
Kolany, Thomas E. and Robbins, John E.
*25th Annual IMPC Workshop
Proceedings*
Apr 8-11, 1979, P 15

*Parking for the Handicapped at
Institutions*
Goldberg, Francis J.
*24th Annual Institutional & Municipal
Parking Cong*
June 11-14, 1978, P 156

*Parking on U. Of Mass Campus Draws
Labor Union . . .*
Campus Law Enforcement Journal
May-June 1973, Vol. 3, No. 3, P 69

Parking Policy Questioned
Sherman, Robert E.
Campus Law Enforcement Journal
Sept-Oct 1976, Vol. 6, No. 5, P 44

Planning for Institutional Parking
Wagner, Robert
*25th Annual IMPC Workshop
Proceedings*
Apr 8-11, 1979, P 159

*Planning Institutional Parking (Panel
Discussion)*
*25th Annual IMPC Workshop
Proceedings*
Apr 8-11, 1979, P 156

Parking Enforcement and Follow-Up
Brophy, John M. and Voccola, Harry W.
*25th Annual IMPC Workshop
Proceedings*
Apr 8-11, 1979, P 203

*Stadium Parking in Gator Bowl—Problems
& Solutions*
23rd IMPC Workshop Proceedings
June 5-8, 1977, 109 pages

The Saturday Afternoon Invasion
Blacklock, Thomas G.
Campus Law Enforcement Journal
Sept-Oct 1974, Vol. 4, No. 3, P 4

*The Student & the University Traffic
Authority*
Finch, Daniel P.
Campus Law Enforcement Journal
Jan-Feb 1979, Vol. 9, No. 1, P 25

Traffic Law Enforcement
Basham, D.J.
Charles C. Thomas, Publisher
1978, 172 pages

Transit-An Aid to Parking
Jones, Bonnie B.
24th Annual Institutional and Municipal Parking Cong.
June 11-14, 1978 P 163

TRAINING

A Campus Plan for Bombs and Bomb Threats
Owens, James
Campus Law Enforcement Journal
May-June 1976
A Factor for Survival: . . . Physical Efficiency
Shanahan, Michael G.
Campus Law Enforcement Journal
May-June 1976
A Giant Step Toward Professionalism
Hudson, Jerry E.
Campus Law Enforcement Journal
Sept-Oct 1976, P 25
A Model for Recruiting and Training Campus Security
Richert
The Police Chief
July 1974, P 76
An Alternative to Roll-Call Training: The Universi
Carcara, William S.
The Police Chief
Dec 1977, Vol. XLIV, No. 12, P 52
Annotated Bibliography of Police History 1900-1972
Cei, Louis B.
Police Chief
Aug 1973, Vol. XL, No. 8, P 52
Bomb Threat Response
Cox, David L. and DeMarco, John M.
Security Management
Jan 1977, P 8
Campus Apprehensions of College Students
Milander, H.M.
Police Chief
Nov 1972, Vol. XXXIX, No. 11, P 70
Campus Concerts . . . Some Guidelines and Precautions
Nielsen, Robert C.
Campus Law Enforcement Journal
Jan-Feb 1976

Campus Police Armed Does Not Mean Dangerous
Campus Law Enforcement Journal
Nov-Dec 1976, P 11
Campus Police Liability
Schmidt, Wayne W.
Campus Law Enforcement Journal
May-June 1978, Vol. 8, No. 3, P 33
Campus Shoplifters-Some Approaches to the Problem
Nielsen, Robert C.
College Store Executives
October 1976
Case Law for College Security Officers
Gehring, Donald D.
Campus Law Enforcement Journal
Sept, Oct 1975
Designing a Slide-Tape Presentation
Low, William C.
Campus Law Enforcement Journal
May-June 1977, Vol. 7, No. 3, P 49
East Texas State Security Dept Completes Firing . . .
Clay, Max
Campus Law Enforcement Journal
March-April 1976, Vol. 6, No. 2, P 7
Educational Aids for Police & Fire Science Instruc
Lansford Publishing Co. PO Box 8711
San Jose, CA
March 1978
Emerging Challenges . . . In a Changing World
Nielsen, Robert C. and Shea, Gordon F.
The Police Chief
Nov 1979, P 28
Excellence a Search . . .
Shanahan, Michael G.
Campus Law Enforcement Journal
May-June 1977, Vol. 7, No. 3, P 22
Field Placement-Its Use at Niagara College
Milligan, Bruce C.
Police Chief
Nov 1972, Vol. XXXIX, No. 11, P 32
First Aid for Emergency Crews: A Manual On Emer . . .
Young, Carl B. Jr.
Charles C. Thomas, Publisher
1970, 192 pages

Fundamentals of Training for Security
  Officers
  Peel, John D.
  Charles C. Thomas, Publisher
  1975, 340 pages
Guidelines for Security Education
  Kingsbury, Arthur J.
  American Society for Industrial Security
Helping Police with Emotional Problems
  Arkin, Joseph
  Campus Law Enforcement Journal
  Apr–May–June 1974, Vol. 4, No. 2, P 6
Hospital Security Guard Training Manual
  Wanat, John A. and Brown, John F.
  Charles C. Thomas, Publisher
  1977, 168 pages
How Big Cities Train for Security . . .
  Creekmore, Edward L.
  Security World
  Jan 1974, Vol. 11, No. 2, P 28
Human Relations Training for Campus
  Police
  Nielsen, Robert C.
  College Management
  Nov–Dec 1973
In-Service Training & the Four Day Week
  Strunk, Daniel M.
  The Police Chief
  July 1978, Vol. XLV, No. 7
Indecent Exposure
  MacDonald, John M.
  Charles C. Thomas, Publisher
  1973
Innovative Program-On Job Training Clev.
  State Uni
  Campus Law Enforcement Journal
  Jan–Feb 1978, Vol. 8, No. 1, P 12
Innovative Training: When? What?
  Hudson, Jerry E.
  Campus Law Enforcement Journal
  Sept–Oct 1978, Vol. 8, No. 5, P 12
Interception of the Alcohol Influenced
  Driver
  Stormer, David E.
  Campus Law Enforcement Journal
  Jan–Feb 1977, P 34
Iona College Hosts Training Institute
  Stump, William
  Campus Law Enforcement Journal
  Sept–Oct 1979, Vol. 9, No. 5, P 33

It's Time to Close the Training Gap
  Weiss, John
  Campus Law Enforcement Journal
  Jan–Feb 1975
Kent State Response: Professionalism and
  Patience
  Malone, Robert and Winkler, Robert
  Campus Law Enforcement Journal
  Jan–Feb 1978, Vol. 8, No. 1, P 6
Law Enforcement Officer . . . Unrecognized
  Minority
  Shaffer, Dale
  Campus Law Enforcement Journal
  Mar–Apr 1977, Vol. 7, No. 2, P 30
Law Enforcement: The Officer as Educator
  McDaniel, William E.
  New Directions in Campus Law
    Enforcement: . . .
  1971
LEEP Funding Threatened
  Guinn, Robert E.
  Campus Law Enforcement Journal
  Oct 1976, Vol. XIII, No. 5
Legal Aspects of Student Dissent and
  Discipline
  Young D. Parker
  Institute of Higher Education Univ of
    Georgia
  1971
Management Development: Filling a Need
  Nielsen, Robert C.
  Campus Law Enforcement Journal
  Sept–Oct 1979, Vol. 9, No. 5, P 26
Management Development: Filling a Need
  Nielsen, Robert C.
  Campus Law Enforcement Journal
  March–April 1979, Vol. 9, No. 2, P 10
Mass. State Police Academy Supports
  Campus Police
  Peckham, Allen
  Campus Law Enforcement Journal
  Jan–Feb 1976
McDaniel Advisor for Training Film
  McDaniel, William E.
  Campus Law Enforcement Journal
  Sept–Oct 1975
Minimanual of the Urban Guerrilla
  Marighella, Carlos
  New World Liberation Front
  1970

Mix It Up—A Simple Training Prescription
Campus Law Enforcement Journal
Jan–Feb 1980, Vol. X, No. I, P 25
Physical Fitness for Police Officers at
Cleveland
Klinzing, James E. and Faraldo, Joseph
Campus Law Enforcement Journal
Sept–Oct 1978, Vol. 8, No. 5, P 23
Police on Campus, Parts 1 and 2
Smith, Eugene N.
Motorola Teleprograms, Inc.
Film, 18 Minutes Each, 1976
Police Training Cooperation
Peterson, John A.
Campus Law Enforcement Journal
May–June 1977, Vol. 7, No. 3, P 30
Police Training The Quest for
Professionalism
Nielsen, Robert C.
Campus Law Enforcement Journal
Apr–May–Jun 1974, Vol. 4, No. 2, P 6
Pre-Service Police Training Academy: One
University's
Wachtel, David
The Police Chief
Dec 1977, Vol. XLIV, No. 12, P 61
Preparing for Disaster with Contingency
Planning
Young, James H. and Smith, Sigmund A.
College and University Business
Aug 1971, Vol. 51, No. 2, P 35
Private Security and Your Local Prosecutor
Salit, Robert-Ian
Security Management
Feb 1978, Vol. 22, No. 2, P 39
Protection of Public Figures: A Challenge
for Univ
Saye, David
Campus Law Enforcement Journal
Nov–Dec 1977, Vol. 7, No. 6, P 6
Quick Quiz on the Subject of Campus Life
Haight, William H.
National Campus Report
621 Sherman Ave, Madison, WI
Rape Crisis Training
Nielsen, Robert C.
Campus Law Enforcement Journal
Nov–Dec 1976, Vol. 6, No. 6
Region 2 Holds Training Session Niagara
Falls, NY
Griffin Lee E.
Campus Law Enforcement Journal
Mar–Apr 1980, Vol. 10, No. 2, P 22

Regional Training Programs
Nielsen, Robert C.
Campus Law Enforcement Journal
May–June 1979, Vol. 9, No. 3, P 18
Rock Festival or Fiasco?
Tuler, Roy A.
Police Chief
Mar 1973, Vol. XL, No. 3, P 34
Roll Call Training: A New Approach to an
Old, Old . .
Lytle, Bonnie J. and Dalton, Dennis
Campus Law Enforcement Journal
June 1978, Vol. XLV, No. 6, P 58–59
Security Education & Training: What Are
the Needs?
Fischer, Robert J.
Security Management
April 1980, Vol. 24, No. 4, P 77
Special Orders for Special Events
Owens, James
Campus Law Enforcement Journal
Jan–Feb 1976, Vol. 6, No. 1, P 37
Special Supplement
Campus Law Enforcement Journal
Jan–Feb 1980, Vol. X, No. 1, P 14
Special Supplement (High Speed Pursuit)
Campus Law Enforcement Journal
Nov–Dec 1979, Vol. 9, No. 6, P 11
Special Supplement: Training Aid
Campus Law Enforcement Journal
Sept–Oct 1979, Vol. 9, No. 5, P 13
Stadium Rock Concerts
McEntee, Andrew P.
Campus Law Enforcement Journal
May–June 1977, Vol. 7, No. 3, P 46
Stress & Its Impact on the Law Enforce-
ment Officer
Wallace, Leann
Campus Law Enforcement Journal
July–Aug 1978, Vol. 8, No. 4, P 36
The American Student Left
Rosenthal, Carl F.
National Criminal Justice Reference
Service
The Crime of Arson
Flanders, David A.
Campus Law Enforcement Journal
Mar–Apr 1977, Vol. 7, No. 2,
The History and Proper Role of Campus
Secty ., PT. I
Powell, John W.
Security World
Mar 1971, Vol. 8, No. 4, P 18

The History and Proper Role of Campus Secty., PT. II
Powell, John W.
Security World
Apr 1971, Vol. 8, No. 4, P 19

The President's Commission on Campus Unrest
U.S. Government Printing Office
1970

The Training, Licensing and Guidance of Private . .
Peel, John D.
Charles C. Thomas, Publisher
1973, P 288

The Well Trained Professional Police Officer
Campus Law Enforcement Journal
Aug-Sept 1975, Vol. 5

Training as a Potential Problem
Morgan, J.P. and Shoemaker, Eric
Police Chief
Aug 1979, Vol. XLVI, No. 8, P 55

Training Efforts Continue
Nielsen, Robert C.
Campus Law Enforcement Journal
Mar-Apr 1980, Vol. 10, No. 2, P 9

Training for Effective Supervision: A Model Program
Jennings, Stephen G. and Dileo Etal, Jean C.
Campus Law Enforcement Journal
Nov-Dec 1978, Vol. 8, No. 6, P 35

U of WA Police Officer Physical Efficiency Battery
Woods, Marella D.
Campus Law Enforcement Journal
May-June 1976

Valuable Material Available for Police Training . . .
Spencer, Claude W.
Campus Law Enforcement Journal
Jan-Feb 1975

Vandalism: Recovery and Prevention
Furno, O.F. and Wallace, L.B.
American School & University
July 1972, Vol. 44, No. 11, P 19

UNIONS ON CAMPUS

Day-To-Day Dealings with the Union
Leggat, Al, and McNamara, Joseph P.
Campus Law Enforcement Journal
Sept-Oct 1976, Vol. 6, No. 5, P 28

Employee Discipline—Punishment or Education?
Thomas, Gerald S.
Campus Law Enforcement Journal
May-June 1980, Vol. 10, No. 3, P 31

Industrial Security for Strikes, Riots and Disaste
Momboisse, Raymond M.
Charles C. Thomas, Publisher
1977, 516 pages

Parking on U. Of Mass. Campus Draws Labor Union . . .
Campus Law Enforcement Journal
May-June 1973, Vol. 3, No. 3, P 69

Police Sue State Union
Shelton, Pat
Campus Law Enforcement Journal
Nov-Dec 1977, Vol. 7, No. 6, P 20

Professors on Strike
Roush, Ronald E.
Campus Law Enforcement Journal
March-April 1979, Vol. 9, No. 2, P 8

Strike Procedures for the Campus Security Dept.
Stump, William
Campus Law Enforcement Journal
Mar-Apr 1978, Vol. 8, No. 2, P 32

The Policeman as Alienated Laborer
Denyer, Tom and Callender, Robert L.
Campus Law Enforcement Journal
Jan-Feb 1976, Vol. 6, No. 1, P 18

VANDALISM

Better Lighting with Less Energy
Meyers, Alan R.
American School and University
Sept 1979, P 30

Bombings, Vandalism & Arson
Powell, John W.
Burns Security Institute

Campus Vandalism—Who Pays?
Gardner, John
American School and University
Jul 1973, Vol. 42, No. 11, P 14

CCTV System Design for School Security
Kravontka, Stanley J.
Security World
Jan 1974, Vol. 11, No. 2, P 22

Designing Security in
Post, Richard S.
American School and University
July 1971

Improved Pedestrian Lighting on Campus
  Molte, John
  Security Management
  May 1977, Vol. 2, No. 2, P 30
Managing Vandalism . . . Parks and Rec Facilities
  Center for Urban Affairs
  1978, P 59
Microwaves Stop School Vandals
  Kolstad, Ken C.
  Security World
  Jan 1974, Vol. 11, No. 2, P 20
Protecting Against Fire and Vandalism
  Reeves, David
  American School and University
  May 1972, Vol. 44, No. 9, P 62
School Security Survey (Vandalism)
  Morton, Roger
  School Product News
  May 1978, P 10
School System Cuts Its Losses—Drastically
  Siden, David M.
  Security Management
  Nov 1978, Vol. 22, No. 11, P 52
School Vandalism Can Be Stopped
  Young, George P. and Soldatis, Steven
  American School and University
  Jan 1973, Vol. 42, No. 11, P 22
Stopping School Property Damage
  Zeisel, John
  AASA . . EFL
  1976
Vandalism . . . Attitudes Toward School Property
  Grealy, Joseph
  Security World
  Jan 1978, Vol. 5, No. 1, P 101
Vandalism: Recovery and Prevention
  Furno, O.F. and Wallace L.B.
  American School and University
  July 1972, Vol. 44, No. 11, P 19
Violence & Vandalism in Public Education . . .
  Ban, J.R. and Climinillo, L.M.
  Interstate Printers & Publishers, Inc.
  1977, 172 pages
Who Is Afraid of the Dark? Vandals That's Who!
  American School and University
  May 1978, P 38

VIP PROTECTION

Countering Terrorism
  Security Suggestions for U.S. Business Rep. Abroad
  Jan 1977
Is FBI Able to Cope with Organized Terror Now?
  Schipp, Bill
  Campus Law Enforcement Journal
  May–June 1978, Vol. 8, No. 3, P 36
Minimanual of the Urban Guerrilla
  Marighella, Carlos
  New World Liberation Front
  1970
Partners in VIP Problems
  Kivett, Jerry
  Campus Law Enforcement Journal
  March–April 1979, Vol. 9, No. 2, P 17
Protection of Public Figures: A Challenge for Univ
  Saye, David
  Campus Law Enforcement Journal
  Nov–Dec 1977, Vol. 7, No. 6, P 6
Terrorist Attacks Present Another Dimension for EM
  D'Addario, Francis M.
  Security Management
  May 1978, Vol. 22, No. 5, P 31
The American Student Left
  Rosenthal, Carl F.
  National Criminal Justice Reference Service

WEAPONS/POLICY/USE

Campus Police Armed Does Not Mean Dangerous
  Campus Law Enforcement Journal
  Nov–Dec 1976, P 11
Correcting the Problem Shooter
  Wilbur, Frank A.
  Campus Law Enforcement Journal
  May–June 1980, Vol. 10, No. 3, P 33
Exertion Shotgun Training Course
  Kelshaw, Robert W.
  Campus Law Enforcement Journal
  Nov–Dec 1979, Vol. 9, No. 6, P 36
Guns on Campus
  Morgan, J.P.
  Campus Law Enforcement Journal
  Nov–Dec 1979, Vol. 9, No. 6, P 16

Searches and Seizures
    Hollister, C.A.
    College Management
    Dec 1972
Should Campus Police Be Armed?
    Yates, Tom B.
    Campus Law Enforcement Journal
    Jan–Feb 1975
To Arm or Not To Arm
    Goldberg, Melvin S.
    Security Management
    May 1980, Vol. 24, No. 5, P 84

WHITE COLLAR CRIME

A Note on Campus Security Transporting Money
    Chafin, Saul
    Police Chief
    Dec 1978, Vol. XLV, No. 12, P 91
Breach of Campus Computer Results in Convictions
    Perry, Gordon
    Campus Law Enforcement Journal
    March–April 1979, Vol. 9, No. 2, P 16
Campus White Collar Crime
    Kleberg, John
    Campus Law Enforcement Journal
    Nov–Dec 1977, Vol. 7, No. 6, P 15
Foozles & Frauds
    Russell, Harold F.
    Institute of Internal Auditors, Inc.
    1972
Management Fraud: The Insidious Specter
    Sawyer, Lawrence B. and Murphy, Albert A.
    Assets Protection
    May–June 1979, Vol. 4, No. 2, P 13
Recognizing the Employee Thief
    Goldsmith, Reginald
    Security Management
    Aug 1979, P 53

WOMEN IN POLICING

Attitudes Relating to the Female Officer
    Drapeau, Robert F. and Cudmore, Mary J.

Campus Law Enforcement Journal
    Nov–Dec 1979, Vol. 9, No. 6, P 32
Campus Police Liability
    Schmidt, Wayne W.
    Campus Law Enforcement Journal
    May–June 1978, Vol. 8, No. 3, P 33
Oct Workshop Sponsored on Women in Law Enforcement
    Hocutt, Deborah
    Campus Law Enforcement Journal
    Sept–Oct 1974, Vol. 4, No. 3, P 32
Police Acknowledge Women's Capabilities as Officer
    Hocutt, Deborah
    Campus Law Enforcement Journal
    Sept–Oct 1974, Vol. 4, No. 3 P 32
She's Just Another Police Officer
    Campus Law Enforcement Journal
    May–June 1973, Vol. 3, No. 3, P 68
UGA Police Sergeant May Be First Woman Supervisor
    Campus Law Enforcement Journal
    Sept, Oct 1975
Woman Likes Job as Cop She Accepted It as a Necess
    Babington, Chuck
    Campus Law Enforcement Journal
    Jan–Feb 1975
Women in Police Workshop Held
    Campus Law Enforcement Journal
    May, Jun 1975

ADDITIONAL READINGS

Off duty weapons—proceed with caution
    Nielsen, Robert C. and Shea, Gordon F.
    Campus Law Enforcement Journal
    Sept–Oct 1980
Productivity and the New Supervisor
    Nielsen, Robert C. and Shea, Gordon F.
    The Police Chief
    Sept 1980
Small Motorcycles: Big Research for Campus Police
    Nielsen, Robert C.
    The Police Chief
    Sept 1978

INDEX

DISCARDED

DISCARDED